AN ACCEPTABLE ABNORMALITY?

FREUD AND THE RIDDLE OF FETISHISM

FIGURES OF THE UNCONSCIOUS 24

AN ACCEPTABLE ABNORMALITY?

Freud and the Riddle of Fetishism

Ednei Soares

LEUVEN UNIVERSITY PRESS

ISBN 978 94 6270 535 7 (paperback)
eISBN 978 94 6166 793 9 (ePDF)
eISBN 978 94 6166 794 6 (ePUB)
https://doi.org/10.11116/9789461667946
D/2026/1869/33
NUR: 770
Typesetting: Friedemann Vervoort
Cover design: Daniel Benneworth-Gray
Cover illustration: Detail from *A Female Nude, Seen From Behind* (1880), Anonymous

GPRC Guaranteed Peer Reviewed Content www.gprc.be

To my family, friends, Marianne and Puk.

Contents

Acknowledgements

I thank Philippe Van Haute (*in memoriam*) for welcoming the research that led to this book at the Center for Contemporary European Philosophy, Radboud University Nijmegen, and Herman Westerink. I also thank Guilherme Massara for his support at the Federal University of Minas Gerais (UFMG). Thanks are due to Ulrike May for research assistance and to Josias Tembo for his friendship in Nijmegen. Finally, I acknowledge the support of my family, friends, and Marianne Anink throughout this project.

Chapter 1

Introduction

Freud's legacy to the field of psychoanalysis encompasses pioneering research on human sexuality, with many philosophers viewing psychoanalytic theory as a crucial contribution to our understanding of human nature. Philosophers of the twentieth and twenty-first centuries have therefore mined Freud's ideas on sexuality in contemporary thought; equally, scholars have also criticized Freud's work (De Vleminck 2010, 9).

This book engages with these debates, but also goes far beyond them in advancing a thesis about the development of some of Freud's ideas on sexuality. In particular, *fetishism* was a powerful driving force for Freud's theories across many decades, and that it was fetishism that caused Freud to rethink, again and again in many different works, some of his most fundamental concepts of psychoanalysis. As just one part of human sexuality, then, fetishism ends up having an outsized influence on Freud's thought, and many of the revisions he makes to his ideas over his career can be traced back, in one way or another, to what Freud called the "riddle of fetishism." (Freud [1909a] 1988, 158)

In 1893, Freud theorized that sexuality is a potential cause of neurosis (Freud and Breuer 1893, 12). Over the next twelve years he evolved his theory of sexuality and eventually formalized it in the 1905 volume *Three Essays on the Theory of Sexuality* ([1905a] 2016). This volume represents the first systematic theory of human sexuality in psychoanalysis. To achieve this systematization, Freud based his theory on a concept of sexual perversions that had already been circulating widely among nineteenth-century scientists with any interest in sexuality.

Compared with his previous work, Freud's 1905 formulation of the theory behind sexual perversions introduced a different clinical and conceptual framework. In addition to sexual perversions such as sadomasochism and inversion, which Freud did describe in *Three Essays*, he also posited the "fetishist" perversion. This would be the focus of his new approach to sexuality theory.

It was in this context that Freud first presented the concept of fetishism as a phenomenon. His use of the term fetishism (*Fetischismus*) conforms to the conventions of the psychiatric and sexological literature of the late nineteenth century (Krafft-Ebing 1893a). He used the concept as a means to develop the notion of perversion as part of psychoanalytical theory. This early definition aligned Freud with the pathologizing frameworks of his psychiatric predecessors. The ambiguities in his later writings, however, complicate this alignment and leave open the possibility that fetishism might not be reducible to pathology alone. This is a tension that subsequent thinkers would amplify, either by reinforcing its pathological status or by contesting it altogether. We shall follow this thread carefully in this book.

Based on the literature on fetishism that Freud "inherited," he initially agreed with his predecessors: fetishism, with its attendant outsized erotic interest in parts of the female body and women's clothing, was a phenomenon that reflected the cultural landscape at the turn of the nineteenth century. The concept of fetishism, pathological or not, was a lens for studying sexuality. For instance, Freud and his predecessors such as Krafft-Ebing knew how the concept of fetishism was evident in modern culture. We see their awareness in discussions of the increasing erotization of female bodies and women's clothing, and particularly in trends that accentuated certain body parts, including women's breasts and hips.

This was to be a preoccupation that never left Freud and it extends to his final writings. Shortly before relinquishing his writing as a result of cancer (Gay 1988, 634–5), Freud drafted two key works, a book and an article, where he redefined his theory on mental illness based on fetishism (Freud 1940a, 275; 1940b, 202).

At the same time, the history of fetishism has always been inflected by questions of gender and sexuality. Nineteenth- and early twentieth-century psychiatry overwhelmingly framed fetishism in terms of male desire for women's bodies and clothing, and so naturalized heterosexual norms by locating pathologies in deviations from those norms. It is not difficult to see how we might invert this emphasis, however, to show how Freud's unstable formulations can be read as destabilizing those very gendered assumptions and the gendered psychopathological environments in which they arose. The persistence of gender as a category of analysis in debates about fetishism reminds us about the extent to which sexed bodies and gendered identities have shaped both the pathologization and the depathologization of the phenomenon. We shall return to this point later.

More than a century later, Freud's thinking on fetishism continues to shape contemporary, non-pathologizing approaches to sexuality. Feminist scholars have drawn on his work to challenge the classification of perversions as deviant, framing fetishism instead as a site of diverse sexual expression (Adams 2002, 258). In queer theory, Freud's ideas inform critiques of heteronormativity and provide a framework for understanding lesbian desire (Campbell 2000, 145). His theory also underpins arguments in trans studies that sexuality is shaped less by anatomy than by the fantasies through which sexual difference is imagined (Dean 2009, 150; Parfitt 2007, 72).

At the same time, Freud's theory of fetishism is not without reproach here, given the gendered assumptions structuring it. His emphasis on *male* development, the absent maternal *penis*, and the fetish as a substitute for *castration* positions the fetishist as paradigmatically *male*, and implicitly frames female sexuality as secondary, derivative, or defined by lack. These points can hardly go unnoticed. Feminist scholars have long observed that this framing risks pathologizing not only certain sexual objects or practices but also femininity itself. As a result, Freud's account both participates in and reinforces a medicalized discourse in which male sexuality is the norm and sexual difference is imagined largely through masculine anxieties, projections, and desires. Queer and trans perspectives, building on these insights, could interrogate how psychoanalysis has historically bundled together questions of gender identity and bodily difference. Sometimes these illuminate the insights, although they just as often constrain or mischaracterize them. We shall return to a number of these issues throughout the book.

Now, these critiques do not diminish the value of Freud's account. They instead challenge us to read it with an eye more attentive to its presuppositions and effects. Fetishism, in this light, becomes more than a clinical category. It is a site where psychoanalysis, cultural ideology, and lived experiences of gender and sexuality intersect, often contentiously, not only for Freud but also for us as well. That intersection is what makes fetishism such a generative concept for contemporary theory, even as its classical formulation requires rethinking. Considering these tensions helps to clarify why Freud's theory remains both useful and unstable: it reflects deep efforts to account for desire's strangeness, but it also reproduces the blind spots of its time. This book takes those tensions seriously and asks not only what Freud said about fetishism but also what his difficulties with the concept might reveal about the deeper contradictions of psychoanalytic thought. In addition, these points will help to illustrate how Freud's unstable formulations made possible two divergent legacies. The first entrenched fetishism within psychiatric nosologies of perversion, and a second has enabled feminist and queer theorists to challenge those very nosologies. The tension between these two trajectories – of the pathologization and the depathologization of fetishism – runs throughout this book, and has a powerful impact on Lacan, as we shall see in Chapter 7.

Clearly, Freud's account of fetishism continues to mobilize arguments about a range of sexualities. We even find a brand-new edition of his writings on the topic, *Schriften zum Fetischismus* (Freud 2025), now available for study; it remains relevant for contemporary debates in psychoanalysis, gender studies, and sexuality theory. This resurgence hints at how fruitful the view is for thinking about sexuality and pathology in many different disciplines.

And yet we are compelled to admit that the account itself is not very clear, rarely consistent, and raises many questions in contemporary application. How exactly, for example, does Freud's thinking on perversions contribute to scholars' reconsideration of whether human sexuality can be understood independently of a sexual object (Van Haute and Westerink 2017, 3–4)? That independence is the *opposite* of what is characteristic to fetishes, where an object is an intrinsic part of the desire. Could Freud's theory of sexuality, then, and his psychoanalytic practice at large, comprise a fundamental part of the movement to normalize human sexuality (Foucault 1979)? What developments lead to his view on fetishes and, more importantly, how did fetishism push back to change many of Freud's other ideas in turn?

This book demonstrates how Freud's exploration of fetishism was for him both a continual source of inspiration and a continual struggle. From the moment Freud begins to treat the topic, fetishism becomes a major problem for his theory of sexuality. His initial concern with fetishism was to demonstrate how the sexual drive attaches itself to various objects; in this regard, Freud challenged his predecessors' idea of an internal, biological norm linking the sexual drive exclusively to the specific objective of biological reproduction. But on conceiving of the object as *not* innate to the sexual drive, Freud's theory of fetishism destabilized his entire theory of sexuality, and most of all his views on perversion and infantile sexuality. Fetishism requires an object, and cannot be conceived independently.

As fetishism became a problem for Freud, he turned to its aetiology. From there arose a theory of fetishism, and by relating the phenomenon to his previous theory of neurosis, Freud adopted a developmental approach. His reformulation of fetishism can be read as an evolution of the same concepts he first appropriated from the literature on perversions. Other characters in our study will therefore include Alfred Binet, Richard von Krafft-Ebing, and many others. Freud's constant reworking of prior ideas culminates in his placing fetishism as the central argument for his theory of psychopathology.

But even here, Freud never managed to settle the question of whether fetishism should be treated as a pathological deviation or as a structural feature of human sexuality. This unresolved conflict is crucial, because it reveals both Freud's reliance on medicalized categories of perversion and his inadvertent opening for later critiques to seize on fetishism and therefore disrupt traditional ideas of sexual normality. It is this conflict – between the psychiatric impulse to classify fetishism as pathology and the critical possibility of reading it otherwise – that will guide much of the analysis in the chapters that follow.

Fetishism did not simply resist Freud's theoretical schemes – it reshaped them. Again and again Freud returned to the fetish in his writings. He sought less to clarify the notion and more to disrupt the very boundaries that he thought he had drawn successfully between symptom and structure, perversion and norm, object and scene. What began as a curious exception to the rules of sexual development gradually revealed itself as a force that unsettled those rules from within. This book traces that disturbance: how the fetish exposed cracks in Freud's thinking and ultimately forced him to revise some of his most enduring concepts. If we follow fetishism through the decades of Freud's work, as this study does, it becomes clear that Freud never resolved its meaning. But in that failure, we can glimpse the full destabilizing power of fetishism, and not just for psychoanalytic theory alone but also for our understanding of sexuality, identity, and desire.

Chapter 2

Freud and His Forebears: Binet and Krafft-Ebing

1. *The Riddle of Fetishism*

Freud's work on fetishism attempts to solve a fascinating but perplexing problem in early neuropathology: how should we understand the circumstances that give rise to fetishism? The argument here shall be that Freud's fetishism theory is a product of his scientific environment. This claim contrasts with twenty-first century thinkers who take the theory as a mere reframing of fetishism, in the sense that Freud expands the definition of the term to include additional sexual practices and more diverse sexual desires, and to accommodate contemporary ideas on gender and sexual identity.

Related views see Freud's psychoanalytic theory of fetishism as being motivated by his personal vulnerability as a Jewish man facing European discrimination (Matory 2018). According to this claim, Freud dealt with fetishism as a means to escape European anti-Semitic oppression, because he distinguished the Jewish race from that of inferior "savages," such as Africans. These positions understand Freud's fetish theory as a masked effort to prove his whiteness, and thus his fundamental acceptability in the eyes of the European bourgeoisie. Indeed, postcolonial critiques have convincingly shown how the category of fetishism could be appropriated in discriminatory ways (Safatle 2010). But it is equally important to recognize a complementary point: in Freud's own debates, fetishism functions not only as a marker of cultural hierarchy but also as a critique of Western norms of sexual and amorous life. In other words, the same theory that seems to reinscribe bourgeois and colonial categories also destabilizes the boundary between normality and pathology. This dual dynamic is central to the argument of this book. Alongside its historical and theoretical reconstruction of Freud's engagement with fetishism, the analysis also traces a second theme – that of the tension between the pathologization and the depathologization of fetishism. These themes are not separate, for Freud's confrontation with fetishism as a "riddle" continually forces him to revisit the very definition of normal sexuality.

To lay the groundwork for my arguments, we begin with the problem of fetishism – or, as Freud thought of it, the "riddle." Freud inherited this riddle from his predecessors, and it would go on to destabilize his evolving psychoanalytic framework in different works and in different ways. In this chapter, we take on the most important of those predecessors, French psychologist Alfred Binet and German psychiatrist Richard von Krafft-Ebing. First, though, let us consider the problem of fetishism in itself to see some of its roots in Freud's thought.

The idea of *fetishism* entered Western thought in the eighteenth century. Charles de Brosses' 1760 work *Du Culte des Dieux Fétiches* is the key text here, as it introduced fetishism into the francophone world. In De Brosses' view of "fetishist" practices, societies classified as "primitive" by colonial European observers were characterized as superstitious and devoted to religious worship. Freud would later take this idea on, as his first mention of fetishism in 1905 acknowledges it as a form of worship. Freud's approach to fetishism therefore follows a tradition in using terminology from religious studies to describe the relationship between the "pervert" or fetishist and the object of the fetish; in such cases, worship and veneration might occur in a sort of cultish environment.

Freud moved these initial ideas forwards by what we can think of as an ongoing internal dialogue with ideas on fetishism first developed by Alfred Binet. Intimations of this view were already apparent in 1905, as instead of sticking to a religious-studies-influenced idea of fetishism, Freud developed a more complex and more broadly applicable definition that included concepts such as overvaluation and sublimation. Accordingly, Freud associated religious cults with a cultural and historical view of perversion that fundamentally differed from any pathological perspective: he was seeking common patterns for both perverse and non-pathological sexualities, without reducing cultural phenomena to mere pathologies.

Interpreters of Freud cannot agree even on this point, however. Scholars of Freud's theory of fetishism (Rey-Flaud 1994; Assoun 1994) acknowledge that he introduced the theory in 1905 by adopting Binet's ideas as well as those of Richard von Krafft-Ebing. But rather than examining Freud's 1905 problems with fetishism, or just framing the subsequent debate as Freud's quest to untangle the riddle, these scholars argue that Freud later redefined or even *invented* the concept of the fetish. These arguments grow out of the French psychoanalyst Jacques Lacan's discussions of Freud's theory (Rey-Flaud 1994; Assoun 1994). To stake out my novel position here, then, it will be necessary to analyze the specifics of Freud's theory, and to look at how Lacan interpreted Freud on fetishes.

Both analyses will show that Freud's original thinking about this issue belongs to a larger theoretical engagement with sexual perversions. In reality, Freud challenged the criteria, established by the sexological and psychiatric literature of the late nineteenth century, which differentiated normal and pathological sexualities.

Now we might indeed read Freud's early theories as critiquing the late nineteenth-century effort to condemn and criminalize sexual pathologies. In the relevant literature of the time, the concept of *perversity* was a common critical target (Krafft-Ebing 1893a, 56–7). In opposition to this view, however, Freud developed his theory of sexuality by making perversions a cornerstone. Freud not only refrains from condemning perversions as either immoral or illegal, though; he identifies them as innate components of human sexuality. In discussing fetishism, Freud shows that the same tendencies present in "perverted" behaviours are also present in the expression of so-called "normal" sexuality: looking, kissing, and scratching, for example (Freud [1905a] 2016, 13). This observation is not merely descriptive but also has a destabilizing effect. If so-called "normal" sexuality shares its structure with perversions, then the distinction between pathology and normality begins to collapse. In this sense, Freud's engagement with fetishism anticipates later critiques of sexual normativity, insofar as it reveals that the very behaviours held up as *natural* are already traversed by the same dynamics as those deemed *pathological*. Fetishism thus functions less as a marginal anomaly than as a pressure point through which Freud was compelled to rethink the very boundaries of "normal" sexuality, and what it would mean to *depathologize* something considered "abnormal."

We can further contextualize Freud's eventual reworking of his ideas within his larger oeuvre. For example, after 1905, when Freud introduced the concepts of the castration complex and the Oedipus complex, he began to understand fetishist pathology as basing itself on an internal norm. Moreover, when trying to develop an aetiology for fetishism, Freud found it difficult to integrate the concept into his own theoretical framework. This destabilizing challenge forced Freud to articulate, repeatedly, his approach to fetishism according to different models, especially those of Binet and, to a lesser extent, those of Krafft-Ebing.

Freud introduced the concept of a sexual perversion as part of his thinking on the role of sexuality in neurosis aetiology. For Freud, some aspects of sexual perversion were "normal" manifestations present in a "normal" sexual life. In fact, perversion entails the *negative* of neurosis, as well as the compulsive and fixed forms of sexual expression in perverse pathologies. A biological argument drives the view here: sexual urges are linked to the sexual excitability of certain body parts, and to sexual stimulation via olfactory and gustatory pleasures derived from organic excremental matter (Freud 1985, 227). As a result, Freud developed his theory of polymorphously perverse sexuality in light of the animalistic features of human sexuality and ancient cults, in which one finds no internal principle of sexual normalization (Freud 1985, 227).

In letters to Wilhelm Fließ, Freud outlined his strategy for dismantling the traditional distinction between "normal" and "perverse" pathology. Here Freud did not discuss perversions in relation to morality, and in *Three Essays* ([1905a] 2016), he explores the role of fetishism and the links between normal human sexuality and perversion. This gesture has far-reaching consequences. If fetishism is continuous with ordinary expressions of desire, then the very criteria by which psychiatry defined pathology lose their coherence. Fetishism thereby becomes a privileged example of how psychoanalysis turns a pathological label into an occasion for rethinking the structure of sexuality as such. In this sense, Freud does not merely critique nineteenth-century sexological categories; he also exposes their fragility, making depathologization an intrinsic possibility of the analytic project. Later chapters will demonstrate how this tension recurs across Freud's work. Fetishism both unsettles Freud's categories and forces him to reconfigure the very distinction between normality and pathology.

Indeed, in 1905, at the very moment Freud was theorizing fetishism as a part of human sexuality, fetishism was also undermining his theory of perversion and infantile sexuality. In continuing to puzzle over this riddle, Freud again drew from his predecessors, including Binet, on fetishism, neurosis, and "splitting."

Thus, while Freud initially considered fetishism as a sexual perversion, his psychoanalytical theory of perversions first arose from late nineteenth-century psychiatric views on perversions (Lantéri-Laura 2012, 76–7; Sulloway 1983, 279–89). In other words, Freud relied here, as elsewhere, on ideas from various academic disciplines – psychiatry, neuropathology, and sexology – to modify his thought on fetishism and other sexual perversions.

To understand all these challenges, then, we must first get to know the role of Freud's predecessors in his thought. The writings of Binet and Krafft-Ebing provide the boundaries within which Freud first explored fetishism, albeit nominally, in 1905. At one time, Freud ([1909a] 1988) cited both Binet and Krafft-Ebing as the leading authors on fetishism and he often referred to them when discussing fetishes and related topics. Their work illuminates how fetishism was a challenge for many authors before Freud took up the subject. But these predecessors did not treat fetishism as a purely pathological anomaly. Both Binet and Krafft-Ebing already recognized that fetishism straddled the boundary between normal and abnormal, appearing at once in the context of ordinary love and in the classifications of sexual perversion. What Freud inherited from them, then, was not only a theoretical riddle but also a conceptual ambivalence. Fetishism simultaneously demanded medical classification and resisted confinement to pathology. This ambivalence would become central to Freud's own difficulties in theorizing fetishism, and it marks one of the key tensions between pathology and depathologization that we shall follow in this book.

And that point is crucial – by exploring the influence of Binet and Krafft-Ebing we shall see that Freud's interest in their work was not limited to fetishism. In fact, his scientific interest in these authors began even before he worked on the concept of perversion. In the late 1880s Freud had already referenced them in thinking about hypnosis, and in the early 1890s, when formulating his aetiology for neurosis, Freud considered the clinical ideas of both authors, and especially Binet's ideas on hysteria.

The ideas are some of the most important ones in the scientific environment in which Freud's theories took shape. For this reason, understanding the background of Binet and Krafft-Ebing will set the stage for the development of Freud's own ideas, as he wrestled with the riddle that would change his view more than once.

2. Alfred Binet and the Riddle of Fetishism

In the course of his career, Freud would progressively undertake a return to Binet's ideas regarding fetishism and "splitting." He does so to solve the challenges fetishism poses to his 1905 theory, and eventually he is able to centre the concept of splitting in his psychopathology in the late 1930s.

Indeed, Freud's early work from the 1880s and 1890s shows Binet's influence, as well as that of his contemporaries in neuropathology, such as Pierre Janet. Freud's scientific environment affected him, but considering how he debated Binet's ideas on fetishism and returned to the ones on splitting, we must make clear the extent to which Freud knew of Binet's writings on the subject. A close look at Binet's views will demonstrate how Freud developed some of them but continued to be challenged by them with his theory of perversion and infantile sexuality.

Freud's theoretical and clinical interest in the field arose when he began to question whether disorders should be taken just as brain diseases. He took a fellowship at the Salpêtrière Hospital in Paris from 1885 to 1886, under the guidance of the eminent French neurologist Jean-Martin Charcot, there encountering a psychodynamic approach to certain psychic disorders. Binet and Janet were disciples of Charcot and were developing his theories. During this time two important concepts were discussed at the Salpêtrière: the idea that the psychological impact of emotionally relevant events can cause pathologies, and the idea that parts of the psyche can become fragmented.

Beginning in this chapter, the influence of these two concepts on Freud's theories will become clear. Freud was studying with Binet under Charcot, with Binet working as one of Charcot's assistants. One of the Salpêtrière's treatments at the time was hypnosis, under which patients appeared to exhibit fragmentation of the psyche; in his retrospective report on those years, Freud (1886, 5, 12–13) described the milieu and noted his interest in French neuropathological theories.

At the Salpêtrière Freud probably observed Charcot's work with hysteric patients, which was undertaken with Binet and his colleague Charles Féré. In 1887, Freud acquired Binet and Féré's book *Animal Magnetism* (*Le Magnetisme Animal*), which documented their experiments. They wished to understand the different psychological states manifested in neuroses and during hypnosis, such as fragmentation of the psyche, and to relate these to sexual and other kinds of sensory excitations (Binet and Féré 1887). Freud first referred to these ideas in 1888 (Freud 1888c), which marked the start of his work on excitability. He hoped that these efforts would help reveal the case of neurosis.

From their experiments with hypnotized hysterical subjects, Binet and Féré emphasized the importance of the erogenous zones (*zones érogènes*). Although they did not specify the location of these zones in subjects, they observed that exciting them led to reflexive reactions and attacks of hysteria as well as genital sensations and states of agitation so intense that patients experienced orgasms. Binet and Féré concluded that the erogenous zones were analogous to the hysterogenic zones (*zones hystérogènes*), which Charcot took as responsible for hysteria and convulsions.

Many years after *Animal Magnetism*, Freud took up a more detailed study of the concepts in trying to develop an aetiological theory of neurosis. He took a stance like Binet's: sexual excitations originating in the erogenous zones corresponded to hysterical and other neurotic symptoms (1985, 212). This insight was fundamental to Freud's psychopathology. And, it turns out, to his concept of perversion in his initial approach to fetishism as well. Thus, the concept of erogenous zones is a foundation for Freud's critique of normal sexuality (Freud [1905a] 2016).

To understand more of how Freud's scientific environment contributed to the riddle of fetishism, we must look at Binet's views in more detail. We turn to those next.

Binet and Doubling

In reporting hypnosis experiments in *Animal Magnetism*, Binet and Féré described a striking phenomenon: "doubling" (*dédoublement*). They cited, for example, doubling of consciousness (*dédoublement de la conscience*), doubling of objects (*objet dédoublé*), and doubling of images (*dédoublement de l'image*). In simple terms, "doubling" refers to the mind's apparent ability to split into two parts that can operate at the same time, but without full awareness of each other. In hypnosis, for example, a person might seem to be fully conscious and responding normally, while another part of their mind is carrying out instructions or recalling memories without their conscious awareness. Binet and Féré used the term to capture how perception, memory, or attention could seem to *divide*, thereby allowing someone to see two versions of the same object, hold two conflicting ideas, or act on thoughts they did not know they were having.

Although the authors offered no explanation for doubling in 1887, Binet returned to the concept in later studies, which Freud then addressed in his search for hysteria's aetiology. In the 1890s, for example, Freud collaborated with Josef Breuer on two works: the article *On the Psychical Mechanism of Hysterical Phenomena: Preliminary Communication* (1893) and *Studies on Hysteria* (1895). Freud and Breuer repurposed therein some of Binet's foundational ideas on *dédoublement* and adopted a German term to describe it, *Spaltung* ("splitting"). In their repurposing of Binet's ideas on doubling, Freud and Breuer perpetuated confusion over the German term's meaning, and even at Salpêtrière they used it to refer to many different phenomena, with Binet's doubling being the most important.

But what did Freud mean by "splitting"? His 1890s references to the idea suggest an altered state of the psyche where consciousness, personality, groups of psychic representations, and the ego all undergo some change. Here, then, "splitting" appears to mean the inability to synthesize mental activity. Freud and Breuer took this inability as a symptom of neurosis and believed it to have a sexual origin.

In his early theories of neurosis, Freud abandoned splitting and Binet's doubling. But he would eventually reintegrate splitting into his theory of psychopathology, which argues for a serious reconsideration of Binet's idea. This took place after 1905, when Freud began to follow Binet's ideas as he explored fetishism.

A closer look at the Freud–Binet connection suggests that, while Freud initially adopted Binet's ideas on doubling, his entire theory of psychopathology in the 1930s was based on the concept of splitting – after dealing at great length with fetishism, Binet's celebrated subject in the field of sexology.

In several works from the 1880s and 1890s, Binet describes psychological phenomena associated with doubling. These studies belonged to a larger debate during this era in France, concerning double-personality, multiple-personality, double-consciousness, and dissociation. Secondary literature (Alvarado 2010; Foschi and Cicciola 2006; Hacking 1995; Ellenberger 1970) has tended to emphasize the differences between Binet's ideas and those of other authors in the French context, in particular the works of Janet. But this scholarship explores the question of how Binet's ideas on doubling influenced Freud in the longer term only fleetingly. This involves the issue of Binet's relationship to Janet, but also goes beyond it, a broader theoretical and historiographical discussion that, while relevant, lies beyond the scope of the present book.

Like Binet, Freud also opposed Janet's ideas. He rejected Janet's claims that hysteria represents an incapacity for psychic synthesis, or as evidence of degeneracy or a restriction of consciousness (Freud 1894; Freud and Breuer 1895, 230–1, 238). In developing his theory of the aetiology for neurosis, Freud also contrasted Janet's arguments with a point fundamental to Binet's theory of fetishism: the aetiological importance of precocious sexual experiences (Freud 1896b, 157). Here we see Freud, after debating Binet's ideas on fetishism, return to a view closely aligned with that of Binet. When Freud and Breuer sought the mechanism behind splitting, they used Binet's work on doubling as a basis and rejected Janet's explanation, which says that splitting comes from a weakness or incapacity of the ego for psychic synthesis and association. They postulated instead a splitting mechanism in which a strong ego acts by suppressing and repressing – which, again, is consistent with some of Binet's earlier views.

This reframing has important implications for the tension between pathology and depathology. Freud's appeal to splitting shifts the emphasis from weakness or defect to a structural duplicity within the psyche. In so, doing fetishism ceases to be a mere sign of pathology and instead becomes an exemplary instance of how psychic life can sustain contradictory attitudes simultaneously. The fetishist's divided relation to the object, at once disavowing and investing it, illustrates a mechanism that is not confined to illness but is rather constitutive of human subjectivity. Splitting therefore allows Freud to theorize fetishism as a "welcome abnormality": sufficiently troubling to challenge nosological categories but productive for understanding the very architecture of the psyche.

Seen in this light, it is not surprising that before defining personality and consciousness in terms of doubling, Binet had already theorized about fetishism and the fetish object. In each case he stressed the inherent duplicity of both the fetishist's psychic attitude and their perception of the fetish object. For Freud's theory of fetishism, these ideas were crucial.

In exploring the sexual aetiology of neurosis, Freud's main reference for splitting was Binet's 1892 work *The Alterations of Personality* (*Les Altérations de la Personnalité*). Here Binet addressed the problem of coexisting personalities in occurrences of ego doubling and consciousness doubling. According to his view, the ego's fragmentation (*morcellement du moi*) lies behind many mental phenomena (Binet 1892, I), but made clear that no existing theory adequately explained doubling. For this reason, Binet described and defined personality and consciousness in terms of doubling and by using results from his studies and experiments (Binet 1892, VIII). Just after this time, in 1893, Freud began to refer to Binet and his discussion of splitting. Freud was harnessing the splitting concept to theorize about neuroses like phobias, obsessional neurosis, and psychoses.

In the same work, Binet concluded that doubling explains how a subject perceives an object as unacceptable or forbidden, and then splits that perception by preserving the object's forbidden features as unconscious perceptions (*perception inconsciente*). To reach this point, Binet examined in detail how perceived objects are modified by mental processes of negation (*négation*), which shares some points in common with Freud's concerns about psychic mechanisms in the 1920s. In this case, Freud came to approach fetishism with the aim of refining his characterizations of forms of negation, refusal, and disavowal. Later topics and terms were also essential to Freud's exploration of neurosis in the 1890s and of fetishism in the 1920s and 1930s.

In fact, Binet coined the terms for many related phenomena, and was also the first to outline the framework Freud used to investigate the sexual aetiology of neurosis. More specifically, developments in psychological studies initiated by Binet, and especially those on ego doubling, were formative influences on Freud's later focus on fetishism, perversions, and neuroses. Indeed, the gradual process of Freud relating his insights from neurosis theory to fetishism culminated in a discussion of the splitting of the ego. Freud described this splitting similar to how Binet had described doubling in 1892. Freud did not merely emphasize the relevance of Binet's work here ([1909a] 1988, 155); he aligned his theory with Binet's view on perception doubling, and claimed that a fetish's formation depended on the splitting of early childhood perceptions. Freud later applied the same concept, but without referring to Binet, in describing how a subject comes to have coexisting yet contradictory attitudes towards perceptions of reality, some of which the subject finds unbearable. Freud's view of splitting therefore intersects with Binet's use of doubling for an unacceptable or forbidden object.

By framing fetishism through splitting, Freud was able to preserve its theoretical significance without fixing it within a pathological category. Splitting transformed fetishism into a model for understanding the coexistence of contradictory psychic attitudes, a mechanism that could apply as much to the so-called normal psyche as to the perverse one. In this sense, fetishism becomes conceptually productive precisely because it resists straightforward medicalization. Its ambiguity forces Freud to use it as an analytic tool rather than to confine it as a disorder. This move illustrates how fetishism functions within psychoanalysis as both pathology and critique of pathology – again, a dynamic that will recur in Freud's later writings.

Some scholars believe that Binet's work *Fear in Children* (*La Peur Chez les Enfants*) was important for the origin behind Freud's idea of the Castration complex (Kern 1975). Binet argued that infantile fear develops via a displacement mechanism; this simple idea had an outsized influence for Freud in thinking about castration, which Freud later claimed ([1914a] 1974, 1927, 1940a, 1940b) was an essential cause of fetishism.

In 1910, in opposition to Freud's and Janet's theories, Binet and Simon (1910) continued developing Binet's concept of doubling along the lines that Binet had laid down in *The Alterations of Personality*. They claimed that the mental state observed in hysteria constitutes a doubling of personality: hysteria manifests as the separation of consciousness, with separate and independent personalities coexisting and alternating in a single individual. Each personality has a particular attitude orienting it towards different goals and pressuring the personalities to ignore each other. By evolving these claims about doubling, Binet and Simon were able to argue that the doubling process underlies various pathologies (Binet and Simon 1910, 126–37). For instance, while acknowledging the diagnostic differences between insanity with conscience (*folie avec conscience*) and manic-depressive insanity (*folie maniaque dépressive*), Binet and Simon still claimed that the process of doubling grounds the aetiology for both pathologies.

In his views on psychopathology from the late 1920s and 1930s, Freud makes a similar assumption. He had struggled to develop a theory of fetishism, and so in the end he followed Binet's reasoning: splitting was to be the foundation of multiple pathologies. Given the influences we have seen here, there is no question that Binet's view of doubling as the foundation for various pathologies was crucial to Freud's later concept of splitting.

Binet's Conceptualization of Fetishism: The Birth of a Riddle

Before turning directly to Freud's writings on fetishism, we need to consider how Binet himself understood the phenomenon. While Binet is more often associated with psychological testing and theories of consciousness, his engagement with sexual pathology, and with fetishism in particular, was both substantial and influential. For Binet, fetishism was not an isolated curiosity but a revealing instance of the broader dynamics of mental doubling he had already identified in work on hysteria and personality. By interpreting fetishism from the lens of dissociated mental states and conflicting psychic attitudes, Binet laid conceptual groundwork that Freud would later draw on – but with different emphases. Understanding Binet's account of fetishism, therefore, not only clarifies the structure of Freud's eventual theory but also highlights the continuity between fin-de-siècle neuropathology and psychoanalysis.

In various works from the 1920s and 1930s, Freud brought together these two ideas from Binet: ego doubling, and the most famous subject in nineteenth-century sexology: fetishism. Here Freud would argue for two contrary, independent attitudes to describe the apparent "splitting" in fetishism; indeed, the connection between the two was to become his ultimate strategy for arguing that the human psychic synthetic function is vulnerable to a great many disturbances. In addition, Freud came to acknowledge, just as did Binet with doubling, that splitting underlies various pathologies. It is no reach to infer that Binet's ideas are the background against which Freud researched into the sexual aetiology of neuroses and problems related to perversions.

Binet's view of fetishism was therefore of major significance to Freud. He referred directly to Binet's ideas, and in particular to those in *Fetishism in Love*. We see this text's great value to Freud even in discussions not directly associated with fetishism. Freud also applied, for instance, Binet's ideas to the aetiology of perversions in general (Freud, 1916–17, 1919). This influence was enduring – it is manifest in the period when Freud was developing his own ideas about topics such as trauma, infantile sexuality, and psychosexual development (1905c, [1914a] 1974, 1916–17).

Binet's *Fetishism in Love* (*Le fétichisme dans l'amour*) was originally published in France in 1887, in the *Philosophical Review* (*Revue philosophique*). The following year, the article was included as the first in a series by Binet published in *Studies of Experimental Psychology* (*Études de psychologie expérimentale*). Here the topic of fetishism is one of several scientific interests for Binet, who also wrote about things as varied as microorganisms, hysteria, the practice of hypnosis, and the intensity of mental images. As his investigations progressed, the studies reflected Binet's diversifying interests in the years following his work at Salpêtrière, part of which he spent at the embryology and zoology laboratories of the Collège de France.

A key feature of Binet's interests in this period was his concern with heredity and reproduction (Wolf 1973, 69), and he wrote about so-called plastic forces (*forces plastiques*). He discussed Ernst Haeckel's concept of "Plastidules," where heredity is understood in terms of how outer conditions influence the inherited undulatory motion of organic molecules (Binet 1888b, 556–7). Binet's (1888a, 8, 23) investigation of fetishism followed suit, as he qualified sexuality and love as possessing "plastic" qualities. Freud, for his part, then found evidence that the sexual drive is characterized by plasticity (Freud 1916–17, 346). Binet's innovation was to propose that pathologies result from the interplay of innate and external factors. It was this thinking that turned fetishism into a riddle for both Krafft-Ebing and Freud.

When Binet published *Studies of Experimental Psychology*, he had not yet formulated his theory on doubling. But in *Fetishism in Love* he had highlighted fetishism and the fetish object as phenomena manifesting contradictory elements. In *Studies*, Binet classified fetishist individuals as sexual perverts and claimed that sexual perversions form early in an individual's life. He knew about fetishism's religious implications, and so imbued the term with a new connotation to describe specifically sexual perversion. According to Binet, sexual perverts' adoration of inanimate (*inert*) objects resembles in every respect the adoration of savages for their religious fetishes. Such a comparison reflects a distinctly colonial and discriminatory gaze. He did distinguish, however, between these fetishisms, stating, "The term fetishism seems to us to suit this kind of sexual perversion quite well. These patients' adoration of inanimate objects such as nightcaps or boot nails resembles in all respects the adoration of the savage or the negro for fish bones or for shiny stones, except the essential difference is that in the cult of our patients, religious adoration is replaced by a sexual appetite" (Binet 1888a, 3).

To differentiate this perversion, Binet used the terms "love fetishism" (*fétichisme amoureux*) and "fetishism of love" (*fétichisme de l'amour*). Fetishism in love life represents the blind adoration (*adoration*) of the beloved's body parts, faults, or caprices. Here Binet studied cases of eye, hand, hair, and olfactory fetishism; the adoration of such objects is evidence of love's plasticity (*amour plastique*). To further investigate the role of such accidental impressions, Binet (1888a, 8, 35, 49) selected and systematized cases involving objects such as costumes, handkerchiefs, nightcaps, boots, and white aprons, and extended this approach to phenomena such as fetishes of psychic qualities and exhibitionism. Binet emphasized that his definition implies the adoration of things unfit to directly satisfy reproductive ends. Notably, in *Fetishism in Love*, Binet offered a strategy for analysing fetishism more precisely: extract information from pathological facts to better understand the psychology of normal love. Freud reflects the idea in *Three Essays*, where he centres Binet's link between (fetishistic) perverse sexuality and normality. As we shall see later, though, Freud could not make the same connection in his theory of infantile sexuality.

Binet's *Fetishism in Love* was foundational to the emerging concept of fetishist perversion and later, to Freud's own theorizing. Binet, while acknowledging the observations of French psychiatrists Jean-Martin Charcot and Valentin Magnan (1882) on various perversions of sexuality, critically shifted the focus from their emphasis on hereditary or "morbid" causes (1882, 317). Binet proposed instead that fetishism arose from "accidental experiences" had in early childhood. For Binet, these seemingly insignificant chance events, when coinciding with early sexual excitement, could profoundly shape an individual's sexuality, thus leading to the specific form of their perversion. Crucially, Binet positioned fetishism as a lens through which to study not only pathology but also the broader psychology of "normal" love, arguing that its object-dependent nature reflected universal aspects of human desire where specific attributes become idealized.

This distinctive aetiological approach directly influenced Freud. Binet's meticulous documentation of patients' early memories and the formative power of these fetish-inducing sexual experiences became essential for Freud's own developing theories, most notably his early seduction theory and the concept of "afterwardsness" (*Nachträglich*), where later experiences imbue earlier, seemingly innocuous events with traumatic significance. Moreover, Binet's argument against heredity as the sole or specific cause of fetishism, emphasizing instead the role of individual accidental experiences, provided a crucial conceptual pathway for Freud to develop a psychological rather than a purely constitutional explanation. In this way, Binet not only defined the phenomenon but also framed a central challenge, part of the riddle we are now exploring: how to explain the origin of fetishism's object-specific nature through early, often traumatic, experiences. The problem would preoccupy Freud for decades.

Binet further refined his understanding of fetishism by analysing cases such as that of Jean-Jacques Rousseau and focusing on what he termed a "cult of psychic quality" (1888a, 49). This form of fetishism centred on an individual's intense focus on a loved one's personality traits or even psychological disturbances, and was often considered to be triggered by early, emotionally charged experiences. Rousseau's self-recounted sexual arousal from being disciplined as a child, for instance, illustrated Binet's concept of the "voluptuousness of pain" and his broader argument that the fetish object could be "double-sided" (*double face*), thus synthesizing contradictory feelings or qualities derived from accidental, early sexual impressions. This emphasis on fetishism as a "dualistic phenomenon" and the fetish object as having "contradictory elements" would profoundly influence Freud's later theory of splitting, where he would similarly argue for split perceptions and attitudes concerning the fetish object (Freud [1909a] 1988, 155; [1914a] 1974, 245; 1915, 150; 1927, 157). Binet's insights into these accidental experiences and their deep, unconscious impact on sexual development also highlighted the erotic role of various senses, such as smell, linking them to non-European religious practices and animal sexuality (Binet 1888a, 25). These connections were pivotal for Freud's own conceptualization of perversion and fetishism (Freud [1905a] 2016, 13; [1909a] 1988, 156) but would ultimately lead him to further problems in relating his theory of perversion to the phenomenon of fetishism itself – the heart of the riddle.

Binet's most significant contribution to the riddle of fetishism and its lasting impact on Freud was his groundbreaking assertion that normal love is the result of a complicated kind of fetishism (*fétichisme compliqué*) (Binet 1888a, 84). By distinguishing between "major" and "minor" forms of fetishism based on intensity rather than on absolute pathology, Binet argued that elements of fetishism were present in all sexual expression, from polytheistic normal love focused on the whole person to monotheistic fixation on a single body part or object. This radical depathologization of aspects of perversion and the notion of a continuum between normal and fetishistic sexuality provided Freud with a crucial conceptual tool. But this continuum also created enduring difficulties for Freud's own project. If normal love is already a form of fetishism, then the category of "pathology" cannot remain secure. Fetishism, in this sense, operates as a hinge. It not only equips Freud with a way to challenge sexual normativity but also simultaneously unsettles his attempts to delimit perversion as a distinct class. This tension explains why Freud would return to fetishism repeatedly across his career, never fully able to stabilize whether it belonged to the realm of pathology or to the broader field of human sexuality.

Indeed, as Freud would articulate in *Three Essays* ([1905a] 2016), he directly appropriated Binet's strategy: fetishism served as a foundational example for his own critique of sexual normativity and demonstrated that the human sexual drive could attach itself to various unsuitable substitutes for the sexual object. This initial Freudian definition, which mirrored Binet's, established fetishism as a key phenomenon for understanding the sexual drive as non-reproductive and non-genital, thus setting the stage for Freud's future theoretical challenges. The scientific context in which Freud was working was crucial; he could not have made these conceptual innovations without relying on Binet.

Binet was not the only such influence on Freud, however. Another figure from that context was also crucial, and would have a similarly powerful impact on Freud's work: the German psychiatrist Richard von Krafft-Ebing, who closely followed Binet's ideas on fetishism as well.

3. Freud, Krafft-Ebing, and the Problem of Perversions

While Binet's pioneering work gave Freud essential conceptual tools for grappling with fetishism, he was not the sole predecessor to shape Freud's early understanding. The German psychiatrist Richard von Krafft-Ebing also played a pivotal role, not only by independently observing the phenomenon of fetishism but also by acting as a crucial conduit for Binet's ideas into the broader discourse Freud would later inherit. Krafft-Ebing's monumental *Psychopathia Sexualis* (1893a) served as Freud's primary reference for the classification of sexual perversions, including fetishism, during his formative years from 1896 to 1904; it thus deeply influenced Freud's initial critique of sexual normativity.

Krafft-Ebing's theorization of perversion and fetishism would, however, further intensify the very challenges Freud encountered in his efforts to integrate fetishism into his evolving theory of infantile sexuality and perversion.

This section will demonstrate how Krafft-Ebing's conceptual framework, particularly his detailed classifications and his understanding of masochism's relationship to the fetish object, provided both an essential foundation and a new set of theoretical hurdles for Freud's "riddle of fetishism." We shall examine Krafft-Ebing's definition of *perversion*, his distinctions between "perversion" and "perversity," and his insights into the object-dependent nature of fetishism. All of these critically shaped Freud's own attempts to define and contextualize this enigmatic phenomenon.

Krafft-Ebing's Classification of Perversions

Richard von Krafft-Ebing's *Psychopathia Sexualis* (1893a) served as Freud's primary reference for the emerging field of sexual perversions. Freud drew heavily on the work when formulating his own theory of sexuality in *Three Essays* ([1905a] 2016), explicitly following Krafft-Ebing's conceptual framework and classifications, which included fetishism as a key perversion. For Krafft-Ebing, perversions, termed *paresthesia*, represented abnormalities of the genital drive that deviated from the natural purpose of reproduction. He famously argued that a distinguishing feature of perversion was the overcoming of *disgust*, an idea Freud himself would later develop in relation to fetishist pathology. Krafft-Ebing identified four major perversions: sadism, masochism, fetishism, and homosexuality, all of which are rooted in what he took to be an abnormal constitution of the central nervous system. In this he implied a heritable, brain-based origin for the conditions.

While emphasizing a constitutional basis, Krafft-Ebing also acknowledged the crucial role of psychological elements, such as fantasies, dreams, and personal history, in understanding sexual perversion. He noted that fantasies could enable coitus even in the absence of the fetish and thus demonstrates a mental component for the fetishist perversion. Moreover, Krafft-Ebing's work addressed the influence of childhood seduction in the aetiology of sexual perversion. This would give an early precedent from which Freud would derive confirmation for his own seduction theory. The reliance on Krafft-Ebing's foundational yet complex framework, which simultaneously posited a brain-based origin and a role for psychological factors, introduced significant conceptual challenges for Freud as he grappled with integrating fetishism into his evolving theories after 1905.

Krafft-Ebing's *Psychopathia Sexualis* also introduced a crucial conceptual distinction between "perversion" (*Perversion*) and "perversity" (*Perversität*). For Krafft-Ebing, "perversion" referred to innate, permanent, and often pathological characteristics of sexuality, understood as deviations from the reproductive norm. In contrast, "perversity" designated temporary, immoral acts that were not necessarily pathological but rather contingent choices or "vice." Krafft-Ebing's aim was to separate the biological reality of sexual deviation from moral or legal judgment. And indeed Freud, as evidenced in his 1896 letters to Fließ, was acutely aware of this distinction. When he later introduced perversion as a universal human condition in *Three Essays*, Freud directly appropriated Krafft-Ebing's gesture of detaching perversion from its moral connotations, embracing it instead as a morally unbiased concept essential to understanding human sexuality. This move aimed to challenge prevailing notions of sexual normativity, but, as we shall explore elsewhere, it also created additional difficulties for Freud's conceptualization of fetishism.

Now although Krafft-Ebing initially considered fetishism to depend on a congenital psychopathic disposition, his understanding developed through his engagement with Binet's ideas. From his 1890 supplement, *New Research in the Field of Psychopathia Sexualis*, Krafft-Ebing (1890b) explicitly incorporated Binet's aetiological theory, acknowledging fetishist pathology as only partially congenital and influenced by individual circumstances. He even attempted to conceive of fetishism as independent of its object, although he ultimately conceded the inevitability of the fetish object. Again, this was to be a persistent challenge: the inescapable fact that fetishism implies an *object*, and thus clashes with any attempt to define sexuality *independently* of its object. This was a riddle that Krafft-Ebing wrestled with before it would similarly preoccupy Freud in his own theorization of infantile sexuality. Moreover, Krafft-Ebing recognized fetishism's forensic importance, noting how a strong "perverse drive" could lead to acts such as stealing fetish objects. In later chapters, this point will become central to Lacan's distinct theorization of fetishism.

Fetishism, Masochism, and Shared Aetiology

Building on Binet's pioneering work, Krafft-Ebing significantly shaped the emerging understanding of the fetish object. His 1890 *New Research* explicitly explored fetishism and viewed it through the lens of *masochism*, a concept he was then introducing into the scientific lexicon. Krafft-Ebing proposed that masochism constituted the very "essence of fetishism," which allowed him to explain how fetish objects, which were often female body parts or clothing, could become central to sexual attraction (Krafft-Ebing 1890b, 6–7). This framing drew directly from Binet's ideas on fetishism and particularly those seen in Rousseau's case, where Binet had noted the masochistic significance of foot and hand fetishism.

Krafft-Ebing's work thus highlighted human sexuality's deep dependence on a sexual object, a fact that would challenge Freud's later efforts to conceptualize infantile sexuality as object-independent. For Krafft-Ebing, fetishism, especially its foot and shoe variations, represented a spectrum of masochistic perversions that were driven by "unconscious masochistic motives" such as the desire for self-humiliation (Krafft-Ebing 1893a, 128–9). This view directly influenced Freud's own aetiological theories of fetishism. Freud, in *Three Essays* ([1905a] 2016), would notably engage with Krafft-Ebing's classification, and in later works ([1909a] 1988, 155; [1914a] 1974, 245; 1927a, 154) he would elaborate on Krafft-Ebing's connection between foot/shoe fetishism and masochism. He even adopted Krafft-Ebing's idea that splitting enables the fetish to synthesize conscious and unconscious elements. Krafft-Ebing's persistent confrontation with the fetish object's inescapable role in perversion set the stage for Freud's own struggles with fetishism, which consistently defied a simple object-independent explanation of sexuality throughout his career.

The pervasive investigation into fetishism before the formal concept of masochism reveals that critical pre-Freudian problem: whether human sexuality should be understood independently of a sexual object. Krafft-Ebing's work, particularly his efforts to define masochism as a core motivation for fetishism, implicitly acknowledged this dependency, employing terms such as *Objekt* and *Gegenstand* (object) in his *New Research*. While Freud would later attempt to theorize the sexual drive as object-independent in *Three Essays*, his engagement with fetishism and masochism, influenced as it was by Binet's ideas, immediately complicated this aim, because any theory of fetishism requires an object.

Krafft-Ebing refined his perspective and eventually classified certain forms of fetishism as a subset of masochism, deeply rooted in the sphere of love (1893a, 141–6). His extensive discussion of foot and shoe fetishism as "midway perversions" (1893a, 123) underscored how an exclusive sexual interest in female feet and shoes expressed a masochistic desire for self-humiliation, driven by those unconscious masochistic motives. Such a sophisticated understanding of fetishism, integrating the physical and psychological dimensions of desire and object-relations, laid conceptual groundwork that would profoundly influence Freud's subsequent efforts to explain the complexities of perversion and the formation of the fetish object.

Like Binet, Krafft-Ebing (1893a, 155) hypothesized that fetishist pathology stemmed from a triggering early childhood event, often related to women. While acknowledging the complex mental processes involved, Krafft-Ebing recognized that identifying the precise origin of such perversions was virtually impossible (1893a, 19). He applied Binet's ideas on sexual impression to his own theoretical framework to emphasize the aetiological role of these early impressions in awakening the genital drive, often even before physical intercourse was possible. This pre-Freudian emphasis on early, potentially traumatic sexual experiences as the root of later perversions, and the riddle of their precise formation, informed Freud's subsequent investigations.

Krafft-Ebing's work further centralized fetishism as a means by which to understand normal human sexuality by elaborating on Binet's concept of its presence in typical love. He argued that the physiological facts of fetishism elucidated individual sexual preferences, and he asserted that a fetish could maintain its significance without being pathological. This claim, separating fetishism from an automatic link with pathology, was decisive for Freud. It not only detached perversion from moral condemnation, which had been a distinction Krafft-Ebing himself insisted on in differentiating "perversion" from "perversity," but also left fetishism suspended between the *normal* and the *abnormal*. Freud inherited the ambiguity: in adopting Krafft-Ebing's framework, he found himself compelled to acknowledge that the fetish might be integral to typical love while still bearing the marks of deviance. This tension was not a weakness in Freud's theory. In fact, it became one of its generative features, as it forced Freud to revisit fetishism as a site where psychoanalysis both pathologizes and depathologizes sexuality.

At the same time, his extensive focus on the physiological processes underlying the sexual drive – distinguishing it from the narrower genital drive, tied solely to reproduction – provided Freud with a crucial conceptual framework. It was through Krafft-Ebing that Freud first adopted the term *Sexualtrieb* (sexual drive), a concept that would become central to psychoanalysis. The distinction between *Sexualtrieb* and the narrower genital drive was not merely technical, as it allowed Freud to theorize desire as exceeding reproduction, which opened space where fetishism could be seen as continuous with ordinary sexuality rather than as its pathological opposite. In this way, the very vocabulary Freud inherited already contained the seeds of depathologization, for it presupposed a sexual drive that could take diverse and non-reproductive objects without losing its claim to normality.

In *Three Essays*, Freud would build directly on this distinction to develop his own critique of the biological norm of reproduction and position fetishism as key to understanding the broad, non-genital nature of the sexual drive. Thus, Krafft-Ebing's detailed analyses of fetishism—incorporating Binet's insights and emphasizing the object-dependent, physiological, and often non-pathological dimensions of sexual interest—provided Freud with a conceptual framework that would both enable his critique of sexual normativity and challenge his own evolving theory of fetishism.

He further distinguished between the sexual drive, which was a continuous function of the cerebral cortex encompassing emotions, ideas, and impulses, and the genital drive, which was narrowly confined to reproductive physiological processes (1893a, 23). His emphasis on the sexual drive's continuous intensity and its role in producing erotic ideas shaped Freud's subsequent critique of the singular, reproductive aim of sexuality. Krafft-Ebing's detailed focus on fetishist pathology, exploring manifestations of both the sexual and genital drives, underscored the fact that fetishism involving body parts does not exceed the limits of the normal stimulation (1893a, 153), even as pathological fetishism was marked by sexual interest limited exclusively to a specific body part or artificial object.

Krafft-Ebing's work, along with Binet's, thus provided the immediate intellectual context for Freud's riddle of fetishism. Their cumulative insights established fetishism as a phenomenon deeply intertwined with both normal and pathological sexuality, driven by early experiences, and fundamentally dependent on an object. This understanding presented Freud with a complex inheritance. As he prepared to publish his *Three Essays* in 1905, Freud drew heavily on Krafft-Ebing's concepts to radically depathologize perversions and position them within the realm of normal human sexuality. He intended fetishism to serve as a central example for this deconstruction of sexual normativity. But this very deconstruction, paradoxically, would immediately undermine his own attempt to categorize fetishism, and would launch him into decades of conceptual struggle to reconcile fetishism with his evolving theories of perversion and infantile sexuality. The enduring riddle was now fully articulated: it set the stage for Freud's profound and often contradictory engagement with the phenomenon throughout his career.

4. Freud's Clinical Framework: The Neurosis–Perversion Opposition

Krafft-Ebing's clinical concepts of neuro-psychosis and psychoneurosis were foundational to Freud's early psychopathology and influenced his understanding of sexuality's role in mental illness (Krafft-Ebing 1893b). Freud adopted Krafft-Ebing's terminology to theorize neuroses as a defence against sexuality and "perverse impulses," and, initially, fetishism itself was categorized as a perversion within this framework. This reliance enabled Freud to establish a clear opposition: neurosis as a consequence of repressed (or defended against) perverse impulses arising from early sexual experiences. However, as this chapter has detailed, fetishism would relentlessly challenge this neat theoretical distinction, and its complexities undermined Freud's early psychoanalytic equation of neurosis as simply the negative of perversion. Krafft-Ebing's work, while providing the initial scaffolding, ultimately bequeathed the very conceptual tensions that Freud would struggle with for decades as fetishism resisted full integration into his rigid early categories.

In this chapter, we have traced the complex evolution of Freud's early aetiological theory. We have shown how his foundational concept of neurosis as the negative of perversion was shaped by, and then eventually challenged by, the phenomenon of fetishism. Beginning with an analysis of Freud's letters to Wilhelm Fließ, the chapter first establishes Freud's emergent ideas on sexual perversion, which he rooted in childhood seduction and the activation of erogenous zones. These early formulations positioned perversions as expressions of non-repressed sexual impulses, while neuroses were conceptualized as their pathological, repressed counterparts.

It has then been shown how fetishism, from its very first explicit mention in Freud's *Three Essays*, began to destabilize this opposition. While Freud initially used fetishism to critique sexual normativity and define the sexual drive as broader than reproduction, fetishism's intrinsic object-dependence and its nuanced exposed inconsistencies in his theory of object-independent infantile sexuality. By examining Freud's evolving concepts of fantasy, childhood sexual theories, and the nascent idea of castration anxiety during this period, we have seen Freud grappling with how fetishism complicated his initial framework.

Crucially, as Freud increasingly engaged with Krafft-Ebing's clinical concepts, including the intricate relationship between fetishism and masochism, he was forced to confront the limitations of his early neurosis–perversion divide. And so it is that Freud's early theoretical scaffolding, while robust for its time, was ultimately inadequate to fully contain the riddle of fetishism. But this inadequacy was itself productive: fetishism repeatedly destabilized the very categories meant to contain it, showing that the effort to pathologize could generate its own depathologization. For Freud, fetishism was never only a deviant exception but also a theoretical hinge through which psychoanalysis could interrogate the unstable boundary between normality and pathology. In this way, the riddle of fetishism persists, although not as a problem to be solved once and for all. It is instead an enduring tension shaping Freud's thought and continuing even now to animate contemporary debates.

Chapter 3

The Neurotic "Negative": Freud's Early Perversion Theory

Although he did not use the term until 1905, we can trace Freud's interest in fetishism to a letter to Wilhelm Fließ from 6 December 1896. There Freud gives an adult female patient's report about her brother's and father's peculiar sexual compulsion:

> A fragment from my [Freud's] daily experience: One of my patients, in whose history her highly perverse father plays the principal role, has a younger brother who is looked upon as a common scoundrel. [...] [T]he brother told her that when he was 12 years old, his sexual activity consisted in kissing (licking) the feet of his sisters when they were undressing at night. In association, she recovered from her unconscious the memory of a scene in which (at the age of 4) she watched her papa, in the throes of sexual excitement, licking the feet of a wet nurse. (Freud 1985, 213)

Just at this time Freud was developing his theory on the causes of neurosis. This passage reveals that he was focused not only on the female patient's hysterical symptoms but also on the behaviours of the patient's brother and father. This insight, described as "highly perverse," aligns directly with what Freud ([1909a] 1988, 158) began to call "*perversen Fussfetischisten*" ("perverse foot fetishists").

Freud's problem with fetishism began in his 1905 *Three Essays*, when his theory of perversion and infantile sexuality did not allow for a comprehensive, consistent understanding of fetishism. But in the context of his December 1896 letters, his concern relates to sexuality in puberty and adulthood. His key interest in linking the aetiological idea of this strong early sexual impression to his patient's account is the fact that this impression is considered a *premature* confrontation with adult sexuality. It was also a traumatic one: the child witnessed her father's sexual excitement when licking a woman's feet. In this context, Freud's theoretical investigation relates to how different pathologies connect to the moment of an early, traumatic encounter with sexual stimulation, usually involving adult sexuality. Freud categorized this as "seduction." (Freud 1985, 212-3). Thus, neurosis and perversion, at least in this circumstance, are different outcomes of seduction.

The contrast between neurosis and perversion that Freud posits here also reflects a broader conceptual split in his early thinking about pathological development. Whereas neurosis was often framed as a conflict internal to the subject, being rooted in repression, guilt, and the return of the repressed, perversion appeared instead as an outward reorganization of desire around a fixed aim or object. It seemingly had no internal ambivalence. This apparent clarity, however, would not hold for long. Fetishism would soon emerge as a phenomenon that unsettled both sides of the binary and revealed that neurosis and perversion were less opposed than Freud had initially imagined. By introducing ambiguity into categories that had before seemed stable, fetishism exposed the fragility of the boundary between pathology and normality.

In connection with these points, and as we noted in the Introduction, queer and trans perspectives could appreciate the fact that such a division often reinforces normative assumptions about what constitutes psychologically "mature" or "resolvable" desire. From these viewpoints, perversion is marked not only by a difference in sexual *aim* but also by its structural resistance to introspection or change, or to an innate malleability in the first place. And these are features that have historically been projected onto queer and trans lives in pathologizing ways. Freud's early seduction theory, with its emphasis on traumatic adult–child encounters and rigid diagnostic outcomes, risks collapsing diverse forms of sexual subjectivity into a fixed aetiological template. It is precisely this rigidity, however, that would soon be challenged by the problems posed by fetishism. And those happened to be the ones that Freud could not easily resolve through either the neurosis–perversion binary or the seduction hypothesis itself.

Freud's idea about perversion resulting from early sexual stimulation follows a different line of thought than the one he would later develop and publish in 1905: this line says that infantile sexuality ought to be understood from the perspective of perversions. But Freud did not anchor his seduction theory in a broader theory of infantile sexuality; in fact, he simply did not yet possess such a view. He embarked on a proper theory of perversion and infantile sexuality only after encountering problems with his seduction theory. It was then that fetishism emerged as a problem.

1. Freud's Early Aetiology of Neurosis and Perversion

Crucially, at this early juncture, these behaviours posed no theoretical problem for Freud. He viewed them simply as a form of adult sexuality, recognizing that sexual interest in an object (like a woman's feet) might emerge in puberty. The specific conceptual challenge posed by fetishism would crystallize for Freud only after 1905, with the publication of *Three Essays*, when his developing theory of infantile sexuality (which he characterized as objectless) directly conflicted with fetishism's inherent object-dependence. We saw the beginnings of this conflict in the previous chapter.

This early understanding of "perverse" impulses was already integral to Freud's developing theory of neurosis in the 1890s. In the 1896 Fließ letter, he linked these behaviours to his concept of abandoned erogenous zones, or sites of early childhood sexual excitation. These excitations, he theorized, persisted into adulthood as perverse impulses when not defended against, and therefore they contrasted sharply with neurosis, which Freud theorized as resulting from the repression of these very impulses. This initial framework positioned perversion as sexual compulsions arising from unrepressed early experiences, thereby casting neurosis as its conceptual "negative." Freud's exploration here paralleled discussions on sexuality and perversion by Binet and Krafft-Ebing, highlighting the intellectual landscape that would soon bring fetishism's conceptual complexities into sharp focus within his own framework.

Freud's understanding of sexual perversion in the late 1890s centred on urges stemming from the earliest bodily sensations, an animalistic tendency focused on various human orifices. He viewed neuroses as a defensive pathology that actively kept those impulses at bay. In contrast, perversions, as articulated in his January 1897 letter to Fließ, were "the negative" of neuroses, a "remnant of a primeval sexual cult" where "perverse actions… are always the same – meaningful and fashioned according to some pattern" (Freud 1985, 227). This analogy to archaic religious cults, such as those associated with Moloch (Molech) or Astarte, allowed Freud to explore perversions not as pathology, but as vestiges of a more archaic organization of sexuality, encompassing bodily eroticisms and aggressive acts. By situating perversions as survivals from archaic sexual cults, Freud effectively normalized them as part of a universal history of sexuality rather than isolating them as mere diseases. This move collapses the distinction between pathology and culture, because what is classified as abnormal in one register becomes legible as an anthropological constant in another. Fetishism will later intensify this ambiguity because it exemplifies how the pathological label itself can reveal structures that also underlie so-called normal sexual life. In this way, Freud's early formulations already anticipate the instability of the boundary between pathology and depathologization, which we have previously noted in various places.

And, as Michel Foucault (2003) notes, Freud's integration of these non-reproduction-oriented behaviours into classifications of sexual disturbances effectively normalized human sexuality. At this early stage, Freud did not yet conceptualize fetishism as what we might call a distinct "problematic" within his theory; its manifestations were simply examples of this broader, naturally perverse disposition, stemming from these archaic eroticizations.

This oppositional relationship between neurosis (defence/repression) and perversion (unrepressed impulse) became fundamental to Freud's early aetiological psychopathology. He theorized that perversion resulted from the absence of defence against premature sexual experiences in childhood, a time before the psychic apparatus was fully formed; such experiences would lead to a compulsive excess of uninhibited pleasure in adulthood (Freud 1985, 210). This conceptual framing, however, began to break down with the formal introduction of fetishism in *Three Essays* ([1905a] 2016). As Freud attempted to contextualize the phenomenon within this framework, its inherent object-dependence and its later emergence as a defensive process challenged his initial definition of perversion as merely unrepressed impulse. To address these growing inconsistencies, then, Freud increasingly turned to Binet's ideas, particularly those laid out in *Fetishism in Love*; in this appeal, we see his persistent struggle to integrate these complexities into an evolving psychoanalytic theory.

2. *Inherited Concepts: Trauma, Splitting, and Defence in Freud's 1890s Work*

As Freud embarked on theorizing sexual perversions, his primary aim was to understand the aetiology of neurosis, drawing heavily on Krafft-Ebing's classifications and engaging with Binet's and Janet's ideas on psychic phenomena such as splitting. His early work until 1896 progressively refined his concept of sexuality and incorporated new neuropsychological perspectives. This foundational period saw Freud develop core aetiological concepts, including affect, trauma, splitting, defence, seduction, and perversion, which he initially articulated to explain neurosis. As we shall see, though, Freud would later remobilize and rework these very concepts to construct his psychoanalytic theory of fetishism, applying models initially conceived for hysterical splitting to understand broader psychopathological phenomena.

Freud originally intended these aetiological concepts to explain neurosis; later, he applied them to his psychoanalytic theory of fetishism. We shall review each briefly to see how they contribute to his thinking in the years of this "negative" period.

In the 1890s, Freud frequently employs the concept of affect, and especially sexual affect, in his thinking on psychopathology, going so far as to define the psyche itself in affective terms. In 1890, Freud characterizes affect as a psychic state that generates various forms of excitement (Freud 1890, 287–8), assuming that all psychic states possess an affective dimension. He argues further that affects can produce pathological outcomes, such as neurotic symptoms (1890, 285). Shortly thereafter, Freud refines his understanding of affect and sexuality in relation to neurosis, emphasizing distress and fright as key affects underlying neurotic conditions (Freud and Breuer 1893, 84). He also introduces "displacement," or the transposition of affects, as a defensive mechanism central to neurosis (Freud 1894, 58). Freud's conceptualization of affect is particularly important here, as he later explains fetishism through the lens of defence by remobilizing this very concept.

Freud began formulating a psychological theory of neurosis by critiquing and ultimately rejecting heredity as its primary cause. Although initially influenced by Charcot's emphasis on hereditary factors, Freud increasingly challenged this view, shifting his focus towards accidental sexual experiences as central to the development of neuroses. Freud's critique echoed Binet's earlier rejection of heredity ([1888a] 1990, 41), particularly the latter's emphasis on trauma as a non-hereditary cause of pathology. Indeed, Freud drew from and expanded on these ideas, increasingly attributing neurotic symptoms to traumatic sexual experiences. This move already destabilized a purely pathological framework, because it implied that the same accidental impressions shaping neurosis could also structure normal development. Binet had made this point explicitly in his account of fetishism, where chance encounters could generate both pathological fixations and the ordinary attachments of love. Freud thus inherited a model in which trauma and sexual impressions bore a double valence: they were at once clinical disturbances and windows into the mechanisms of psychic growth. Fetishism, as Freud would later realize, condensed this ambiguity in its most striking form.

It is in this light that we can better understand the origins of Freud's theory of trauma. Binet's ideas on fetishism, in particular, already linked sexuality and childhood impressions to outcomes that could appear either pathological or normal. Freud would take up this framework when stipulating that traumatic childhood experiences could lead to neurotic symptoms later in life. The shift brought psychological concepts such as memory, representational conflict, defence, repression, and especially the notion of "afterwardsness" (Freud and Breuer 1895, 169) to the forefront of Freud's theorization of neurosis. Although hereditary factors were never fully dismissed, they became less important as Freud emphasized psychological explanations more and more.

To understand the origins of Freud's theory of trauma, we must first recall that Binet's ideas on fetishism precede the connection Freud stipulated between sexuality and traumatic childhood experiences that would lead to neurotic symptoms later in life. The idea first appears in Binet's *Fetishism in Love* (1888a, 18–9, 51–4), and although Freud and Breuer refer to Binet in the same works where they theorize about this same idea, they do not refer to Binet nor to his *Fetishism*. But it is crucial to recognize that Freud, in applying the framework he used for the aetiology of neurosis to fetishism, came to appropriate Binet's ideas in his own framing of trauma.

Freud and Breuer describe a clear causal link between hysterical symptoms and precipitating traumatic events, and they also emphasize that accidental occurrences play a significant role in the development of hysteria. They argue, however, that it is not the traumatic event itself but the distressing affects (particularly fright, anxiety, shame, and physical pain) that directly trigger illness. Freud and Breuer underscore fright (*Schreckaffekt*) as particularly central, and so position psychic trauma as the primary factor in traumatic hysteria. This trauma, often connected symbolically to the precipitating event, may consist of a single powerful experience or multiple partial experiences. These shape not only the emergence but also the persistence of symptoms. Freud's early adoption of Binet's concept of intense sexual experiences influenced his theorization significantly here; throughout the 1890s, he reinterpreted trauma as fundamentally *affective*. This led him later to explain fetishism in terms of affective trauma, particularly through notions of "frightening away" (*Abschreckung*) experiences (1914a [1974], 244) and the "frightening affect" (*Schreckwirkung*) (1940b, 256).

Far and away the most significant reflection of Binet's influence in Freud's early aetiological thinking, however, is the concept of splitting, which we have seen before. In this case, though, Freud and Breuer repurposed the concept.

In the 1890s, Freud gradually bolsters his arguments about splitting by using the notion of ego defence. Just as Binet treats splitting in hysteria in the work *The Alterations of Personality* (1892), Freud in 1895 explores the assumption that the psyche is divided rather than unified. Freud and Breuer also investigate the formation of a second personality as a result of splitting (Freud and Breuer 1895f, 287), thus linking the different strata of the ego to the notion of personality itself (1895f, 299). Indeed, in Freud's works of the 1890s, splitting implies the formation of a psychic group separated from the ego (Freud and Breuer 1895, 133). This formation indicates different levels of functioning and different sets of representations and memories. Already here we can see how splitting complicates the distinction between normal and pathological psychic life. Freud does not treat splitting as degeneration or weakness, but rather as an active defence available to a strong ego; it is a structural capacity of the psyche rather than a mere symptom of illness. This means that what might first appear as an abnormal mechanism is in fact constitutive of psychic functioning more broadly. Fetishism would later embody this ambiguity. It becomes intelligible to Freud precisely as an instance in which such structural duplicity is concentrated, but it cannot be confined to a pathological register alone.

In this light, Freud and Breuer's account appears consistent with Binet's framing of "doubling," because splitting is not a defect of psychic synthesis but rather a fundamental element of mental life that becomes especially visible in hysteria (1893a, 12). They describe splitting as resulting from hysterical patients' efforts to suppress or repress distressing memories and associated traumatic affects. Unlike Janet and others who view splitting as evidence of psychic degeneration or ego weakness, Freud and Breuer emphasize the ego's active strength in employing defensive mechanisms. In the 1890s, however, Freud did not yet connect splitting with perversion or fetishism, as his initial theorization focused primarily on hysteria. Only later, in his final theory of psychopathology, did Freud explicitly link splitting to fetishism, when he was able to conceptualize fetishism as a model of defensive processes. We shall explore this point later. By contrast, Lacan incorporated fetishism as a perversion directly into his psychoanalytic framework from the outset, by building on Binet's concept of doubling.

We now turn to *defence*. From 1893 to 1895, Freud and Breuer use the terms "suppression" and "repression" interchangeably with "defence," without defining them precisely (Strachey 1962, 10). They regard these processes as intentional responses by the patient. Splitting, in their account, occurs when traumatic memories reach a certain intensity and are excluded from associative processes, leading to a dissociation of consciousness. Freud and Breuer also link splitting to sexual content and the onset of puberty (Freud and Breuer 1895, 245–6).

In the cases Freud examined, sexual life frequently appeared as the source of neurotic symptoms, which he came to understand as defensive in nature. He argued that sexual excitation, when disrupted, is transposed into neurotic symptoms. As he put it, "a perpetual defence is going on against sexual ideas that are continually coming up afresh – a piece of work … which has not yet come to completion" (Freud 1894, 53–4). For Freud, the defence mechanism serves to ward off morally troubling sexual representations, often rooted in real experience (Freud 1894, 47).

Furthermore, he states that sexual experiences and sensations (*sexuelles Erleben und Empfinden*) cause the emergence of incompatible representations (Freud 1894, 52). He writes:

> In all of the cases that I have analysed, it was the subject's sexual life that gave rise to a distressing effect of precisely the same quality as that attached to his obsession. Theoretically, it is not impossible that this effect should sometimes arise in other fields. I can only report that so far, I have not come across any other origin. Moreover, it is easy to see that it is precisely *sexual life* that brings with it the most copious occasions for the emergence of incompatible ideas. (Freud 1894, 52)

Freud connects the splitting of consciousness to other forms of psychopathology by grounding it in psychological rather than hereditary causes, and specifically in the ego's attempt to avoid incompatible representations. He links this process to both obsessional neurosis and hallucinatory psychosis (Freud 1894, 48–9). In *Studies on Hysteria* (1895), Freud and Breuer continue their engagement with Binet and Janet's ideas, arguing that the distressing representations behind splitting are sexual in nature. These representations stem from early, pre-sexual experiences that initially have no traumatic effect but later gain traumatic force as memories (Freud and Breuer 1895, 133). Freud suggests that the splitting off of psychic material may be a normal feature of adolescent development, but its later return through recollection creates frequent potential for psychic disturbance (1895, 134).

Freud and Breuer investigate the defence process and its relation to sexuality through clinical case studies. They trace the hysterical mechanism Freud had outlined in 1894, and argue that while the sexual needs of hysterical patients are no greater than those of healthy individuals, these patients fall ill precisely because of their struggle against such needs – a result exactly of their defence against sexuality (Freud and Breuer 1895, 247). Freud thus distinguishes between affect as a brief, reactive state triggered by external stimuli and neurosis as a sustained response to internal excitation, which functions as a constant force (*konstante Kraft*) (Freud 1895b, 112). This shift in emphasis sets the stage for his later engagement with the concept of perversion.

Freud's early writings reflect a sustained effort to understand persistent somatic sexual excitation, and its relation to neuroses, in both men and women (1895b, 108–9, 115). He introduces terms such as "sexual libido" (*sexuellen Libido*), which he defines as the psychic manifestation of bodily sexual pleasure (Freud 1895b, 107), as well as "genital drive" (*Geschlechtstrieb*) and "sexual drive" (*Sexualtrieb*), but without clearly defining either (1895b, 108–9). These conceptual explorations highlight Freud's early alignment with Krafft-Ebing's views and his emerging interest in perversion. Freud also investigated sexuality in neurological terms, as seen in his *Project for a Scientific Psychology* (1895e), where he links pathological defence to sexual processes (1895e, 409–10). In this context he sketches an early model of the symbol-and-substitution process by an example of fetishism. Notably, before the *Three Essays*, Freud saw no major theoretical difficulty with fetishism; it was only after 1905 that the complexities of symbolic substitution in fetishism demanded closer scrutiny.

In *Project for a Scientific Psychology*, Freud, despite not yet using the term "fetish," illustrates normal symbol formation through the example of a knight who fights for a lady's glove. The knight understands that the glove's significance lies in its association with the woman, and his reverence (*Verehrung*) for the glove does not prevent him from recognizing or serving the lady in other ways. By contrast, hysterical symbols function differently: they replace rather than represent. Freud explains that when a hysterical patient reacts emotionally to a recalled element of an event, the patient is unaware that this response stems from its association with a broader, distressing memory (Freud 1895e, 407). In such cases the symbol fully displaces the original content.

Freud then presents fetishism as a normal model of symbolization and substitution – an idea already taking shape in 1895. At this stage, Freud does not yet see fetishism as pathological; rather, he treats it as a useful conceptual model. This moment is striking because fetishism here appears not as a deviation but rather as a paradigm for understanding how symbols function in ordinary psychic life. Freud treats the knight's glove and the fetish object as operating through the same mechanism of substitution, and so he collapses the boundary between normal and pathological processes. Only later would he reclassify fetishism as a specific perversion, but this early framing already reveals the ambivalence that defines his engagement with the phenomenon. Fetishism serves simultaneously as pathology and as a model of psychic function, which demonstrates a theme we have encountered a number of times now, about the continual destabilization of the line between pathology and depathologization.

As later arguments will show, Freud deepens this view through his engagement with Binet, initially aligning fetishist symbolization with hysteria and eventually developing a more specific account of symbolization and substitution in fetishism. This culminates in his evolution of Binet's theories of defence and trauma.

It is precisely against this background that Freud first began to introduce the broader concept of perversion through his theorization of sexuality's role in neurosis. Undefined at first, perversion was linked to acts of sexual stimulation involving children. This is what Freud, in his correspondence with Fließ, called "sexual seduction" (Freud 1896c, 207–8; 1985, 342). At this stage he viewed neurosis as one possible consequence of such early experiences, with perversion as another. Freud proposed that premature sexual stimulation in childhood, particularly when not followed by repression or guilt after puberty, could lead to perversion (Freud 1985, 163). He claimed that beneath every case of hysteria lay one or more early sexual experiences, recoverable through psychoanalysis, and saw this as a foundational discovery in neuropathology (Freud 1896c, 203). The one is the negative of the other, which Freud took as a major advance in understanding.

Freud argued that childhood seduction occurs during a phase of sexual immaturity, with its effects surfacing only after puberty, when the memory of the experience produces "unpleasure" and defensive symptoms (Freud 1896a, 1896b, 1896c). This model shaped his later theorization of fetishism, which he traced to early seduction and understood as a defensive response. While explicit references to Binet fade in these texts, that influence persists in Freud's terminology: terms such as "sexual impressions," "primary pathogenic impressions," and "original impressions" echo Binet's emphasis on early imprinting.

Freud also associated perversion with the lasting effects of such impressions, in line with Binet's aetiological thinking. But Freud's theory began to shift when he questioned whether the seduction events reported by his patients had actually occurred. The idea that children could experience pleasure from seduction, particularly in cases of obsessional neurosis, led him to doubt the literal truth of these memories and to reinterpret them as fantasies (Freud 1985, 239, 261). This turn introduced new elements into his framework, such as fantasy, impulse, infantile sexuality, and erogenous zones, which would become central to his later efforts to theorize fetishism.

This section has traced how Freud's early work on affect, trauma, splitting, and defence, which were all initially developed to explain neurosis, laid the conceptual groundwork for his later theory of fetishism. By drawing on the ideas of his predecessors, Freud adapted existing models of psychological conflict and symbolic substitution to shift gradually away from hereditary explanations to a dynamic theory rooted in sexuality and psychic defence. While Freud began by framing fetishism as a normal process of symbolization, he increasingly recast it as a pathological outcome of unresolved childhood experiences. His evolving views on seduction, trauma, and fantasy reveal the deep influence of Binet's thinking, even where explicit references faded. Together, these developments mark the transformation of concepts first designed for hysteria into foundational tools for theorizing fetishism.

3. The Nascent "Riddle": Fetishism's Challenge to Freud's Early Framework

When Freud first used the term *perversion*, it carried strong moral overtones, often describing deviant character traits or misconduct in the context of hysteria – what he called "moral perversion," "perversion of the will," or "perversion of character" (1888b, 52; 1892–3, 123–7). These early usages aligned with broader medical and moral discourses of *degeneration*, and echoed themes already present in Binet's *The Alterations of Personality* (1892). However, by the mid-1890s, Freud began to move away from this moral framework. His correspondence with Fließ in 1896–7 marks a turning point, as he began to redefine perversion *biologically*: as the persistence of infantile sexual impulses in adulthood. He was thereby able to distinguish it from Krafft-Ebing's concept of *perversity*, which emphasized immoral acts. Freud's goal was not to pathologize immoral conduct but rather to trace perversion to structural patterns in human sexuality. This distinction, inherited from Krafft-Ebing, was decisive. By separating perversion from perversity, Freud broke the direct link between sexual non-conformity and moral condemnation. The move did not amount to a wholesale celebration of sexual diversity, but it did introduce depathologization as a structural possibility: if perversion was to be explained as a developmental outcome rather than an immoral vice, then its analysis had to be conducted on psychological rather than moral grounds. Fetishism, as Freud would soon recognize, exemplifies this shift. It was not a question of criminality or immorality, but rather one of understanding how sexuality itself resists simple categorization into normal and abnormal forms. In so doing, he also set aside Krafft-Ebing's nosographic model, which grounded psychoneuroses in constitutional weakness, and instead pursued a developmental account of perversion rooted in the dynamics of pleasure, repression, and psychic conflict.

Freud, then, began this work in early 1896, when he outlined the possible outcomes of sexual stimulation in childhood. According to Freud, perversions refer to infantile sexual patterns of pleasure that endure in adulthood in the form of a compulsion without repression (Freud 1985, 209–10). But Freud is not always consistent with terms here, and so we face the question of how his later ideas concerning the association between perversion and immorality may have changed. These later developments relate to his exploration of sexuality, where he considers perversion to be the permanence of infantile patterns of sexuality in adulthood (Freud 1985, 209–10).

In 1905, Freud introduced the idea of fetishism to argue that childhood patterns of perverse sexual arousal characterize normal sexuality in adulthood. At this stage, Freud granted fetishism the status of unrepressed, impulsive sexual behaviour, as he had initially characterized perversion. The goal of differentiating *perversion* from *perversity* is also crucial, given that it underlies the contrasts between Freud's and Lacan's theories of fetishism. Contrary to Freud's theory, Lacan's view of fetishism and perversion departs from theories on the constitution of perversity as immorality.

According to Freud, there can be no repression of sexual experiences before the age of four, given that the psychic apparatus required to do so has not yet developed sufficiently prior to that time (1985, 209). In perversion, the defence against premature sexual experiences does not take place before the development of the psychic apparatus; alternatively, it may not take place at all. He writes, "Another consequence of premature sexual experiences is perversion, of which the determinant seems to be that defence either does not occur before the psychic apparatus is completed or it does not occur at all" (Freud 1985, 210).

When recalled later, these premature sexual experiences generate displeasure in some people – bringing on normal repressive forces – but pathological defence symptoms in others. They also persist as a sexual compulsion in some individuals, understood as perversion. Indeed, pathological defence is determined by repression. Repression, in turn, occurs only based on traces of memory from an earlier stage; these traces have not yet been "translated" into the next phase of development. Ultimately the process leads to the emergence of sexual psychoneuroses, such as hysteria, obsessional neurosis, and paranoia. Freud concludes that "hysteria is, in fact, not repudiated sexuality but rather, it is a repudiated perversion" (1985, 212). This striking formulation makes the porousness of Freud's categories unmistakable. If hysteria is nothing other than repudiated perversion, then the boundary between neurosis and perversion collapses into a matter of degree or perspective. What appears pathological in one register reappears as the negative form of the other. In this sense, Freud's own language undermines the stability of the neurosis–perversion binary, foreshadowing the difficulties fetishism would pose for his attempts to preserve such categorical distinctions.

This aetiological reasoning grounded Freud's theory about the relationship of opposition between neurosis and fetishism. Thus, while perversions refer to the persistence of infantile sexual patterns in adulthood as *compulsions*, neuroses are linked to defences (repression) *against* these patterns in the form of *symptoms*. This idea is crucial; we must understand it to account for the difficulties fetishism would later pose for Freud's concept of perversion. As time goes on for Freud, the phenomenon of fetishism challenges this fundamental opposition between neurosis and perversion.

There are a few other points to discuss in connection with this challenge. We shall finish this section with these points.

Freud's growing emphasis on biology in his theory of perversion led him to adopt and revise elements from Krafft-Ebing's work, particularly the idea that psychoneuroses stem from innate constitutional factors. One key development was Freud's theory of abandoned erogenous zones, which are regions of the infant body capable of producing sexual pleasure but that are later subjected to repression. This marked a turning point in Freud's understanding of infantile sexuality: he came to see sexual impulses in early infancy as stronger and more complex than previously assumed, and began to interpret early sexual experiences as normal developmental events rather than purely traumatic ones (Freud 1985, 212, 255, 274). In 1897, Freud extended this idea further by linking perversions to persistent erotic sensations associated with bodily excretions. He focused in particular on olfactory and gustatory pleasures tied to urine, faeces, and the body's surface (Freud 1985, 223). These observations closely echo earlier work by Binet and Krafft-Ebing, and reflect Freud's broader argument that perversions have a phylogenetic and even animal character. He emphasized the anus, mouth, and throat as sites of sexual excitation in both humans and animals, and suggested that the emergence of disgust and repression, linked to evolutionary changes such as upright posture, marks the shift to "normal" development.

Perversions, then, result when these zones are *not* abandoned or repressed. While Freud did not claim a one-to-one correspondence between infantile sexual behaviour and adult perversion, this framework laid the foundation for the difficulties he would soon face when attempting to locate fetishism within his theory of sexual development.

Freud's concept of repressive forces, especially disgust, also emerged in the late 1890s as a key mechanism for sexual development. They became central to his theory of perversion. He saw reactions such as disgust, shame, and morality as normal responses to sexual stimuli, rooted in both psychological and evolutionary development (Freud 1985, 163–4). Phylogenetic shifts, he argued, triggered the abandonment of erogenous zones and the emergence of higher affective responses, such as disgust. Freud's reasoning here makes explicit the instability of moralizing distinctions. As Blass (2017, 24) emphasizes, disgust and shame are not moral categories but organic reaction-formations, onto which cultural codes of normality are later grafted. What one generation condemns as "disgusting" may become the ordinary practice of another.

This contingency suggests that Freud's analysis of disgust does more than relativize cultural taboos. It undermines the idea that stable boundaries can be drawn between pathological and non-pathological sexuality. If disgust itself varies historically and socially, then the clinical categories on which it is built cannot claim fixed validity. Freud thus found himself relying on a criterion that was at once indispensable and unstable, a sign of how the mechanisms he sought for classification already blurred the lines they were meant to police.

For Freud, the abandonment of erogenous zones formed the developmental basis for *repression*, which could then result in either neurosis or perversion. Adapting Krafft-Ebing's idea that perversions involve the overcoming of disgust, Freud instead used disgust as a clinical marker for both neurosis and perversion, which for him were both outcomes of failed or incomplete repression (Freud 1985, 280–1). As we shall see, though, Freud's later theory of fetishism disrupts this model, as fetishism eludes a disgust-based framework.

In this chapter, we have seen how Freud's early theory of neurosis and perversion emerged through his engagements with affect, trauma, defence, and sexual development. These concepts, shaped in dialogue with figures including Binet, Krafft-Ebing, and Janet, initially served to explain neurosis, with perversion conceived as its conceptual "negative": an expression of unrepressed, persistent infantile sexuality. Within this framework, fetishism appeared to pose no special difficulty. Freud regarded it as one among many perverse outcomes of seduction or developmental arrest. This was a result entirely understandable within the broader structure of early sexual impressions and abandoned erogenous zones.

But as Freud's thinking evolved, fetishism began to exceed the bounds of this early system. Its resistance to repression, its symbolic structure, its compatibility with both pathology and "normal" sexual life – these features rendered fetishism increasingly anomalous. The very concepts that had once clarified its origins now struggled to contain it. Freud returned repeatedly to the tools developed in this early period, especially Binet's work on splitting and symbolic fixation, in an effort to resolve what became, for him, a persistent conceptual crisis. Fetishism thus transformed from a subclass of perversion into a riddle: one that disrupted the coherence of Freud's model of sexuality and compelled him to rework its foundations. This disruption is also what makes fetishism central to the second major theme of this book. Freud's efforts to classify it as a perversion continually generated the conditions for its depathologization: the very features that marked it as "abnormal" also revealed structures that underlie so-called "normal" sexuality. Fetishism therefore functions as both a clinical anomaly and a theoretical contact point, as it exposes how fragile the boundary might be between pathology and normativity.

In closing this chapter, we can already see how Freud's confrontation with fetishism ties his historical-theoretical elaborations to his ongoing struggle with the unstable line between pathologization and depathologization.

The next chapter traces how this riddle takes centre stage in Freud's *Three Essays on the Theory of Sexuality*, where fetishism ceases to be a peripheral example and becomes a pressure point for the entire theory.

Chapter 4

The Initial Confrontation: Fetishism in Freud's Three Essays and Early Revisions (1905–8)

The previous chapter traced how Freud's early theories of neurosis and perversion, rooted in trauma, repression, and the persistence of infantile sexual impressions, laid the conceptual groundwork for his emerging understanding of fetishism. In that context, fetishism appeared relatively unproblematic: it could be situated within the larger structure of unrepressed infantile sexuality and explained in terms of early impressions or failures of repression. But with the publication of *Three Essays on the Theory of Sexuality* in 1905, this apparent coherence began to unravel.

In introducing a new developmental model of sexuality – one that emphasized objectless drives, autoeroticism, and the eventual organization of perversions into a "normal" adult sexual trajectory – Freud inadvertently destabilized the very conceptual framework that had previously made fetishism intelligible. The phenomenon no longer fit cleanly into the oppositional structure Freud had drawn between neurosis and perversion. Its persistent attachment to specific objects as well as its symbolic nature, to say nothing of its connections to pathological and normative sexual development, posed immediate theoretical challenges.

It is important to recognize, however, that the 1905 edition of the *Three Essays* has long been a "missing object" in Freud studies, overshadowed by the later 1924 version that introduced Oedipal and developmental materials not present in the original text. The 1905 text was radically different: it theorized infantile sexuality in non-Oedipal, polymorphous, and autoerotic terms, treating pathology not as a deviation but rather as a magnification of universal tendencies. Hysteria, in particular, became for Freud a "pathoanalysis" of sexuality itself and showed how the study of symptoms revealed the very structures of ordinary sexual life (Westerink and Van Haute 2016, xxxvii). Read in this light, the *Three Essays* already deconstructs the normal/pathological binary dominating nineteenth-century psychiatry. Fetishism, which Freud identifies here as a peculiar but persistent riddle, will become the privileged site at which this destabilization is most apparent.

This chapter, then, examines Freud's initial attempts to respond to the riddle's challenges in the years immediately following the publication of *Three Essays*. It argues that from 1905 to 1909, Freud began to reframe fetishism not as a straightforward perversion but rather as a phenomenon that exposed deeper structural tensions in his theory. This reorganization took place primarily around the notions of object-choice, repression, fantasy, and infantile sexual theories. Drawing heavily once again on Binet's work on external impressions and symbolic displacement, Freud began to shift away from models of unrepressed perversion towards frameworks grounded in internal conflict and developmental trauma. As we shall see, this period marks the beginning of a long and ultimately unresolved struggle to account for fetishism's theoretical excess as what Freud would come to describe, more and more, as a persistent riddle.

1. Fetishism and the Breakdown of Freud's 1905 Framework

In *Three Essays*, Freud finally sets forth a theory of human sexuality (to situate the discussion in the broader context of Freud scholarship, reference is made to the work's first edition.). We can read this theory as a critique of both sexual normativity and nineteenth-century theories of sexual psychopathology. *Three Essays* documents the evolution of more than ten years of Freud's thought on the aetiology of neurosis; for the first time, he presents human sexuality as the *cause* of neuroses. This point leads to the assumption that neurosis is the negative of perversion. In 1905, while Freud was determined to explore human sexuality, his overarching goal was to understand that cause.

Three Essays also uses the term "fetishism" for the first time. He opens the discussion by criticizing the psychiatric conceptualization of fetishism as a pathology, or a sexual perversion. The phenomenon of fetishism itself, however, works right away to destabilize Freud's own concept of perversion.

In this regard, Freud came to identify three specific problems. First, he treats the aetiological theory of fetishism as an exception. Second, he clearly acknowledges the difficulty of classifying fetishism, according to the book's own criteria, as a sexual deviation. Third, he admits that it is not possible to posit fetishism as the *positive* of neurosis; this admission occurs on Freud's first mention of neurosis as perversion's negative.

These difficulties should not be seen merely as technical obstacles in Freud's classification but rather as symptoms of fetishism's refusal to remain within the framework of pathology. As Van Haute and Westerink (2021) emphasize, Freud in 1905 began not with the "normal" but with the so-called perversions as his point of departure for conceptualizing sexuality, thereby overturning the normative order of psychiatry. Fetishism made this reversal most explicit, as its resistance to being neatly assimilated revealed how Freud's own theory blurred the boundary between normality and abnormality. This is why, as others have noted (Van Haute and Westerink 2016, xviii–xxi), later interpolations into the *Three Essays* attempted to stabilize fetishism through Oedipal and developmental narratives. But these were revisions that retrospectively imposed a framework of normativity absent from the original 1905 text.

In the text's original form, the overarching strategy for theorizing about perversions relies on his understanding of the notion of a biological norm. That notion tended to presuppose an unbreakable bond between the sexual drive and its *object*. Here Freud is engaging directly with contemporaneous medical thought on sexuality, on its classifications, and on its concepts. He begins with the notion of a sexual drive and then focuses on the four main types of sexual perversion: sadism, masochism, fetishism, and inversion (homosexuality). He criticizes the view of a binding link between the sexual drive and its object. As a result, and given that Freud studies the human sexual drive in terms of its various sexual aims and objects, his conception of fetishism ends up being essential to his argument. He further states that in most normal sexual processes, one can detect elements that might or will lead to perversions.

In the first essay, "The Sexual Aberrations," Freud begins by exploring features of the sexual drive in sexual maturity, perversion, normal adult sexual life, and neurosis. In the second, "Infantile Sexuality," he characterizes the namesake phenomenon and argues that it develops *perversely*, that is, as both polymorphous and perverse. He also claims that infantile sexuality is *objectless*. Finally, he discusses the role of the changing sexual drive during puberty ([1905a] 2016, 61). In these discussions, we can see the problems that the riddle of fetishism would pose for him.

Indeed, Freud closes the first essay by summarizing his view on the sexual drive, normality, neurosis, perversion, and infantile sexuality. He confesses that fetishism had already appealed to him within his broader theoretical undertaking in 1905:

> Thus, the extraordinarily wide distribution of the perversions impels us to suppose that the disposition to perversions is itself nothing rare and special, but it is bound to form a part of what passes for the normal condition. It is, as we have seen, debatable whether the perversions go back to innate conditions or if they arise as a result of chance experiences as Binet has shown for the case of fetishism. The conclusion now presents itself to us that there is indeed something innate lying at the basis of the perversions but that it is something innate in all human beings, though as a disposition it may vary in its intensity and may lie dormant, waiting to be brought to the fore by life experiences. It concerns the innate, constitutional roots of the sexual drive. (Freud [1905a] 2016, 32)

This passage reveals that Freud took Binet's aetiological theory of fetishism as an exception; it was a contrast to his own explanation, which he based on his exploration of sexuality and perversions.

In 1905, in the course of exploring the innate sexual disposition towards perversions, Freud discusses the constitutional roots of the sexual drive in terms of partial drives and erogenous zones and the part they play in perversion ([1905a] 2016, 29). Freud argues that the tendency towards perversion is connected to the pervasiveness of a particular erogenous zone or a partial drive. This connection hinges on the perverse disposition (*perversen Veranlagung*) of human sexuality (Freud, [1905a] 2016, 31). However, in the first edition of his *Three Essays*, Freud does not explain which infantile constitutional roots of the sexual drive, partial drive, or erogenous zone constitute the innate disposition that explains fetishism.

As he traces the sexual drive's development, the second essay turns to the sexual life of children to determine the origin of perversion and neurosis and to explore what constitutes normal sex life in infant sexuality. Freud describes the notions of partial drives and erogenous zones; he determines that the general human disposition towards perversions, to which he ascribes the human sexual drive, is sometimes observed in childhood as non-functional sexuality and non-genital pleasure-seeking. It is in this context that he writes:

> It would then turn out that sexual excitation in children springs from a multiplicity of sources. Satisfaction arises first and foremost from the appropriate sensory excitation of what we have described as erogenous zones; any part of the skin and any sense organ could probably function as an erogenous zone [...] The excitations from all these sources would not yet be combined at that stage, but it would seem that each follows

> its own separate aim, which is merely the attainment of a certain sort of pleasure. In childhood, therefore, the sexual drive is without an object, that is, autoerotic. (Freud 1905a [2016], 82)

Here we see an inconsistency with Binet's model of fetishism, which proposes that it results from chance events. Freud argues that, in childhood, the sexual drive exists without an object, whereas Binet's idea of childhood impressions requires an object. This contrast becomes more and more evident as *Three Essays* progresses, and later Freud distanced his theory of fetishism from the idea of an innate polymorphous disposition. We shall return to some of these points both in this chapter and later.

In this light, we see Freud collapsing the distinction between perversion and normality, because the very features psychiatrists classified as pathological prove to be constitutive of sexuality as such. As Westerink (2017, 33) notes, Freud sharpened this point with deliberately provocative examples, such as describing kissing as a "perverse" act, even though it is celebrated in ordinary love. What counts as normal or abnormal is thus revealed to be a matter of cultural convention rather than medical essence. Similarly, Freud's insistence on autoeroticism, exemplified by sensual sucking as the paradigm of infantile sexuality, undermined functionalist definitions of sexuality that tied its value to reproduction (Van Haute and Westerink 2016, xliii). In these moments, the *Three Essays* make explicit what is a central theme of this book: Freud's encounter with fetishism does not simply pathologize sexual difference but destabilizes the boundary between pathology and normativity.

In light of this contrast with Binet, it is notable that *Three Essays* does not focus on the fetish object's formation. Freud addresses that object in the third essay only, in the course of explaining puberty transformations. There he explains how, at the start of puberty, sexuality becomes directed towards an object in the psychological sphere. Freud thus assumes that the oral autoerotic infantile sexual pleasure, once uncoupled from the act of ingesting food, prepares newly pubescent children to choose an object that may restore the original lost bliss. But he does not explain how this works.

In connection with this object focus, Freud claims that a sexual disposition exists in infancy. He calls it the "polymorphously perverse disposition" (*polymorph perverse Anlage*) and assumes that children can experience sexual pleasure in erogenous zones (1905a [2016], 51, 82). This means that the polymorphous-perverse aspect of infantile sexuality is a given disposition of the sexual drive; and so, according to Freud, the seeds of all perversions can be found in children.

At this point, however, there is yet another inconsistency. He has not established a link between sexual deviance, as categorized in the book, and infantile sexuality. In *Three Essays*, fetishism and other perversions do not constitute clear clinical evidence of perverse polymorphous infantile sexuality. In 1905, after all, Freud had not shown that something like infantile fetishism existed.

Another challenge from fetishism is that of showing it to be the opposite of neurosis. As we have seen, Freud's model of perversions still depends on the non-repressed sexual content stemming from erogenous zones. In *Three Essays*, however, Freud claims that perversions result from the insufficient *repression* of the innate disposition, which is found in the sexual drive's innate constitutional roots. In contrast to neurosis, then, perversion, including fetishism, is not seen as a neurotic repressed defensive structure. More generally, rather, perversions are attributable to fixations on specific kinds of pleasure. Freud suggests that all variations on the listed perversions present in the sexual drive of neurotics.

But in this work Freud does *not* show how an erogenous zone or the unconscious aspect of neurosis relates to fetishism. As a result, even when Freud was dealing only with his fledgling theory of perversion in 1905, fetishism could still defy the oppositional relationship between neurosis and perversion. Freud was not unaware of this: "Among the unconscious trains of thought found in neuroses, there is nothing corresponding to a tendency to fetishism" (Freud [1905a] 2016, 28). But this exclusion exposes the fragility of Freud's binary. If hysteria provided him with a model in which pathology magnified universal psychic tendencies, fetishism functioned as a limit case that made the overlap between neurosis and perversion unavoidable. Hysteria showed Freud that the mechanisms of illness were continuous with the mechanisms of ordinary psychic life. Fetishism sharpened the point by refusing to conform, as it could not be neatly assimilated as either the "positive" of neurosis or a deviation entirely outside it. In this way, fetishism crystallizes the tension at the heart of Freud's project – a tension between pathologization and depathologization.

In various of its aspects, therefore, fetishism challenged Freud in 1905. What, exactly, is pathological about it? How does it relate to neurosis and perversion? Unlike neurosis, which causes the individual to suffer, the fetishist perversion does not induce suffering. So, what is a theory to do with it?

The problem is compounded as fetishism also defies categorization in other ways. In his study of perversions in *Three Essays*, Freud introduces the technical terms "sexual object" and "sexual aim" to describe and conceptualize deviations with respect to "normal" human sexuality. He writes that "scientifically considered experience will show us numerous deviations in terms of both the sexual object and sexual aim whose relation to the accepted norm requires thorough investigation" (Freud [1905a] 2016, 1).

Freud's conceptualization of "sexual object" and "sexual aim" thus allow him to theorize that the sexual drive is a disposition that can bypass the aim of copulation; that is, it can *reject* the *normative* function of reproduction. He comments: "But even in the most normal sexual process, we may detect some elements whose development would lead to those aberrations that have been described as perversions" ([1905a] 2016, 12–13). Note, though, that when Freud uses fetishism to prove the point, this conflict has not gone away. He concludes by admitting that the concept of fetishism complicates the classifications given in these technical terms. This leads to the problem of whether his theory of perversion allows human sexuality to be understood without reference to a sexual object. It is the riddle of fetishism, confronted time and time again.

In response, Freud asserts that particular facts of normal sexuality show that, initially at least, sexuality is not directed towards a specific object or an innate aim. Then, after discussing deviations towards sexual objects, he concludes by refuting the existence of a close connection between the sexual drive and the sexual object. According to Freud, in fact, the regularity in normal sexual configurations, where sexual drives orient around a specific object, is only an *apparent* correspondence (Freud 1905a [2016], 12).

But this appears only to kick the can down the road a bit. If the object is not essential to the sexual drive, then how can we discuss fetishist *perversion*, when the latter intrinsically involves an object?

Freud introduces fetishism in *Three Essays* under the heading "Unsuitable Substitutes for the Sexual Object," presenting it as an aberration that resists classification within his new technical terms. While he officially lists fetishism as a deviation from the sexual *aim*, he concedes that it would have made more sense to treat it as a deviation from the sexual *object* – because the fetish, by definition, centres on an inappropriate or symbolic object of desire (Freud 1905a [2016], 16). This uncertainty reflects Freud's broader theoretical difficulty: even as he insists that the sexual drive is independent of any inherent object or aim, fetishism depends precisely on object-specific fixation. He attempts to reconcile this tension by linking fetishism to "sexual overvaluation" and treating it as evidence that the sexual drive can abandon its reproductive aim while still investing in substitute objects. In this way, Freud casts fetishism not as an anomaly, but rather as proof that perversions help to reveal the flexibility, as well as the instability, of the sexual drive itself.

To support this claim, Freud emphasizes the continuity between perversions and normal sexuality. Like Binet and Krafft-Ebing before him, he argues that the very features that define fetishism, such as an interest in non-genital body parts, symbolic objects, or sensory associations, also appear within "normal" adult sexual behaviour. Concepts such as "anatomical extensions" and "sexual overvaluation" serve to bridge the gap: they allow Freud to frame fetishism as an exaggerated version of tendencies already present in normative sexuality (Freud [1905a] 2016, 13–16). But while this move offers a partial resolution, it also reinforces the riddle. Fetishism cannot be cleanly located as either deviation or norm, perversion or neurotic symptom. Instead, it exposes a fault line in Freud's theory. He attempts to manage it here, but it will continue to widen in the years ahead.

This ambivalence is not incidental but structural. By treating fetishism as both a deviation and a normal extension of sexuality, Freud collapses the criteria by which psychiatry sought to distinguish pathology from normativity at all. What makes fetishism so troublesome for Freud is precisely what makes it central for our analysis here. It demonstrates how efforts to pathologize sexuality tend, in one way or another, towards their own depathologization. At least in these early years, fetishism functions less as an exception to Freud's theory than as the point where we butt up against its deeper contradictions.

Freud's concept of anatomical extensions includes excitations and the activities of partial drives, which are neither purely genital nor purely copulative. Indeed, he claims that anatomical extensions are used in all normal sexual foreplay. The introduction of fetishism therefore follows Freud's discussion in connecting elements found in perversions and those in a normal sexual life. Freud highlights elements of the normal sexual process developed in perversions as preliminary sexual aims. Examples include pleasurable activities such as touching, looking, and kissing. He notes that these activities have a high sexual value in normal sexual life, and the body parts involved therein do not belong to the genital apparatus.

Seen from the perspective of anatomical extensions, Freud says that perversions are fragments of normal sexuality that are neither pathological nor perversities (Lantéri-Laura 2012, 91–5). It is here that he introduces the notion of anatomical extensions, which allows him to more precisely define a perversion:

> Here, then, are factors which link the perversions to normal sexual life, and which can also serve as a basis for their classification. The perversions are either (a) actions of *extending* anatomically beyond the regions of the body designed for genital union or (b) actions of *lingering* over the intermediate relations to the sexual object normally rapidly traversed on the path toward the final sexual aim. (Freud [1905a] 2016, 13)

In other words, because sexual interest extends beyond the genitals of the sexual object (in this case, a person), and because the actions mediating the connection to the sexual object are both facts of a normal sexual life, Freud draws two conclusions. First, the aim of the sexual drive is rarely limited to the genitals of the sexual object; this implies that the sexual drive could extend across the entire body of the sexual object, including all accompanying sensations. Second, these facts produce a psychic overvaluation of the sexual object.

Freud's use of fetishism in *Three Essays* can be read as a development of Binet's earlier claims. For Binet, normal sexuality was already a composite of varied excitations, and fetishism exemplified this integration. The concept of anatomical extensions helped to explain how sexual gratification could centre on non-genital body parts in both perversion and normative sexuality. Freud appears to follow this line of thinking, which raises the question of whether his theory marks a true break from Binet and Krafft-Ebing, or simply elaborates their assumptions. He does reinforce the continuity between perversion and norm, noting that "no other variation of the sexual drive verging on the pathological is as clear to us in every respect as this one" (Freud [1905a] 2016, 16). By extending their connection between substitution, symbol, and fetishism, Freud observes that the fetish object is often a body part like a foot or hair – "hardly appropriate for sexual purposes" – yet still central to adult sexual interest (Freud [1905a] 2016, 16). Fetishism, then, remains bound to non-genital bodily focus, and blurs the line between deviation and norm.

In this context, Freud's central argument criticizes the criteria for distinguishing between normal and pathological sexualities, as these had been established by the sexological and psychiatric literature of the late nineteenth century (Davidson 1987, 266). As the sexual drive has no internal natural aim, deviations from the aim of genital intercourse lose their pathological status as genuine perversions; because Freud has therefore emptied the conceptual space within which perversion functions, *there are no genuine perversions*.

With perversion no longer a legitimate psychiatric concept, Freud can then challenge the assumed role of fetishism in human sexuality – but how?

After *Three Essays*, Freud needed a solution to this problem. As we shall see later, reception of Lacan's psychoanalytic interest in this subject highlighted fetishism as a perverse construct par excellence.

Consider how this question and its presuppositions look as against *disgust*. In his 1905 work Freud also developed a theory of disgust. The "dam of disgust" was a barrier to certain kinds of behaviours, and transgressing the barrier could be a means to measure deviations from the normal, or deviations constituting perversion. Freud remarks that the limits of disgust are purely conventional, and so the libido can overcome disgust to maintain the overvaluation of the sexual object: "The strength of the sexual drive loves actively overriding this sense of disgust" (Freud [1905a] 2016, 15). Now, though, that we have concluded that perversion in its genuine form is no longer a legitimate concept according to *Three Essays*, Freud's theorization of reactions such as disgust and shame cannot be an independent criterion for classifying some sexual phenomena as perversions (Davidson 1987, 271). It is similar for fetishism as a perversion. Freud cannot include it in his indexes for the repression characterizing perversion. As Freud argued both in his letters to Fließ and in his 1905 writings, the model of reaction formation appears to be an insufficient explanation for fetishism ([1905a] 2016, 15). This is particularly the case because Freud sees fetishism on a continuum of normal sexuality as understood by means of anatomical extensions – the normal cherishing of the objects belonging to the beloved is neither disgusting nor shameful.

Because Freud argues in *Three Essays* that sexual overvaluation arises from abandoning the sexual aim, we see that the idea of perversions such as fetishism lead to inconsistencies in Freud's theories. The same applies to his ideas on infantile sexuality, which he characterizes as lacking an object. In short, Freud cannot show that there is an overvaluation of an *object* in infantile sexuality when there is no object! The concept of sexual overvaluation thus makes it difficult to study fetishist perversion exclusively as a *deviation* from the normal sexual aim, because there must be an object to be overvalued in the first place. In Chapter 4, we shall see how Freud attempts to resolve this issue in the years following *Three Essays*.

Let us close this section by tying up a few more loose ends. If, according to Freud's understanding in 1905, the bond between the drive and the object cannot be formed by a biological norm, how then can the fetish object be explained? Freud returns to Binet's aetiology:

> As Binet first claimed, and as was later confirmed by ample evidence, the choice of fetish reveals the continuing influence of a sexual impression mostly received in early childhood, comparable with the proverbial "stickiness" of first love under normal circumstances (*on revient toujours à ses premiers amours*). [...] It is a symbolic association of ideas, of which the person concerned is usually not conscious, that has led to the replacement of the object by a fetish. (Freud [1905a] 2016, 17)

Freud's discussion of fetishism in *Three Essays* ultimately questions the foundation of the sexological and psychiatric literature established by his predecessors. But he follows the categorization of perversions established in that very same literature. The ambiguities resulting in his own theory show that he was, in some sense, a prisoner of the very conceptual space he was trying to transcend (Davidson 1990, 320). Without yet knowing how to integrate fetishism into his theories following *Three Essays*, Freud made an increasingly strong connection between fetishism and his own insights into neurosis.

For example, in the 1906 *My Views on the Role of Sexuality in the Aetiology of the Neuroses*, Freud assesses his aetiological thinking from the 1890s to 1906. He affirms his confidence in the biological arguments of *Three Essays*, and claims that his work had revealed that disturbances of the organism's sexual processes (*Störung der Sexualvorgänge im Organismus*) overlap with the aetiological importance of hereditary, constitutional, and accidental factors. These would then form the core for his aetiological thinking (1906a, 279). But the very next year, the topic of fetishism was to clash with his reasoning on organic sexual processes.

He would turn to Binet for help, and to begin to solve the problems that fetishism had given him in *Three Essays*.

2. *Childhood Impressions and the Turn to Fantasy*

In his 1907 essay *Delusions and Dreams in Jensen's Gradiva* (henceforth referred to as *Delusions and Dreams*), Freud approached the problem of fetishism and infantile sexuality. Where does the fetish object originate? As we shall see, there are problems here that forced Freud to change his views. He would have to re-engage with Binet's groundbreaking idea that the fetish object originates in childhood.

In fact, from 1907, Freud attempts to deepen Binet's aetiology of fetishism through the theoretical models and clinical insights he himself had developed to that point. Whereas Freud had previously stated that neurosis is the negative of perversion, he now tries to solve the origin of the fetishist perversion by relating it differently to the very same concept of neurosis.

The move in *Delusions and Dreams* is different from what goes before, however. Here Freud begins shifting his focus away from the innate elements of the sexual experience. His ongoing adoption of Binet's idea, namely that fetishism is explained by an external object, makes it impossible to theorize about fetishism by deepening the topics of internal dispositions (understood as erogenous zones or the components of the sexual drive). In 1906 Freud assumes that the organic disturbances in sexual processes overlap with the aetiological importance of hereditary, constitutional, and accidental factors; but in 1907, by building on Binet, Freud privileges the influence of an external event (*Einfluß einer äußeren Einwirkung*) (1907a, 34). That is, he privileges a stimulus from the external world (*Reiz aus der Außenwelt*) (56) and the chance impression (*zufälliger Eindruck*) (46). Thus, in contrast to 1906, Freud is not now exploring fetishism from the point of view of disturbances in either the synthesis of the sexual drive's components or in the perverse polymorphic infantile disposition (1906a, 277). Freud now regards an enquiry into those components to be irrelevant, and he is now more directly taking on the fetishism debate in psychiatry at the time. Rather than being part of normal sexuality, fetishism is now associated with psychosis.

This shift illustrates how unstable Freud's classificatory project remained. In one moment fetishism serves as a variation continuous with normal sexuality; in the next, it is reabsorbed into the language of psychiatric pathology. The ease with which Freud could relocate fetishism across these conceptual boundaries hints at why it resists definitive placement. Again and again, it unsettles the line between what counts as illness and what counts as an ordinary mode of human sexual desire.

In this view, fetishism no longer stood apart as an unrepressed perversion but was reclassified as part of the same psychic economy that produced neurotic disorders. Drawing explicitly on Binet's notion of childhood impressions, Freud emphasized that the psychic consequences of repressed early erotic experiences, including fetishist delusion, were structurally continuous with the formation of neurotic symptoms. This marks a significant departure from his 1896 view, where fetishistic behaviour was understood to result from the absence of repression (Freud 1985, 209–10). In contrast, Freud now treats fetishism as a product of repression, applying to it the same mechanisms he had originally developed to explain neuroses. This conceptual shift reveals his growing difficulty in maintaining a strict division between perversion and neurosis.

Delusions and Dreams is an analysis of German writer Wilhelm Jensen's novel *Gradiva*, and covers psychic manifestations such as delusions (*Wahn*), fantasies, and dreams. Arguably these phenomena respond to sexual overvaluation, which Freud had linked to fetishism in *Three Essays*. Discussing fetishism in 1907 as related to delusion and fantasy, therefore, leads to a question already framed in 1905: where does the fetishist overvaluation originate? By taking adult fetishism back to childhood and linking it now to delusion and fantasy, Freud seeks the origin for the unreasonable judgement that the fetishist overvaluation sets on the sexual object.

Hanold, the main character in *Gradiva*, is intensely attracted to a sculpture of a walking female figure. In his essay, Freud associates the love for statues with fetishism: Hanold's interest in women's feet and their gait represents a singular derivation of fetishism (*der Ableitung der merkwürdigen Erscheinung des Fetischismus*). Freud remarks that Hanold's attraction manifests in delusions and fantasies derived from the repressed childhood memories of his youthful love, Zoe Bertgang. Freud notes that Hanold's interest in real women has been displaced by his focus on the sculpture. The approach here is psychiatric:

> A psychiatrist would perhaps place Norbert Hanold's delusion in the great group of "paranoia" and possibly describe it as "fetishistic erotomania" because the most striking thing about it was his being in love with the piece of sculpture and because in the psychiatrist's view, with its tendency to coarsen everything, the young archaeologist's interest in feet and the postures of feet would be bound to suggest "fetishism". (Freud 1907a, 45)

In this way Freud finds an important insight to fill theoretical gaps in the relationship between childhood and the overvaluation of objects. It happens by children's early propensity to fantasize. According to Freud, the protagonist's precondition for fetishism is explained by the need for erotic fantasies. Although the novel itself is not concerned with a disposition explaining the need for erotic fantasies, Freud says that Jensen recognized childhood erotism (*Erotik des Kinderlebens*) as a basis of fetishism. Freud acknowledges his agreement with Binet's ideas on fetishism, and argues that Jensen's descriptions of Hanold are a remarkable, scientifically accurate example of the phenomenon:

> [W]e cannot avoid tracing the interest back to the memory of his childhood playmate. For there can be no doubt that even in her childhood, the girl showed the same peculiarity of a graceful gait, with her toes almost perpendicularly raised as she stepped along; and it was because it represented that same gait that an ancient marble relief acquired such great importance for Norbert Hanold. Incidentally, we may add that in his derivation of the remarkable phenomenon of fetishism the author is in complete agreement with science. Ever since Binet, we have in fact tried to trace fetishism back to erotic impressions in childhood. (Freud 1907a, 46)

In this passage we see that, by connecting childhood and the fetish object, Freud links Binet's aetiological ideas to the formation of the delusion. The delusion's development begins when a chance impression awakens the traces of forgotten childhood erotic experiences. Again, in line with Binet, Freud notes children's ability to fantasize. He stresses that early childhood impressions determine the products of one's imagination in the form of fantasy; fantasies are reverberations of forgotten childhood memories.

On the origins of fetishist sexual overvaluation, Freud takes Hanold's fantasies about the sculpture as echoes of the erotic value of Zoe Bertgang's foot posture, as it appears in his childhood recollection. Rocha (2010, 292) points to a link between fetishism and Hanold's aesthetic pleasure as well as his scientific curiosity for the sculpture. This link shows the reasoning behind Freud's earlier mechanism of sublimation, as elaborated in *Three Essays*. Freud claimed that parts of the body can be sublimated in art if the sexual interest towards the genitals shifts (Freud [1905a] 2016, 18–19). Indeed, sublimation implies modifying the aim of the sexual drive that turns sexual satisfaction to other non-sexual purposes, such as artistic creativity.

Thus, in his 1907 work, Fred emphasizes Hanold's submission to his intellectual activity and his dedication to science as fixed satisfactions. Bearing in mind his lack of interest in real women, Hanold avoids a psychic conflict related to sexually desirable (and immoral) women through the compromise between psychic currents. In other words, by means of fetishism, he can satisfy his eroticism by fantasizing about Gradiva as a woman endowed with moral and socially valued attributes. And, as we shall see shortly, Freud would then try to explain fetishism through the concept of sublimation to solve the problem of the link between childhood and overvaluing the object.

Freud argues that fantasies function as precursors to delusions, with the crucial difference that fantasy, unlike delusion, does not block access to reality. This distinction would become central to his later theory on fetishism. Freud interprets Hanold's psychological transformation as a process in which childhood erotic memories, initially repressed, resurface in fantasy and gradually harden into belief. While Jensen labels Hanold's experience a "fantasy," Freud prefers the psychiatric term "delusion" to underscore its pathological weight (Freud 1907a, 41). Drawing on Binet's emphasis on the power of early impressions and external triggers, Freud attributes Hanold's fixation on the sculpture to the reactivation of unconscious erotic material from his childhood encounter with Zoe Bertgang. These repressed memories, distorted by resistance to eroticism (*Widerstand gegen die Erotik*), re-emerge in symbolic form as fantasies, dreams, and ultimately delusions (Freud 1907a, 34, 48–49). Freud does not yet explain, however, why a child would resist eroticism in the first place. Thus, even in an otherwise smooth application of his theory to the novel, this absence reveals lingering conceptual gaps among the connections between fantasy, repression, and fetishistic structure.

This section has shown how Freud, drawing on Binet, began in 1907 to locate the origins of fetishism in repressed childhood impressions and the fantasies they generate. Moving away from his earlier understanding of fetishism as unrepressed perversion, Freud now positions it within the same psychic economy as neurosis, governed by repression and symbolic substitution. Through his reading of *Gradiva*, Freud explores how erotic memories from early life can be displaced onto symbolic objects and revived in fantasy and delusion. In so doing, he frames fetishism as a compromise formation: it is an imaginative solution to the tension between repressed desire and psychic conflict. But even as he advances this model, Freud leaves important questions unanswered, particularly regarding the child's resistance to eroticism. The explanatory gaps in this account point to the continued instability of fetishism within Freud's broader theoretical framework, underscoring the riddle that remains unresolved as he turns next to a greater focus on infancy.

3. Infantile Theories, Castration Anxiety, and the Object

In 1907, by attempting to relate adult fetishism to childhood, Freud tried to explain the origin of the object with delusion and fantasy. Missing in 1907, though, was a concept of infantile "theories" and infantile fantasies. Thus, Freud's next step in 1908 was to develop the theoretical connection between childhood and fantasy. In this regard, he would argue that children's elaborations, or "theories," have an essential function in the psychosexual constitution. This function is similar to that of fantasy. By returning to the vestigial problems from his thinking on fetishism in 1905, Freud changed his previous views: the object may already be part of infantile sexual life. This would be the starting point for thinking about the overvaluation and idealization of the object, to which Freud would then connect fetishism in 1909.

It is significant that this theorization occurred entirely outside the Oedipal framework that would later dominate Freud's thinking, and that was not present in the original text of *Three Essays*. Theories of sexual difference and birth were imaginative constructions but not yet anchored in the law of the father or the logic of castration. Only in later editions did Freud retrospectively impose Oedipal structures, partly as a way to normalize what in 1905 had been a more radical critique of sexual normativity. Fetishism, theorized in this early context, reveals Freud grappling with sexual development without the stabilizing reference points of Oedipus or castration anxiety. In this grappling we find a reminder of how precarious his categories remained at this stage. We shall continue to see this precarity in this section.

Following *Delusions and Dreams*, Freud extended the aetiological potential of fantasies in 1908. In his article *Creative Writers and Day-Dreaming*, he explores the role of fantasy in the development of childhood imagination. In this and in other work from 1908, we see Freud's strategy for justifying the motives behind infantile fantasies. The strategy works by recovering aetiological topics he had discussed as early as the 1890s, such as defence of the ego and splitting. Now Freud will argue that, during a child's development, fantasizing recalls an earlier infantile (erotic) experience. Fantasies, in his view, are the immediate mental precursors of symptoms, and can act as conduits to pathologies such as neurosis and psychosis. Freud (1908d, 148) adds that fantasizing recalls the erotic infantile experience that needs to be fulfilled as a wish.

Building on Binet, Freud in 1908 links fantasy to the ego's sense of invulnerability and to the creative capacities of writers, who split their egos into partial selves to express inner conflicts (Freud 1908d, 149–50). He describes fantasy as a corrective mechanism that offers security and psychic protection, especially in childhood development. Revisiting the idea of splitting, Freud now frames fantasy as both a source of psychic stability and a structural division within the ego. Although he had previously set aside splitting to emphasize sexuality's role in neurosis, he now reactivates it as a way to theorize how fantasy shields the ego. This sets the stage for his later efforts to explain fetishism through the same framework.

In his subsequent essay *Family Romances* (1908e), Freud returns to the link between childhood and psychological overvaluation by adding that children can overvalue prominent figures in their lives. This overvaluation belongs to the child's psychosexual constitution and development. According to Freud, the influence of the most intense sexual impulses grounds a child's relationship with their parents and finds expression in fantasies (1908d, 237–9). He also argues that the child's fantasies are connected to an overvaluation of his parents (*die kindliche Überschätzung der Eltern*). This non-sexual overvaluation later survives in the dreams of normal adults (241).

In another 1908 work, *On the Sexual Theories of Children*, Freud introduces the notion of infantile sexual theories (note that the word "theories" in this sense refers to fantasies and ideas children form, in this case about sexual matters and objects). Freud of course had to make a modification here, as infantile sexuality lacked an object. Thus, in 1908 he argues that children's typical elaborations, or "theories," are necessary for the psychosexual constitution (Freud 1908b, 215). Freud identifies three such theories: the theory of the neglect of the differences between the sexes, the cloacal theory of birth, and the sadistic theory of coitus. Although these sexual theories, inasmuch as children believe them, are factually false, Freud takes them as correct with respect to the components of the sexual drive, which have already begun to incubate in the infantile organism (Freud 1908b, 215). In childhood, the components of the sexual drive lie at the origin of children's elaborations about the enigmas of adult sexuality. This means that the organic sexual processes of childhood, such as autoerotism, coprophilic inclinations, and anal erotism, involve the typical elaboration of the infantile understanding of sexuality. Once again, Freud falls back on the arguments concerning defence, splitting, and the idea of modification of perceptions similar to that discussed by Binet in terms of doubling.

In 1908 Freud argues that defence is the reason for the genesis of infantile theories. In constructing these theories, children aim to prevent the onset of feared events (1908b, 213). According to Freud, the first occasion of a child's psychic conflict is the confrontation of his theories and fantasies based on sexual-drive preferences, with the views of grown-ups. Freud also argues that this psychic conflict soon leads to a psychic splitting (*psychische Spaltung*) (Freud 1908b, 214). Thus, Freud compares splitting to doubling in the context of modifications of perceptions, as discussed by Binet. In his late theory of psychopathology, Freud's idea of fetishism would become the phenomenon by which he connected splitting and the change in unwanted perceptions. We shall have more to say on this point in Chapter 6.

The first infantile theory mentioned in *On the Sexual Theories of Children* is the frequent attribution of a penis to all human beings, including females. Freud theorizes that children have fantasies about (sexual) objects, and he reasons that the penis's status as the main erogenous zone and the central autoerotic sexual organ results in the child's appreciation of it. Consequently, the child is unable to imagine a person lacking a penis – a remarkable change from his earlier, object-independent views. In addition, in Freud's 1905 theory of sexuality, the penis was not the child's leading erogenous zone. The genital zone was merely one such zone among others.

So, in 1908 Freud adds this wrinkle: the inability to accept genital difference in childhood. In Freud's interpretation of erogenous zones and autoeroticism, human sexuality (and infantile sexuality) exists in reference to a sexual object. In Freud's theory of infantile sexuality in *Three Essays*, there was no place for an object or fantasy, or for the knowledge of sexual differences in childhood. In contrast, in *On the Sexual Theories of Children*, Freud suggests that children's wonder upon realizing that women lack a penis demonstrates that children already have a strong prejudgement distorting their perception (*um die Wahrnehmung zu beugen*) (Freud 1908b, 215–16). Indeed, modifying the perception of the penis lack in the female would become a fundamental idea in Freud's ultimate theorization of fetishism.

Once Freud connects the child's inability to accept the genital difference between the sexes to his view of the penis as the child's leading autoerotic zone, he is able to introduce another important concept: the threat of castration (*Kastrationsdrohung*) (1908b). It appears here as a prop in the description of a defensive operation in the child's economy of excitation. Once a child is dominated by excitations in the penis, the effect of the castration threat is proportional to the value set on that excitement. But Freud would also later endow this castration with greater aetiological relevance.

In 1909 Freud presented clinical evidence for infantile fantasies (recall these sexual "theories"), asserting that there is already an interest in objects in early childhood and that these objects can be overvalued. In *Analysis of a Phobia in a Five-Year-Old Boy*, best known as "Little Hans," Freud (1909b) deals with a specific case history to explore the infantile psychosexual constitution and its connection to fantasies. He argues for the existence of the infantile fantasy (theory) leading children to presuppose a universally monosexual human anatomy; this is part of infantile fantasies on how sexuality grounds the child's love for his mother.

Rather than experiencing sexual pleasure in connection with sexual reproduction, Little Hans's pleasurable sensations of urinating and touching his penis are consequences of his auto-erotic sexual activity and the sexual constitution of the genital zone. This means that, among his erogenous zones, the genital zone was the one providing the most intense pleasure. Freud connects this fact to the sexual pleasure Little Hans experienced when looking at his parents' genitals (sexual scopophilia), as well as when exhibiting his own genitals (1909b, 106–7).

More directly, by analysing the boy, Freud finally shows that finding an object does not occur in puberty, as he had claimed in *Three Essays*. With Little Hans's special interest in "widdlers" (*Wiwimacher*), Hans's word for penis, it becomes clear that children's interest in certain parts of the body can become *over*developed. According to Freud's account of Hans's ideas, everybody has a widdler, and there is therefore no sexual difference between boys and girls. Little Hans disregarded the fact that his sister had no penis and simply predicted that she would grow one.

Castration anxiety plays a role here too. Although Freud considered castration when exploring the formation of the patient's main symptom, which was a phobia of being bitten by a horse, Little Hans disregards his mother's threat to cut off his widdler and responded without any guilt. Furthermore, when Hans saw his sister naked in the bath, he initially ignored the idea of castration and instead predicted the growth of a penis. A mere fifteen months after his mother had threatened him with castration, Little Hans appeared to experience a deferred effect: he intensified his fantasy that his mother possessed a penis, according to Freud. Freud says that the increase in Hans' fantasies was protective and defensive in nature (Freud 1909b, 120).

Freud's turn towards fantasy and infantile theory in 1908 and with this case study reflects a growing awareness that childhood sexuality must be approached on its own terms, rather than as a defective version of adult desire. This insight coheres with later phenomenological approaches, such as those developed by Merleau-Ponty, who emphasized both the structural asymmetry between child and adult and the need for a full description of the child's lived experience, experienced qua child and not qua adult. As one commentator notes (Eilenberger 2020), Freud and Merleau-Ponty represent complementary efforts to develop a more nuanced account of childhood: Freud by identifying the child's sexual theories as structurally formative, and Merleau-Ponty by attending to the concrete embodiment and temporality of childhood experience. Recognizing this asymmetry bolsters the view that fetishism, tied as it appears to be in Freud to childhood impressions, substitutions, and misunderstandings, cannot be fully theorized through adult categories alone. Freud's increasing difficulty in accounting for fetishism reflects, in part, the limitations of adult models applied retrospectively to a fundamentally different psychic terrain.

Nevertheless, as we have seen, Freud's writings from 1908 and 1909 already contain the seeds of ideas he would later develop in his theory of fetishism, and particularly the neglect of sexual difference and fear of castration as key defensive mechanisms. Building on Binet, Freud begins to refine the concept of early impressions by narrowing their causal role: not all childhood sexual impressions lead to fetishism, only those involving the traumatic discovery of sexual difference. In this shift, fetishism becomes less a fixation on an overvalued object and more a defensive response to a specific kind of psychic trauma.

This chapter examined the emergence of fetishism as a disruptive force in Freud's evolving psychoanalytic framework from 1905 to 1909. Beginning with *Three Essays on the Theory of Sexuality*, Freud's initial attempt to systematize perversion ran aground on the peculiarities of fetishism, which resisted classification within his new technical distinctions between sexual aim and object. Fetishism defied his opposition between neurosis and perversion, challenged his notion of objectless infantile sexuality, and unsettled his assumptions about normal development. In response, Freud returned to the work of Binet, whose model of early childhood impressions provided a developmental path for thinking about the origins of fetish objects. Through his readings of *Gradiva* and his development of concepts such as fantasy, splitting, and infantile sexual theories, Freud began to reframe fetishism as what we might call a compromise formation—rooted in repression, structured by fantasy, and entangled with the child's discovery (and denial) of sexual difference. Across this period, fetishism moved from a puzzling aberration to a key test case for the limits of Freud's theories on human sexuality and development.

What makes fetishism such a persistent riddle is precisely its capacity to destabilize Freud's categories at every turn. Freud's pathology is always already anthropology: what appears as a perversion is simultaneously a magnification of universal sexual tendencies (Van Haute and Westerink 2021, 10). This is why *Three Essays* could so forcefully overturn psychiatric normativity, treating perversion not as an aberration but rather as the lens through which sexuality becomes intelligible in the first place. But the text also wavers, as later editions impose Oedipal and developmental frameworks to normalize what the 1905 edition had left radically open. Blass (2017) has shown that fetishism condenses these unresolved tensions. It is sometimes theorized as objectless substitution, sometimes as structured by early object-relations, but never fully one or the other. The question of which Freud we are to "return" to in considering fetishism – the radical critic of 1905, or the more normative theorist of later editions – is in this sense crystallized in the phenomenon of fetishism itself. It is here, perhaps more than anywhere else in Freud's early oeuvre, that his struggle with the unstable line between pathology and depathologization comes most clearly into view.

The remainder of Freud's work from this period would see fetishism cast not only as a defensive structure rooted in fantasy but also increasingly as a response to trauma and castration anxiety within the Oedipal framework. The next chapter traces how Freud, from 1909 through 1920, sought to integrate fetishism into his broader model of psychosexual development. But even as he expanded his conceptual toolkit, the riddle of fetishism stubbornly persisted.

Chapter 5

Deepening the Riddle: Fetishism, Trauma, and the Oedipus Complex (1909–20)

In the previous chapter we traced how Freud's early theory of fetishism began to shift under pressure from the phenomenon itself. Fetishism resisted Freud's initial classifications in *Three Essays*, exposing tensions between perversion and neurosis, sexual aim and object, and fantasy and repression. Through renewed engagement with Binet, Freud began to reframe fetishism as a product of early childhood impressions and unconscious conflict, and he linked it to neurosis by mechanisms such as repression, splitting, and symbolic overvaluation. But while this early period clarified some aspects of fetishism's structure, it left unresolved the central riddle: why the fetish takes the form it does, and how its symbolic content relates to the developing sexual and moral life of the child.

This chapter examines Freud's efforts from 1909 to 1920 to deepen his understanding of fetishism by integrating it into his broader theory of psychosexual development. Through key texts, including the 1909 foot fetishism case, *Totem and Taboo* (1913a), and *A Child Is Being Beaten* (1919), Freud attempts to resolve the explanatory gaps left by earlier models. Fetishism is now treated as a defensive structure that wards off psychic threats, particularly the trauma of sexual difference and castration. But even as Freud introduces increasingly elaborate theoretical scaffolding, fetishism continues to destabilize his conceptual system. It troubles the neat boundary between neurosis and perversion, and refuses to be fully absorbed into the Oedipal framework. As this chapter shows, the riddle of fetishism persists not despite Freud's theoretical development, but because of it.

At the same time, these developments foreground a central tension of this book: whether fetishism must be pathologized as a defensive aberration or can instead be read as a mode of attachment that undermines the very notion of normal sexuality. This double movement, towards classification and towards critique, runs throughout Freud's writings of this period, and it is precisely in this tension that the riddle of fetishism gains its critical force. As noted in the Introduction, a broader discussion lies beyond the scope of the present book, which situates its historical reconstruction in view of contemporary debates without developing them exhaustively.

From a contemporary perspective, indeed, the instability of fetishism within Freud's system opens space for rethinking how sexual and gendered subjectivities form outside linear or normative developmental paths. We saw this issue arise in Chapter 3, and it shall arise again here – the fetish's resistance to integration into the Oedipal narrative, that is, its refusal to cleanly signify or to resolve psychic conflict, could make it a particularly rich concept for theorizing from queer and trans perspectives. Rather than interpreting fetishism as a failed or incomplete traversal of psychosexual stages, we might treat its symbolic density and structural tenacity as signs of a totally alternative logic of desire. This logic, quite apart from traditional norms of desire and desire expression, would be one less interested in resolution than in sustaining attachment through imaginative means. For trans identities especially, the fetish's capacity to revalue bodily signs and transform psychic threat into erotic form demonstrates the power of a willingness to negotiate a gendered embodiment beyond the binary models that Freud presupposes. In this light, the continued "riddle" that fetishism causes for Freud is not a defect of theory. It is a sign of the concept's disruptive vitality. It is a sign of its capacity to unsettle the very categories that psychoanalysis would otherwise hope to contain it.

1. On the Genesis of Fetishism *(1909)*

During the scientific meeting of the Vienna Psychoanalytic Society on 24 February 1909, Freud presented a case history of fetishism in a paper entitled *On the Genesis of Fetishism* (1909a). This composite history represents the first time Freud had ever systematically explored cases of perverse pathology. The work was published only in 1988, and was based on handwritten minutes of the meeting, long thought to be lost. In attendance were psychoanalysts, medical doctors, psychologists, psychiatrists, and writers.

Freud's paper illustrates how fetishism continued to challenge his theoretical efforts. After his work of 1905 and 1907, he had still not worked out how to categorize fetishism. Even so, he was continuing to relate fetishism to his own ideas on neurosis. As Freud tried to articulate the concepts, though, new problems arose. *On the Genesis of Fetishism* is paradigmatic of the way Freud faced those problems in trying to apply his own theoretical framework: he recognized, even if he did not rely on, Binet's work and, to a lesser degree, that of Krafft-Ebing, as relevant literature (*einschlagige Literatur*) (Freud [1909a] 1988, 150). And Freud tries to go beyond them.

Freud begins by expressing his hesitation about his theory of fetishism. He had previously acknowledged this uncertainty in *Three Essays*, and in *On the Genesis of Fetishism* Freud attributes it to an insufficient number of psychoanalytic clinical observations. He insists that his efforts must not be considered a solution and he presses the point that his theoretical attempts should not be applied in medical or psychoanalytic practice. Before accepting his ideas as a theory, he says that one should first wait until other psychoanalysts have brought forward their own observations, so that his own could be supported or refuted ([1909a] 1988, 150).

Freud also reverted to Binet's distinction between major and minor fetishism. This was a useful way of distinguishing the normal prerequisites for love and reminiscences (memories) to certain fetishes that are not as striking as the pathological ones (Freud [1909a] 1988, 151). This is a development of Binet's insight from *Fetishism in Love*. Binet had connected his assertion that everyone is to some extent a fetishist (in normal sexuality) to his concepts of major and minor fetishism.

In this distinction, Freud also leaves open a crucial ambiguity. By extending Binet's insight that everyone is to some extent a fetishist, Freud underscores the instability of the line separating normality from pathology. What appears, on the one hand, as a technical attempt to categorize the minor from the major fetish can, on the other hand, be read as a concession that fetishism itself resists stable medicalization. Insofar as the fetish is both prerequisite for love and potential sign of illness, it calls into question the coherence of any boundary between healthy and pathological sexuality. This tension reveals how Freud's theory, while seeking to pathologize, at the same time supplies tools for a depathologizing reading. On this reading, fetishism functions as a critique of the norms of sexual and amorous life that psychiatry claimed to safeguard.

In addition, *On the Genesis of Fetishism* addresses a number of Krafft-Ebing's ideas ([1909a] 1988, 151–2). Among them is the claim that fetishism is caused by psychic impotence in which the fetish is considered a sexual prerequisite (*Bedingung*). This implies that without the fetish, the fetishist individual's sexual potency fails. Another of Krafft-Ebing's ideas concerns foot and shoe fetishism constituting a masochist symbol ([1909a] 19888, 152, 164). In addition to expressing his approval of these observations, Freud notes that Krafft-Ebing's *Psychopathia Sexualis* rests on puzzling notions of sexual constitution and of nervousness in general. Thus, by clarifying the obscure points in Krafft-Ebing, Freud begins to address his own theoretical attempt to understand fetishism, and he proposes a specific mechanism for it.

In 1909, Freud adapted Binet's distinction between minor and major fetishism by applying the model of hysterical reminiscence to cases of fetishism. While hysterical symptoms arise from repressed memories of traumatic affect, typically distress or fright, Freud now described the fetish as a direct reminiscence of normal childhood experiences of love (Freud [1909a] 1988, 153). Unlike hysterical reminiscences, these memories are not repressed, and the fetish object remains consciously accessible. Crucially, Freud argues that such fetishes originate in early affective bonds, often with the mother, and function as *Liebesbedingungen* – prerequisites for love. This marks a shift from earlier associations with pathology: the fetish is no longer linked to disgust or reaction formation, but to idealized and affectionate memories. In this light, fetishism is not the opposite of neurosis, as Freud had once suggested, but rather structurally related to it through shared mechanisms of reminiscence. Drawing on Krafft-Ebing's notion of the fetish as a sexual prerequisite, Freud introduces the idea of a maternal aetiology (*Mutterätiologie*), positioning the fetish within the intimate dynamics of early love rather than as a perverse deviation. This reframing is crucial for the major themes of this book. By relocating the fetish within the dynamics of early love, Freud breaks down the medicalized division between normal attachment and pathological perversion. The fetish no longer appears solely as a deviation to be diagnosed but also as a trace of intimacy and memory cutting across the categories of health and illness. In this sense, Freud's maternal aetiology both pathologizes and depathologizes, as it marks fetishism as a clinical problem while simultaneously providing the conceptual tools to read it as an extension of ordinary affective life. As he puts it, "A large number of cases prove to be reminiscences, along the model of the mechanism of hysteria – reminiscences of earlier, perhaps normal affects of love [...]. As 'fetishes', they are [...] direct reminiscences of beloved persons" (Freud [1909a] 1988, 153).

Freud admits that the model of the fetish as a reminiscence of the beloved person's characteristics cannot be applied in cases of genuinely perverse pathology: "It is otherwise in cases that genuinely deserve the name fetishism. We cannot suppose that they are reminiscences; neither can we account for them as a prerequisite for love" (Freud [1909a] 1988, 153). In addressing these "puzzling cases," Freud more than ever carries out Binet's methodological idea: to draw attention to childhood events to locate the origin of the fetish. In

1909, insofar as Freud addresses problems in his theory of (infantile) sexuality left unresolved in *Three Essays*, here Freud assumes that the search for a sexual object does actually take place, and it happens in childhood.

This ambiguity in Freud's treatment, between the fetish as a desexualized, exalted object and as a source of unambiguous sexual arousal, finds an echo in recent attempts to reposition fetishism within the domain of aesthetics. For instance, a twenty-first-century psychological study (Høgh-Olesen 2018) proposes that fetishism involves attraction to species-specific "key stimuli," perceived as especially beautiful or exciting, and that such stimuli function as "power objects." This model shifts the explanation away from defensive structures or developmental trauma and towards an aesthetic impulse, rooted in innate sensibilities. Viewed in this light, Freud's oscillation between sublimation and raw erotic charge may reflect not a theoretical failure, but rather an unresolved tension within the nature of fetishism itself.

This tension is evident in Freud's presentation of a case of a male clothes-fetishist patient whose sexual interest in women was displaced (*verschoben*) onto female clothing (Freud [1909a] 1988, 154). Freud describes the patient's early sexual recollections of routinely watching his mother undress. According to Freud, the mother and son had begun to live in an atmosphere of physical intimacy, and thus the mother fell in love with her son. In this intimate setting of mother–son love, there was no oversight of the mother's behaviour and so no one to reproach her. Freud claims that the outcome of the child's interest was voyeurism. After the groundwork for the patient's adult voyeuristic tendencies had been set in his childhood, his sexual inclination towards voyeurism and towards his mother were repressed. Thus, the fact that the patient became a clothes-fetishist was a result of repression.

This case once again highlights that fetishism, for Freud in 1909, cannot be classified as a perversion. Instead, he frames it as the result of repressing a perverse tendency, and thus treats it within the model of neurosis. Notably, Freud does not connect the childhood origins of the fetish to the infantile sexual theories he explored in 1908, such as the denial of sexual difference or fear of castration. He focuses instead on the child's fascination with the mother's nudity, and specifically the moment her underpants fell. While he does not fully explain why this interest was later repressed, he suggests that the fetish, centred as it was on the underpants, emerged through displacement and transferred the erotic charge from the mother's nudity to the object itself.

At the scientific meeting in 1909, Freud applied the mechanism of repression to the development of the innate components of the sexual drive. By trying to explain fetishism, Freud described a specific type of repression involving fetishism. Repression came after childhood; the patient repressed his sexual inclination towards his mother as well as his drive to look (*Sehtrieb*) and the pleasure he once took in looking (*Schaulust*). As with other defensive neurotic symptoms, the mechanism of repression is responsible for the displacement of the patient's interest in his unclothed mother onto the clothes that fell to the floor in his remembered scenes of her undressing.

The question remains from *Three Essays*, though, of how to explain sexual overvaluation in fetishism. Freud acknowledged that the patient's interest in the fetish object does not stem from normal love-affects for parents. Considering the material Freud had available on the patient's childhood memories, the model of reminiscence presented at the beginning of the scientific meeting cannot explain why the overvaluation was not suddenly or unexpectedly (*plötzlich*) directed at the mother but was instead directed at artificial objects.

According to Freud, as a consequence of repression, the individual places a high value (*Hochschatzung*) on the element of the situation that becomes the fetish. Freud adds that the displacement of this patient's interest in his unclothed mother onto her clothes explains why the patient worships (*verehrt*) clothes in adulthood. Here Freud connects repression to the notion of splitting (*Spaltung*) and claims that repression was initiated through a splitting of particular elements of infantile sexuality.

Freud notes that the same patient also exhibited a boot fetish and uses this case to introduce sublimation into his theory of fetishism. He explains that repression can function as an intermediary between total repression and sublimation, and that so-called perverse impulses are common in childhood as sources of pleasure (Freud [1909a] 1988, 156). The patient recalled early experiences of anal erotism, including digging between his toes to produce a strong-smelling secretion and inserting his finger into his anus to smell it. Freud argues that, through splitting, the olfactory component of anal erotism was repressed while the foot, an odourless object, was idealized. This mechanism, he suggests, illustrates a partial repression of perverse impulses, mediated by idealization and sublimation (Freud [1909a] 1988, 156).

Sublimation, for Freud, involves redirecting the sexual drive towards non-sexual aims, effectively desexualizing its satisfaction. Idealization similarly transforms the object by magnifying its value and distancing it from direct sexual gratification, resulting in veneration or "worship" (Spruiell 1979, 779; Rocha 2010, 301–2). Freud reinforces this link by referencing Christian Mariology: the repression of sensuality in the Middle Ages, he argues, coincided with the idealization of women in the figure of the Virgin Mary (Freud [1909a] 1988, 155). This analogy highlights Freud's belief that both sublimation and idealization offer a model for understanding how the fetish, while no longer overtly sexual, retains its libidinal charge through exaltation of the object.

From the perspective of this book's arguments, the Virgin Mary analogy also demonstrates how Freud's categories blur the boundaries between religious idealization and pathological sexuality. Sublimation and idealization, presented as mechanisms of psychic defence, also echo broader cultural strategies of regulating desire through moral and religious imagery. But fetishism disrupts this regulatory framework. It insists on the erotic charge of objects, *even when* they are "exalted" or sanctified. In so doing, fetishism exposes the instability of distinctions between the pure and the impure, or between the holy and the pathological. Fetishism becomes a point of resistance to disciplinary powers, such as psychiatric, moral and theological forces, which sought to define "normal" sexuality.

By arguing in 1909 that the concepts of idealization and sublimation (partial repression) imply desexualization, and that both concepts help to understand fetishism, Freud introduced a new problem into his evolving theory of fetishism. After all, fetishism is a sexual activity. This is clear in the case history of clothes and boot fetishism. In fact, after presenting this case study, Freud proceeds to apply to other pathological cases of fetishism the same splitting mechanism of repression through sublimation and idealization.

First, Freud deploys his notion of partial repression by means of sublimation and idealization in examples of foot fetishism. Here he does not identify the pervert's relationship to the fetish object as anything other than sexual, and so we see the evolving idea of fetishism challenging Freud's theoretical framework: while the odourless foot is indeed idealized, the foot fetishist's overvaluation of the object is a sexual, rather than a desexualized, idealization. Freud then applies the same notion of partial repression to a pathological case of hand fetishism described by Krafft-Ebing. Again, the problem here is that instead of the hand being a desexualized object, such as the object of aesthetic appreciation or scientific curiosity, for instance, the hand is the sexually *overvalued* object.

Later Freud would affirm that the assumption he made in characterizing partial repression confirms the positive aspect of fetishism in the perversions. This point enabled Freud to show how, in line with Krafft-Ebing, the perverse impulses manifest a graduation conditioned by the clinical index of disgust. Here Freud gives an example of the kind of foot fetishist who prefers to lick prostitutes' dirty feet: "The chief confirmation of the description which has been given lies in the positive aspect of fetishism, in the perversions. Thus, for example, it [has been] long known from perverse foot fetishists that they prefer to single out for themselves a young prostitute with quite dirty feet, which they then lick. Here the suppressed drive of disgust is striking" (Freud [1909a] 1988, 158). Freud acknowledges the variability of foot fetishists being either disgusted or aroused by dirty feet or odourless feet. He also acknowledges that, in the act of overvaluing female feet, the foot fetish does not represent a deflected sexual aim, as implied by the concepts of sublimation and idealization; rather, the foot fetishist engages in an explicitly sexual activity.

As fetishism acquired the status of a neurotic symptom, Freud wondered whether fetishism could be understood without considering repression (Freud [1909a] 1988, 161). Furthermore, unlike his theory in *Three Essays*, Freud's central argument in 1909 was that in adult cases of fetishism, the infantile anal erotism was directed towards an object. In his presentation Freud asked, "Does not repression belong to impotence, and is there also fetishism without repression? Or if the instinct to smell had not been directed toward an object which later was to be repressed, would there have been no precondition for a fetish?" (Freud [1909a] 1988, 161). He concluded that fetishism required him to rethink his own theory of repression, and to assume the existence of various types of repression in this context. "After what has been said, it is probable that it is actually the solution to fetishism insofar as it expresses itself in the pathological form to which we have called special attention: suppression of instinct, partial repression, and elevation of a portion of the repressed complex to an ideal" (Freud [1909a] 1988, 157–8).

So far, we have seen Freud attempt to understand fetishism by applying concepts from his theory of neurosis. At this point it is worth questioning whether the ideas of sublimation and idealization actually helped him resolve the problem. Both concepts remained loosely defined in Freud's writings (Spruiell 1979, 777–8, 790), and after 1909 he rarely returned to them. *On the Genesis of Fetishism* is his only text where he explores these ideas in detail. Closing his 1909 presentation, Freud acknowledged that fetishism remained an enigma (*das Rätsel des Fetischismus*) and suggested that only further case studies might resolve it: "If five or six more similar observations of fetishism … are brought forward, then we will have solved the riddle of fetishism" (Freud [1909a] 1988, 158). As the next section will show, however, neither sublimation nor idealization ultimately offered Freud a stable framework for explaining fetishism.

2. *The Role of the Fetish in* Totem and Taboo

This section examines Freud's treatment of fetishism in *Totem and Taboo* (1913a), where he confronts a new problem: the challenge of integrating religious fetishism into his evolving theory of the Oedipus complex. Since 1910, Freud had developed the Oedipus complex as a stage in which the child directs erotic wishes towards the parents and experiences hostile feelings towards them. With the addition of the castration complex, triggered by the child's discovery of anatomical difference, Freud positioned infantile sexuality as object-directed. But this framework raises a problem: how can fetishism, especially religious fetishism, fit within a theory that requires the sexual object to be a parent?

Freud's handling of religious fetishism in *Totem and Taboo* is notably cautious. He does not fully elaborate it, probably because he could not reconcile it within his existing model of sexual fetishism. Although both religious and sexual fetishism involve the idealization of an object, Freud does not link religious fetishism to either the substitution of the father figure or the child's Oedipal development. Freud avoids theorizing fetishism in this context precisely because it threatens the coherence of his broader psychoanalytic claims. The specialized literature on which he drew offered no clear link between fetishism and parental figures, further complicating any attempt to construct an Oedipal theory of fetishism.

Placing the Oedipus and castration complexes at the centre of his reasoning in *Totem and Taboo*, Freud (1913a, 130) claims the two complexes form the core of all neuroses – and that these complexes comprise the foundation of culture and religion. However, as of 1913, Freud had not devised an integrated theory of fetishism. The same holds true for his concept of the Oedipus complex. Thus, the passing reference that Freud makes to religious fetishism in *Totem and Taboo* supports the idea that, by 1913, he still lacked an Oedipal theory of fetishism. There are two reasons for this. First, Freud links the belief in objects to the replacement and overvaluation of people, and not to objects that qualify as fetishes, such as body parts or artificial objects. Second, unlike Freud's previous theory, where he understood fetishism as concerning a sexual overvaluation of objects of the opposite sex, Freud's 1913 theorization posited a non-sexualized overvaluation of the father figure.

In contending that the Oedipus and castration complexes ground the creation of culture and religion, Freud explores the anthropological notion of *taboo*. This entails the so-called prohibitions associated with non-European societies, imposed by an authority and directed against human desires.

In *Totem and Taboo* he highlights the process of object-choice by advancing an anthropological and psychological theory comparing forms of non-European religious worship to the mental life of neurotic patients. He notes that the taboo's peculiar magical power can be transmitted through an inanimate object, and he describes how societies labelled "primitive" by European colonial observers endow inanimate objects with human characteristics (Freud 1913a, 75).

In this connection, Freud considers the link between non-European beliefs in the power of objects and a child's love toward its parents from a psychological and anthropological standpoint. Here he argues that this love is an incestuous desire, and Freud asserts that the defence against incestuous desires is comparable to the taboo's power manifested in inanimate objects. According to Freud, the taboo of inanimate objects protects unborn babies and young children against the consequences of certain actions as well as against harm, dangers, and the wrath of gods and spirits. Hence incestuous desires dominate children's relationships with their parents, and come to form the backbone of neurosis. It is precisely here that Freud engages with the literature of religious studies and anthropology to discuss the cultural function of the father and the prohibition against incest.

In *Totem and Taboo* Freud briefly discusses religious fetishism, drawing on anthropological literature that treats the worship of inanimate objects as a psychological phenomenon associated with societies described as "primitive" by European colonial and anthropological authors, and as persisting in modern superstition and belief. His primary reference appears to be Max Müller, who argued that fetishism is a rudimentary form of religion tied to object worship, but not one sufficient to constitute a religion in its own right (Müller [1878] 2002, 216). Freud had already made a racialized comparison between so-called "savage" worship to sexual overvaluation in fetishism, and the anthropological sources he engages, including Müller, Binet, and Krafft-Ebing, convey scepticism about fetishism's place in structured religious systems. Unlike totems, which Freud (via the anthropologist James George Frazer) (1913a, 103) defines as part of an organized class linked to animals or plants, the fetish is portrayed as a randomly chosen inanimate object, often arising from superstition or accident. Other sources Freud references, such as William Robertson Smith (1889) and James Atkinson (1903), treat fetishism as a vague or inferior kind of worship and further distance it from patriarchal or totemic systems.

What emerges from Freud's review is a consistent theme: fetishism, as understood in this anthropological context, is not connected to the father figure or any symbolic substitution of parental authority. Instead, it appears as an arbitrary, individual attachment to material objects that are overvalued without system or rule. This presents a significant obstacle for Freud's psychoanalytic framework. The anthropological literature provides no support for linking fetishism to Oedipal structures, and so leaves Freud unable to integrate religious fetishism into his broader theory of perversion. That theory depends on object-choice shaped by familial dynamics. In this sense, in 1913 totemism, rather than fetishism, was more appropriate for Freud's theory of sexuality.

In 1913, Freud placed the Oedipus and castration complexes at the centre of his reasoning, and he approached the totemic system in relation to the substitution of persons; the totem replaces the father. It can therefore be argued that Freud could not use religious fetishism to claim that the fetish *replaces* the father. The reasons for this will be explained below. First, consider the father–son relationship in *Totem and Taboo*; this cannot be characterized as sexually fetishistic. As late as 1913 Freud had described cases of fetishism where the sexual overvaluation is of an object of the opposite sex, that is, a male person who overvalues a female object (part of the female body or an object of woman's clothing). In contrast, in *Totem and Taboo*, the anthropological or religious elevation of the father to a totem does not concern merely a part of the father. In this sense it does not fit the concept of fetishism. Second, consider also that these issues concern a father–son relationship based on fear and respect. The father functions as the prohibition against incest and thus represents the fundamental symbolic pact and rules that constitute society (Freud 1913a, 5, 128–9). This overvaluation and elevation of the father to a totem is not a sexualization of an object. According to the religious-studies literature referenced by Freud in 1913, religious fetishism is not connected to the idea of a system of substitution, and so his previous thinking on fetishism did not align with his theoretical undertaking in this book.

In sum, *Totem and Taboo* reveals Freud's struggle to integrate fetishism, and especially religious fetishism, into the Oedipal framework he was developing in the early 1910s. Although he had previously treated fetishism as involving the sexual overvaluation of objects, he found no way to align religious fetishism with his newer ideas about object-choice, the castration complex, and the symbolic function of the father. The anthropological literature Freud consulted further complicated matters by characterizing fetishism as an arbitrary, individual attachment to material objects, untethered from familial or patriarchal structures. Consequently, Freud largely avoids theorizing fetishism in *Totem and Taboo*, a telling omission that underscores the continued theoretical instability fetishism posed for psychoanalysis.

From the standpoint of issues on pathology and depathology, Freud's avoidance of religious fetishism does more than reveal a theoretical shortcoming. It also teaches us about how fetishism possesses a structural resistance against being folded into the Oedipal framework. The resistance destabilizes the project of psychoanalysis as a pathologizing discourse, because it uncovers how certain forms of attachment, be they arbitrary, excessive, or non-familial, cannot be explained away as deviations from a normative sexual trajectory. It refuses integration. Fetishism reopens the question of whether "normal sexuality" can ever be coherently defined. It teaches us that Freud's silence on this and related issues is itself a site of depathologization.

In the next section we shall examine how Freud, in response to this instability, returned to Binet's theory of childhood trauma in an effort to ground fetishism more firmly in psychoanalytic terms. Freud's renewed emphasis on trauma, memory, and repression would shape his evolving approach to fetishism during the 1910s, as he sought to reframe the fetish object not through symbolic systems like religion or totemism, but through individual psychosexual histories rooted in childhood experience.

3. Freud's Development of Binet's Theory of Childhood Trauma

On 11 March 1914, Freud presented another paper on fetishism to the scientific meeting of the Vienna Psychoanalytic Society, this one shorter. Freud elaborated on the case of his 47-year-old male patient who was a foot fetishist, and who experienced "psychic [sexual] impotence" linked to his fetish. Freud had attempted to treat the patient's fetishism for a short time but had not succeeded.

But why present this case? As argued in the previous section, in *Totem and Taboo* Freud could not integrate religious fetishism into his evolving conceptualization of the Oedipus and castration complexes. In *A Case of Foot Fetishism* Freud relies on Binet's theory as he begins to think about fetishism in terms of the castration complex. In the scientific meeting of 1914, Freud then develops Binet's idea that fetishism is caused by a sexual impression, as he argues that this is the impression of *sexual* difference; this is a development of Binet's idea of early impression in childhood into a traumatic sexual impression (Freud [1914a] 1974, 244). In his ongoing shift from a theoretical framework first developed in the aetiology of neurosis to that of fetishism, *A Case of Foot Fetishism* depicts fetishism no longer as a matter of sublimation, nor of sexual overvaluation, but as a defensive structure. We must therefore discuss how Freud came to understand fetishism as a defence, and no longer saw it as the opposite of neurosis, in his psychoanalytic theory.

In 1914 Freud thus shifted focus in exploring the precondition (*Bedingung*) of fetishism. In 1909 he had adhered to Krafft-Ebing's idea that the fetish is a sexual precondition of the fetishist's sexual potency. But in *A Case of Foot Fetishism*, Freud focuses on the notion of precondition to clarify the constitutional and accidental facts of sexual development required for any culmination of perversion in adulthood. Here again we see Freud using and evolving Binet's ideas: he says that the constitutional and accidental preconditions (*akzidentellen Bedingungen*) found in the case history give the basis for Binet's aetiological ideas about fetishism. And so, while intending to argue that the early childhood sexual impressions at the origin of fetishism can be considered traumatic experiences, Freud ([1914a] 1974, 244) coined the phrase "Binet's childhood trauma" (*Binetschen "Kindheitstrauma"*). As part of the 1914 presentation he says: "The case in question is that of a 47-year-old foot fetishist with psychic impotence who was treated for a short time but without success. His peculiar traits made it possible to cast a new light onto the genesis of this perversion, and to point out the constitutional and accidental preconditions of this attitude. These are at the bottom of Binet's 'childhood trauma,' which shows the perversion already fixated" (Freud [1914a] 1974, 224–5). In this remark we can see that, by adopting Binet's ideas, Freud is able to make an assumption that had not yet been available to him in *Three Essays*: he could assume the existence of fetishism in childhood.

Given that part of my argument references Freud's use of different clinical and theoretical models to explore fetishism, it is worth covering in more detail the differences in Freud's approach to his psychoanalytic case histories of fetishism up to this point. Freud's 1909 case study aimed to investigate how fetishism is a result of sexual pleasure stemming from constituents of the anal perverse disposition of the sexual drive, and how fetishism connects to individual parts of the female body or to specific pieces of female clothing. This case study also led Freud to examine the transition from the normal to the pathological in fetishism.

This transition also highlights a broader, often overlooked aspect of Freud's clinical practice and theoretical orientation. As Freud himself remarked in a 1913 meeting of the Vienna Psychoanalytic Society, analysis was not intended to "make people normal," but rather to "make them harmonious and to solve their conflict" (Freud [1913b] 1974, 186). Such a position situates psychoanalysis at a critical distance from juridical or moralizing discourses, and demonstrates that its task was not the eradication of perversion but rather the alleviation of psychic suffering. In this light, the 1914 case study not only prompted Freud to consider the threshold between normality and pathology but also, more subtly, pointed towards a depathologizing orientation. Fetishism would emerge as a form of sexual life to be understood and integrated, rather than condemned or cured. This stance reinforces how Freud's engagement with fetishism complicates medical and psychiatric assumptions about normal sexuality.

In that 1914 case study, by relying on his psychoanalytic investigations into the patient's sexual development, Freud establishes explanations for the origin of perversions in general and for foot fetishism in particular. He articulates two major points regarding sexual development: erogenousity (*Erogenität*) and sexual intimidation (*Sexualeinschüchterung*) (Freud [1914a] 1974, 244).

Freud first claims that the erogenous aspect of the patient's sexual development is responsible for his selection of the foot as a sexual object (*den Fuss zum Objekt genommen*). During the patient's childhood, the foot carried an excessive erogenous charge; here Freud is applying his early aetiological ideas of sexual stimulation (seduction) and heredity, which we saw him develop in 1896 and 1897. In fact, in his letters to Fließ, Freud had already referred to Krafft-Ebbing's idea that the experience of sexual stimulation in childhood could retain its erogenous force. This would lead to perversions instead of neuroses (Krafft-Ebbing 1895, 223, 279). In his 1914 paper, though, Freud claims that the patient had experienced early, abnormal sexual stimulation (*Sexualreizung*) from the mother, who was herself sexually abnormal (*der sexuell selbst stark abnormen Mutter*). This is important for two reasons. First, in rehabilitating his earlier theory of seduction, Freud reverts to his predecessors' ideas about the origin of perversion. He does it here in his ongoing effort to build his psychoanalytic theory of fetishism. Second, given the unending riddle of fetishism, Freud found it necessary to renew his earlier conceptualization of neuroses.

Part of this effort involved the phenomenon of sexual intimidation. Freud had been interpreting Binet's ideas about fetishism and trauma theory by relating the concept of trauma to the notion of early childhood impressions. In 1914 Freud highlights two traumatic scenes: one during the patient's childhood and another during the patient's puberty. Freud uses the term "traumatic scene" (*traumatische Szene*) to denote the trauma as it relates to the events remembered by the patient (Freud [1914a] 1974, 244). He interprets the scenes as terrifying experiences (*große Abschreckung*) and notes that the first occurred when the patient was six years old. In this scene, Freud associates the notion of trauma with the patient's intense interest in the foot of his English governess. According to Freud, this traumatic scene remained latent until puberty. The second scene took place during sexual intercourse in puberty, when the patient became extremely frightened on seeing the female genitals.

According to Freud ([1914a] 1974, 244), the sexual intimidation triggered by the traumatic scene of seeing his sister's genitals created a precondition for his patient's foot fetish. Freud also connected this frightening experience to the patient's experience of his father's threats, and claims that the patient's terror in the puberty scene was a re-experiencing (*Wiederbelebung*) of these threats. Consequently, Freud demonstrates that the aetiology of fetishism results from a defence mechanism; furthermore, as in a typical description of the development of a neurotic defensive symptom, Freud affirms that the patient created a fetish by defending (*verteidigen*) his penis after the terrifying experience of seeing female genitalia (Freud [1914a] 1974, 245). The focus here is on the genital erogenous zone as a way to theorize about the fetish object as a defensive symptom. We conclude, therefore, that from the time of *Three Essays* onward, fetishism presents obstacles not only for Freud's general theory of human sexuality and sexual behaviour but also for Freud's psychoanalytic theory even more broadly. Previously, in Freud's 1905 theory, fetishism as a defensive pathology would have been inconceivable; at that early juncture, the genital zone was considered to be as important as the other erogenous zones. Not so any longer.

Freud's effort to isolate the fetish object by tracing it to a single scene of trauma or substitution was continually frustrated by the object's symbolic excess and narrative instability. As Emily Apter (2018) has argued, the fetish in fin-de-siècle French literature was less a fixed sign of male anxiety than a "feminized" structure: a recursive, obsessive narrative space where desire, power, and femininity converged. In this context, the fetish is not simply the male child's defence against the absent phallus, but a cultural form that reflects wider anxieties about gender and symbolic loss. Apter's reframing casts further doubt on Freud's ability to contain the fetish within a developmental sequence. It appears instead as a persistent disruption, where female figures and feminized objects haunt the male subject's effort to stabilize meaning.

Emily Apter's analysis of turn-of-the-century French literature highlights how fetishism emerged not only as a clinical puzzle but also as a narrative and symbolic obsession. It was often entangled with ideas of femininity and the repetition of experience. In Apter's account, the fetish becomes a feminized site of narrative looping – haunted by excess, resistant to closure, and saturated with displaced meanings. This reading complements the difficulties Freud faced in theorizing fetishism within a strictly developmental frame. Rather than pointing to a discrete traumatic cause, fetishism in these years repeatedly returned him to scenes of lingering ambiguity among his theoretical tools. This emphasis on scenic return and narrative entrapment helps to contextualize Freud's eventual recourse to regression as a theoretical solution. That regression formed part of an effort to describe how the fetishist reactivates earlier scenes of desire and anxiety instead of moving forward along a normative sexual path.

Apter's account provides insight into how fetishism resists the closure Freud sought through trauma theory and regression. By framing fetishism as a recursive, feminized narrative space and not just some developmental error, Apter makes clear its capacity to sustain desire outside the linear teleology of normal sexuality. In this way, Freud's difficulty becomes revealing. The more he attempts to reduce fetishism to defensive mechanisms, the more apparent its alternative logic of attachment becomes. That logic is not one of pathology, but rather one of persistence. It is an insistence on forms of erotic life that exceed the categories of cure, completion, or normality, and that live at the heart of hoped-for but fleeing balances between pathology and depathology.

Indeed, in 1914 Freud uses the concept of regression to understand the cause of the disturbance in the patient's sexual development. For Freud, regression is a consequence of sexual intimidation during childhood. That he would apply regression to understanding how fetishism signals a shift in the theoretical framework he used, from the aetiology of neurosis to that of perversion. In this Freud uses the concept of regression quite specifically, positing that a "topical regression" or "geographical regression" took place during sexual development (Freud [1914a] 1974, 245) as the patient regressed to the circumstances of his early interest in feet, which involved crawling on the floor below a table to look at genitals.

In 1914, Freud explicitly identifies the foot as a symbolic substitute for the absent female penis, linking it to the sight of a sister's genitals and the resulting castration anxiety ([1914a] 1974, 244). The foot becomes a fetish that both acknowledges and defends against the threat of castration. Freud draws evidence for this symbolic reading from a dream in which the patient's wife had a penis. While he had already explored the connection between infantile fantasy and fetishism in his 1910 essay on Leonardo da Vinci, it was not until 1914 that he introduced the symbolic function of the fetish object in response to traumatic scenes of anatomical difference. Is it notable here that Freud now views fetishism as a psychic defence accommodating castration while simultaneously denying it. This marks a shift from his earlier theory, where fetishism was treated as the opposite of hysterical defence. Instead, Freud now uses the model of substitution and symbolism to construct a new theory of fetishistic defence. This one continues to draw on and reshape his predecessors' insights, especially concerning the link between fetishism and masochism.

In his concluding remarks on foot fetishism in 1914, Freud theorizes about the origins of another perversion: masochism. According to Freud, the behaviour of the foot fetishist is grounded in the masochistic perversion; early sexual intimidation could ultimately reveal not only the cause of foot fetishism but the cause of masochism as well. In *A Case of Foot Fetishism*, Freud identifies the dual attitude of the child vis-à-vis traumatic sexual intimidation as the most significant factor in the fetishist case. By becoming passive in his relationships with women, the child thereby reconciled himself to a female role (Freud [1914a] 1974, 245). This view was a self-conscious development of ideas we have already seen from Binet and Krafft-Ebing.

Freud also echoed Binet's doubling once again by examining the connection between fetishism and the child's dual attitude. To set the stage for this argument, he posits a link between fetishism and masochism and a primary bisexual disposition (*bisexuellen Anlage*) in humans (Freud [1914a] 1974, 245). Both concepts appear in Krafft-Ebing's *Psychopathia Sexualis*. Krafft-Ebing emphasized that both foot and shoe fetishism are a type of masochism, and although Freud did not refer to Krafft-Ebing in 1914, he agreed with him with respect to the idea that foot fetishism is a subcategory (*Unterart*) of masochism.

The bisexual disposition in humans, Freud says, determines whether the patient develops a neurosis or a perversion ([1914a] 1974, 245). For foot fetishism, Freud asserts that the decisive factor in an individual's bisexual disposition veering towards a passive (masochistic) stance in his relationships is the instance of traumatic sexual intimidation during childhood. A person who at an early age has been intimidated by a man, develops a tendency to be masochistic in relation to women. Freud formulates a synoptic understanding of this behaviour: "The briefest formula for the foot fetishist would be: a masochistic secret voyeur" (Freud [1914a] 1974, 245). Freud would later develop more of Binet's ideas as well, as he aimed to understand the libido's propensity for fixation depending on external accidental factors.

Thirty years earlier, Binet had shown a similar interest in pointing to the fixation of erotic ideas as linked to fetishes in the development of fetishistic perversion (1888a, 20–1, 40, 58). Freud later acknowledged this and explains that before the existence of psychoanalytic research, Binet explored whether the libido in perverts remains attached to an object or trend throughout their lives owing to very early impressions (Freud 1916–17, 348).

This point will be addressed in the next section. It will examine how, in the course of enquiring into the origin of all perversions, Freud again refers to Binet's "accidental causes" as the primary triggers. As of 1917, as we have seen, Freud was still unable to theoretically link fetishism and the Oedipus complex. In 1919, he tried once again to solve this conceptual problem. This will be examined in the section below.

4. The Oedipus Complex and the Aetiology of Perversions

With all the arguments we have seen so far, we are now in a position to better assess Freud's attempt to apply his concept of the Oedipus complex to fetishism. In 1919 he tried to formulate a general theory of the causes of perversions; these ideas come forth in *A Child Is Being Beaten: A Contribution to the Study of the Origin of Sexual Perversions*. Since 1913 Freud had avoided theorizing about fetishism in connection to the Oedipus complex. But in his 1919 work, he set the concept of the Oedipus complex as key to understanding fetishism.

One of Freud's goals in *A Child Is Being Beaten* is to advance Binet's founding ideas on fetishism. Freud also aims to elaborate on them to explain the cause of all sexual perversions. It is striking that Freud's effort here, while occasionally acknowledging female cases, does not extend to theorizing feminine fetishism. Instead, he reverts to Binet's male-oriented framework and thus reproduces the asymmetry that casts fetishism primarily as a riddle of male desire. This omission is not incidental. It reflects a broader psychoanalytic tendency to equate perversion with male sexuality. The absence of feminine fetishism from Freud's account reinforces the norms of sexual difference that fetishism itself might otherwise be used to disrupt. From the vantage of the major themes in this book, this selective treatment exposes how Freud's project both resists and reinscribes pathologizing categories. While fetishism destabilizes the line between normal and abnormal, the refusal to consider female fetishism *constrains* the destabilization, preventing the critique from reaching its full, potentially far more radical, potential.

This limitation makes it all the more telling that, in 1919, Freud returned to Binet's framework to ground his claims about the origins of perversion. Rather than expanding his account to encompass the untheorized terrain of feminine fetishism, Freud doubled down on the Oedipal model as a universal explanatory key. In so doing, he redirected the debate over fetishism towards the broader question of how perversions might be systematized under the same developmental logic as neuroses. His contribution to Binet's argument is to promote the main cause of neuroses, which he took to be the Oedipus complex, as the source of sexual perversions in mature stages of life (Freud 1919, 204). While in 1919 Freud initially had the ambition to discuss the Oedipus complex as a cause of all sexual perversions, he instead now focuses on the masochistic perversion.

These ideas, and how they strengthen this interpretation of Freud's development, will now be examined.

In a direct reference to Binet's assumptions, Freud writes that "long before the days of psycho-analysis, observers like Binet were able to trace the strange sexual aberrations of maturity back to similar impressions and to precisely the same period of childhood, namely, the fifth or sixth year" (Freud 1919, 181–2). Freud is assuming that patients' actual experiences with perversions, recalled in the clinical setting, could be considered manifestations of the Oedipus complex. Interestingly, Freud's stance in this context is rather tentative: to claim the Oedipus complex as the source of all perversions would require additional investigation, he tells us, and such a claim could not be made on the basis of Freud's work alone (Freud 1919, 192). He also admits to an opaqueness in the connection between the aetiological theory of perversions and the Oedipus complex (1919, 193).

Why was Freud so tentative about his conclusions here, in *A Child Is Being Beaten*? Freud points out that masochism as well as fetishism demonstrate that the Oedipus complex is in fact a determining factor in perversions (1919, 192). But Freud lacks, or at least does not give, a detailed explanation for how this occurs in fetishism. Indeed, arguably if not obviously, Freud could not explain how the fetish object is connected to the love of parents as the object of erotic wishes.

This is a striking point. From 1905 until 1920, Freud was self-consciously systematic and persistent in hewing to Binet's idea that (psycho)pathologies can be explained by indelible sexual impressions occurring in childhood. Binet's ideas on fetishism prompted Freud to confront the contradictions, inconsistencies, and other problems in his own theories, including and especially those relating to trauma, infantile sexuality, and psychosexual development. By reviewing Binet's ideas in *Fetishism in Love*, Freud was led to revise his view in *Three Essays* that infantile sexuality lacks an object. He then formulated a theory in which the fetish object already originates in infancy.

Freud's increasing emphasis on the Oedipus complex as the central explanatory mechanism for both neuroses and perversions reveals his larger theoretical ambition, namely, to integrate all forms of psychopathology under a unified developmental model. However, as fetishism continued to resist easy assimilation, Freud's attempt to generalize the Oedipus complex became strained. In *A Child Is Being Beaten*, the persistence of childhood fantasies centred on scenes of punishment and erotic humiliation point towards the sexualization of power relations and the transformation of parental figures into ambivalent objects of desire. Yet, even here, Freud falls short of clearly identifying how such fantasies generate fetishist fixations on objects, and particularly non-human ones, without undermining the very notion of object-choice he had built into the Oedipal narrative.

Moreover, Freud's increasing focus on masochism as a "prototype" for other perversions subtly displaces fetishism from the gravitational centre of his explanatory project. While he remains committed to Binet's idea of early impressions as formative, he now frames these impressions within an emotional economy of punishment and gratification; he shifts the aetiological emphasis away from material objects and towards internalized relational dynamics. The fetish object, in this view, becomes a trace or compromise formation, as something that stands in for a repressed desire and its prohibition. But, again, this formulation does not resolve the earlier question: why is a specific object, such as a boot or a piece of underclothing, erotically overvalued rather than symbolically dismissed or desexualized?

This ambiguity only underscores Freud's ongoing difficulty. The Oedipus complex presupposes a coherent trajectory from infantile desire to adult object-choice, but fetishism repeatedly interrupts that narrative. Rather than progressing from polymorphous desire to genital heterosexuality, the fetishist's development appears to veer off course, but without the kind of repression that would make this detour intelligible by means of the neurosis model alone. In this way, fetishism becomes the clearest example of what Freud's "compromise formation," a persistent anomaly that reflects the failure of psychic integration. Despite Freud's efforts to contain this anomaly within the Oedipal framework, his theoretical language in *A Child Is Being Beaten* suggests hesitation and unresolved contradiction rather than resolution.

Ultimately, *A Child Is Being Beaten* stands as both an extension of and a departure from Freud's earlier thinking. It extends the reach of the Oedipus complex into the realm of perversion but does so by redirecting attention away from the material fetish object and towards fantasy, repetition, and masochism. In so doing, it leaves open the central problem posed by fetishism: how to explain the persistent erotic charge of a specific, non-genital object without collapsing into either a purely symbolic account or a simplistic developmental error. The unresolved riddle continues to loom.

5. Fetishism and the Riddle

This chapter has traced Freud's efforts between 1909 and 1920 to integrate the phenomenon of fetishism into his psychoanalytic theory, especially in relation to trauma, the Oedipus complex, and perversion. Freud's early attempts, notably in *On the Genesis of Fetishism* adapt Binet's ideas of reminiscence and the importance of early sexual impressions to argue that fetishism emerges from the repression and displacement of childhood erotic experiences. Here the fetish object becomes a symbolically charged substitute formed through mechanisms such as repression, sublimation, and idealization. But Freud encounters contradictions in this framework: the fetish retains a distinctly sexual character, undermining the notion of sublimation, and challenging the opposition between neurosis and perversion. His discussions in *Totem and Taboo* (1913) reveal further conceptual tension. Freud attempts to relate religious fetishism to the Oedipal and castration complexes but ultimately avoids developing a theory, finding no support in anthropological literature for linking fetishism to familial or patriarchal structures.

In the second half of the chapter, we saw how Freud's thinking shifts more decisively towards trauma and the defensive function of fetishism. His 1914 and 1919 writings emphasize early experiences of sexual intimidation and the psychic mechanisms transforming those experiences into fetishist symptoms. By positioning the fetish object as a compromise formation, or a defence against castration anxiety, Freud takes up and refines Binet's idea of childhood trauma. In *A Child Is Being Beaten*, he attempts to generalize the Oedipus complex as the root of all perversions, but again struggles to explain fetishism's precise mechanism. Freud gravitates towards masochism and fantasy as explanatory models, subtly sidelining fetishism even as he insists on its importance.

Fetishism thus remains unresolved. It is a conceptual outlier, as it were, that exposes the limits of Freud's dream of integration as well as the enduring tension between material object and symbolic life-narratives in psychoanalytic theory. This unresolvedness becomes significant in its own right. Freud's inability to stabilize fetishism within the categories of either neurosis or perversion implicitly imbalances the binary of normal versus pathological sexuality on which psychiatric discourse relied. Although it might appear to be a weakness in the theory, it is not. In this context, the riddle of fetishism can be read as a critical resource for exposing the instability of the norms it was meant to police. Feminist and queer perspectives could seize on this point and treat Freud's difficulty not as a failure to domesticate fetishism but rather as evidence of its capacity to resist domestication altogether. In short, the riddle itself becomes an opening for depathologization, by offering a framework for rethinking desire beyond the strictures of medical and moral evaluation.

The unresolved theoretical tensions explored in this chapter set the stage for Freud's later efforts to explain fetishism in the 1920s and 1930s. We next turn to Freud's late writings, where the "riddle of fetishism" is revisited with new conceptual tools, particularly the theory of the splitting of the ego. As Freud attempts to stabilize his account of fetishism within the broader architecture of psychoanalysis, he increasingly draws on structural models of the psyche to explain how incompatible beliefs, such as the simultaneous disavowal and acknowledgement of castration, can coexist. The next chapter explores how these late formulations reveal both the evolution and the limits of Freud's thought on fetishism, and how they crystallize his long-standing struggle to make sense of its enigmatic hold on the psyche.

Chapter 6

Freud's Late Works on Fetishism

In the preceding chapters, we traced Freud's shifting attempts to explain fetishism within his psychoanalytic theory. From his early work in *Three Essays*, where fetishism appeared as a puzzling deviation from normative sexuality, through his engagement with Binet's aetiological model of childhood trauma and doubling, Freud wrestled with the theoretical and clinical challenges fetishism posed. As the previous chapter showed, Freud's efforts to connect fetishism to the Oedipus complex remained inconclusive, and the problem of fetishism persisted as an unresolved "riddle." In his 1919 essay *A Child Is Being Beaten*, Freud advanced his thinking by turning more directly to the Oedipus complex and began to foreground the defensive aspects of perverse formations. Even then, however, fetishism remained resistant to complete integration within his developmental model of sexuality. The central theoretical tension, which is whether fetishism represented a perversion, a neurotic defence, or something else altogether, continued to destabilize Freud's framework.

This current chapter examines how, in the 1920s and 1930s, Freud responded to this destabilization by redefining fetishism not as a clinical deviation in need of aetiological explanation, but as a privileged site for exploring the ego's capacity for psychic splitting. Returning once again, though now implicitly, to Binet's model of doubling, Freud recasts fetishism as a defensive solution to intolerable perceptions, particularly those related to sexual difference and castration. He is no longer interested in classifying fetishism as perversion. Freud instead uses it as a theoretical tool to revise key psychoanalytic concepts: defence, disavowal, and the splitting of the ego. This chapter thus tracks the emergence of fetishism in Freud's later work as a conceptual bridge between neurosis and psychosis. It argues that Freud's final contributions, and particularly in *Fetishism* (1927), *The Splitting of the Ego in the Process of Defence* (1940a), and *An Outline of Psychoanalysis* (1940b), represent a shift away from sexual aetiology and towards a structural model of ego instability. In doing so, Freud retroactively aligns with Binet's theory of doubling as a general psychopathological mechanism, closing a theoretical arc that had begun more than three decades earlier.

This transformation also marks a decisive shift for one of the throughlines we have been following in this book. By no longer treating fetishism as a perversion requiring classification and instead using it as a theoretical tool in analysis, Freud repositions the phenomenon outside the strict boundaries of pathology. Perhaps surprisingly, especially because of his early struggles with the concept, fetishism for Freud becomes a resource for conceptual innovation. We shall see it now as a case through which psychoanalysis can interrogate the limits of normality and abnormality, rather than just reinforce them.

1. Freud on Fetishism: Early and Late

In his late work, Freud confirms the occurrence of fetishism in infancy and argues that even in early childhood the child defends itself against the dangerous and distressing conditions imposed by the external world. By having directly engaged with many cases of fetishism in practice and research, Freud by this time had acquired considerable experience with fetishist patients. From that knowledge he could conclude that fetishism is devoid of therapeutic significance. He also reconsidered the idea that the choice of the fetish as a sexual object was intransigent. We shall analyze these arguments below.

Another way Freud's late theory of fetishism differs from his earlier approach is how his examination of the drives gives way to a discussion of affects. In the 1920s, Freud shifted focus in his drive theory, framing *Eros* as a unifying, narcissistic force (1920, 52) and introducing the *Id* as the unconscious reservoir of drives (1923a, 23–4). These revisions moved away from the non-functional, autoerotic model of infantile sexuality presented in *Three Essays*. Further, unlike the examination of the drives' internal demands, Freud now focuses on fetishism to theorize about the role of perceptions of the external world. In this sense, Freud's approach to fetishism is, once again, linked to Binet's ideas on doubling, and specifically to Binet's view on the fetish object as a double-sided or a dual-character phenomenon, together with Binet's conceptualization of ego doubling. This will be crucial later.

The main feature of Freud's approach to fetishism in this period is his consideration of fetishism as a convenient phenomenon to which he could apply concepts from his earlier theoretical developments about neurosis, as well as a subject through which he could continue debates about psychic mechanisms. Towards the end of the 1920s and into the 1930s, after removing fetishism from his initial theory of perversion, Freud's conceptual framework for fetishism and the aetiology of neurosis became clearer. This was the case from 1926 onwards, specifically with regard to his re-engagement with an earlier view on defence. In fact, this was the same framework through which Freud elaborated on Binet's ideas about doubling. Thus, Freud's study of fetishism aimed to further develop his ideas on splitting and his theoretical framework of defences. The challenge here, then, is to interpret what these changes in the psychoanalytic theorization of fetishism mean for Freud. Specifically, in his late works, fetishism fundamentally undermined his previous idea that neurosis is the negative of perversion. With this idea no longer valid, Freud next comes to see fetishism as a defensive phenomenon. In doing so, Freud eclipses entirely his early conceptualization of perversion.

In exploring Freud's work on fetishism, this chapter focuses on *Fetishism* (1927), *An Outline of Psychoanalysis* (1940a), and *The Splitting of the Ego in the Process of Defence* (1940b). A few more comments here will prepare the ground for my analysis of these important writings.

As discussed before, Freud had used fetishism to theorize about sexual difference, castration, and the centrality of the genitals in his theory of sexuality. In the 1920s these topics became a key focus in his work. During the development of infantile sexuality, Freud claims, the child's interest in the genitals and their activity takes on a determinative significance lasting until sexual maturity. This then leads to the "primacy of the genitals" (*Primat der Genitalien*) (1923b, 142). Having resumed his evolution of Binet's ideas on doubling in the 1920s and 1930s, therefore, Freud endeavours to examine psychic mechanisms that serve to solve psychic conflicts caused by representations of events experienced as unbearable. Here the centrality of the genitals becomes the basis of Freud's argument; he places the female's perception of the lack of a penis as fundamentally unbearable, and as linked to the castration complex.

From there Freud could develop, in 1924, a more effective characterization of the mechanisms by which the ego detaches itself from the external world as a means to solve such psychic conflicts. To explore these mechanisms Freud distinguished between two major clinical conditions: neurosis and psychosis. This distinction corresponds to a conceptual differentiation between the two main psychic mechanisms; in *Neurosis and Psychosis* (1924a), Freud argues that both conditions stem from ego conflicts. In neurosis, the ego defends itself through repression, producing symptoms; in psychosis, the ego breaks from reality, resulting in delusions and hallucinations (1924a, 149, 151–2).

Freud then stipulates the existence of a specific mechanism, similar to repression for psychosis, in which the ego detaches itself from the external world (1924a, 152). But how could the ego find a way to avoid a break with reality? Although perversion was not central to this discussion, Freud did include it as a phenomenon that called for further investigation of these mechanisms to resolve psychic conflicts. It is in the course of Freud's investigation of psychic mechanisms that we see why fetishism and splitting captured his attention in the 1920s: this phenomenon was, in his mind, ideal for exploring these mechanisms.

Indeed, Freud posits sexual perversions as a possible mechanism through which individuals avoid repression at the expense of the ego's disintegration. In sexual perversions, he suggests, such a process can take place by means of the cleavage (*zerklüftet*) or division (*zerteilt*) of the ego (Freud 1924a, 152–3). Given that Freud is not specific, we may ask which sexual perversion(s) he is referring to in this case. Freud had only just taken up again the idea of splitting as linked to perversion. In this work, though, it is important to note that as late as 1924, Freud was still conceiving of perversions as fragments of normal sexuality rather than transgressive perversities. He likened perversions to acceptable eccentricities (*Verschrobenheiten*), follies (*Narrheiten*), or mere inconsistencies (*Inkonsequenzen*) in human nature: "In this way the inconsistencies, eccentricities and follies of people would appear in a similar light to their sexual perversions, through the acceptance of which they spare themselves repressions" (Freud 1924a, 153). This comparison to eccentricities and follies underscores how Freud was already loosening the conceptual boundary between pathology and variation. By placing sexual perversions in the same category as harmless idiosyncrasies of character, Freud suggests that fetishism may be less a disorder to be cured and more simply an expression of human inconsistency. As we noted in the introduction to this chapter, here we see fetishism being reframed as a tolerable feature of psychic life, and as just one more part of the spectrum of ordinary difference rather than a deviation demanding medicalization. Freud's perspective on fetishism in 1927 takes fetishism as displaced from a therapeutic concern, that is, not as an abnormality to be experienced as suffering.

For the purposes of this chapter, Freud argues that, in neurosis and psychosis, the mechanisms for dealing with psychic conflict affect the experience of reality in different ways. The mechanism for the psychotic reaction in facing a conflict is disavowal (*verleugnen*) of reality (1924b, 184) and results in an attempt to replace or reconstruct it. In neurosis the mechanism responsible for solving the psychic conflict is the repression of the drives' demands (183).

Later, when Freud chose fetishism as the ideal phenomenon by which to reopen the discussion of disavowal as a mechanism, he referred to precisely the idea he established in 1924. These are the kinds of problems Freud was trying to solve when he addressed fetishism in his late work. At this point, fetishism takes on a new conceptual role. No longer framed primarily as a pathological deviation, it becomes for Freud a perspective by which to study the ego's basic defensive operations. In this shift, Freud begins the gradual withdrawal of fetishism from the domain of strict pathology and situates it instead as an exemplary case for investigating psychic mechanisms more broadly. As we have seen elsewhere in this book, fetishism ceases to be only a diagnostic problem and emerges as a theoretical resource that challenges the categories of normality and abnormality. We also see here how Freud had re-established in his own mind the importance of splitting, just as Binet had done in discussing fetishism.

Following this insight, Freud's thinking aligned even more closely with Binet's, especially in his 1925 work on psychic mechanisms of negation. Echoing Binet's studies on dissociation and reality-testing, Freud explores how intellectual functions can detach from affect, allowing for the partial return of repressed content via the "symbol of negation" (Freud 1925, 235–6). He argues that representations of reality can be reshaped by ego interests, leading to omissions and fused elements in perception (1925, 236–8). With this return to Binet's ideas on splitting, then, Freud also re-engages his earlier focus on defence mechanisms – particularly in relation to fetishism, Binet's most enduring topic in sexology.

Freud's arguments establish the link between fetishism and splitting of the ego beginning in 1926, a year before his essay on fetishism. Freud (1926, 88) highlights disturbances (*Störungen*) of a fetishist nature (*fetischistischer Natur*) as a model to investigate how disturbances of the sexual function connect to disturbances of the ego. He also revisits various issues originally discussed in the 1890s in connection with Binet's notions of doubling, namely, the concept of defence and its link to external perceptions and ego modifications. Freud discusses how the ego avoids danger by both withdrawing from dangerous perceptions and by refusing to perceive danger; Binet had made similar remarks. In fact, Freud's interest in fetishism as linked to ego disturbances runs parallel to his discussion of psychic mechanisms. More specifically, in 1926 Freud initiated a debate with the French psychoanalyst René Laforgue about psychic mechanisms; this debate culminated in the essay on fetishism in the following year.

One final comment is fitting before reaching that essay. Freud's description of perversions as "acceptable eccentricities" is especially telling. By likening them to ordinary inconsistencies or follies, he implicitly reframes fetishism as part of the continuum of human variation rather than a pathological condition. His reference to disturbances of a fetishistic nature likewise suggests a loosening of the boundary between illness and peculiarity, pointing to fetishism as a manageable, even tolerable, mode of desire. Read in this way, Freud's 1926 formulations anticipate the depathologizing thrust of his later writings, where fetishism no longer belongs to a separate nosological class but instead illustrates the ordinary operations of psychic defence.

2. Fetishism *(1927) and Other Works*

In 1927 Freud turns once again to Binet. Now, however, his motive is no longer to find an explanation for fetishism; rather, Freud's intention is to reconceptualize splitting. This reconceptualization builds directly on Freud's 1926 reflections on the protective object in child development, which he described as shielding the child from danger and psychic helplessness (1926, 154, 167–8). In 1927, Freud effectively transfers this protective function onto the fetish object itself. The fetish now appears as a defence against the trauma of castration anxiety. In this continuity we see a structural move that takes fetishism from an eccentric symptom to a mechanism of psychic preservation, as a way of negotiating vulnerability rather than marking pathology. In this sense, Freud formulated fetishism in 1927 differently from the way he had in previous decades.

Freud's essay *Fetishism*, published in 1927, represents his first published work to focus exclusively on this subject. Here Freud proposes a theory of fetishism that, arguably, diverges completely from the one he had developed in 1905; in 1927, Freud thought that a young child can be a fetishist. Now more than ever, we can observe the crucial flaws in Freud's initial concept of perversion as applied to fetishism. Indeed, it is remarkable that in the work of 1927, there is no mention at all of "perversion."

Freud knew the existing psychoanalytic landscape on the subject, and presented what he called a simple solution (*einfache Lösung*) to the subject (Freud, as quoted in Timms 1995, 126). A different perspective on the controversial passages in *Fetishism* is proposed here. In fact, the solution Freud published in 1927 had already been presented: perhaps most fully in *A Case of Foot Fetishism*, but also in several other publications, as well as in footnotes added to later editions of *Three Essays*. We shall see that Freud's 1927 essay points to his interest in fetishism as a suitable subject for pursuing the broader theories he was developing during the 1920s, and with which, in accordance with Binet's development, he could incorporate the idea of splitting. Rather than re-engaging with Binet's focus on the origin of fetishism, Freud (1927, 152) stated explicitly his preference *not* to show how accidental circumstances contributed to the choice of fetish.

In *Fetishism*, Freud views the phenomenon as he did in 1924 – as an "eccentric," yet acceptable, part of human sexuality. He states that in the last years of his clinical practice, he had the opportunity to analyze cases of male patients whose object-choice was dominated by a fetish: in most cases, patients were quite content with their fetish, even when they perceived it as an abnormality. In Freud's clinical experience, it was not the fetish that motivated his patients to seek psychoanalytic treatment. The fetish was instead an incidental discovery in the course of the treatment. Patients rarely perceived their fetish as a symptom that causes suffering; in fact, they appreciated the relief (*Erleichterungnen*) that the fetish brought to their love lives.

Equally significant here, though, is what Freud *omits*. In the 1927 essay the term "perversion" disappears altogether, signalling a conceptual withdrawal of fetishism from its former pathological classification. His clinical reports reinforce this shift. Patients rarely sought treatment for their fetishism, and when the topic surfaced incidentally, it was often described as a source of relief, as we have seen. Later archival studies by Franz Alexander (1954) and David J. Lynn confirmed this clinical pattern and noted that fetishism typically appeared not as a primary complaint but rather as an incidental dimension of otherwise functional love lives. These findings highlight how Freud's late thinking relocates fetishism outside the boundaries of pathology.

At the same time, Freud's account remained conspicuously limited. While he occasionally drew on female cases to develop aspects of his theory, he never provided a sustained analysis of feminine fetishism. He instead continued to rely on Binet's male-oriented framework, with its focus on phallic primacy and the male child's perception of female castration. In this context it is worth noting, however, that Freud once sent a nose-fetishist patient to Franz Alexander after two years of treatment, and Alexander continued the analysis for another two years. The two psychoanalysts corresponded about the case, Alexander later provided a detailed account of its course (Alexander 1954, 12–16). In Alexander's reconstruction, the patient reported a childhood seduction in which an older woman had compelled him to stimulate her genitals with his mouth (1954, 14–15). This detail underscores the divergence between

Freud's 1927 emphasis on castration anxiety and the alternative aetiological factor of seduction, and highlights the clinical complexity surrounding fetishism at this time. In some ways, the absence of feminine fetishism limits the depathologizing thrust of Freud's later thought, and constrains its critique of sexual norms, at least to some extent, to a predominantly male register.

This clinical perspective supports Freud's renewed interest in the concept of splitting. First, by presenting the fetish as a tolerable abnormality that brought relief rather than distress, Freud avoided placing it within a strict diagnostic category. Second, this allowed him to use fetishism as a focused case for exploring specific psychic mechanisms, particularly splitting. Throughout the 1930s, Freud placed splitting at the centre of his theory, using fetishism to illustrate the ego's vulnerability to disruption. In this context, Freud treats fetishism as a gateway to understanding the defensive structure of the ego. This is an approach that aligns fetishism more closely with neurosis than with perversion.

While Freud did not express clinical concern about the patients in his therapy practice, the riddle of how to contextualize fetishes yet remained. We see it in Freud raising a case of nose fetishism in his essay. Supplementary information on the case was provided by the American-Hungarian psychoanalyst Franz Alexander, who took over the patient's care.

In contrast to his earlier assertion that fetishists tended to be content with their fetishes, this nose case suggests otherwise, as it frames the fetish as a serious symptom that caused suffering. This unnamed patient's primary reason for seeking treatment was to rid himself of this fetishist perversion (Alexander 1954, 12–17). Fetishism, in this case, also presented Freud with a contrast between the aetiological factors of perversion, like seduction, which diverge from those he presented in 1927, which were defence against castration and sexual difference. Another problem emerging here is the insufficiency of disgust as an effective marker for distinguishing the pathological degree of (fetishist) perversion, given that both pathological perversion and a strong sense of disgust coexisted. This point is important. In the case of fetishism, Freud's initial conceptualization of perversion no longer applies in the 1920s. On the one hand, this contrasting case is evidence of the challenge to Freud's theorization on fetishes as well as to his clinical practice. In particular, it indicates Freud's awareness of at least one fetish as a symptom of major pathological significance. On the other hand, as Freud has confirmation that fetishism does align with the presence of disgust, we can conclude that Freud does discuss fetishism in order to theorize on perversion. He does not aim to integrate the fetish into any major nosological class.

This is the situation, then, in 1927. Citing as an example the nose-fetishist case, Freud says that for all cases of fetishism, the psychoanalytic method provided the same answer to the fetish's meaning and purpose. Freud (1927, 153) linked his theoretical solution to earlier ideas on the primacy of the phallus:

> When now I announce that the fetish is a substitute for the penis [...] I hasten to add that it is not a substitute for any chance penis, but for a particular and quite special penis that had been extremely important in early childhood but had later been lost. [...] To put it more plainly: the fetish is a substitute for the woman's (the mother's) phallus that the little boy once believed in and – for reasons familiar to us – does not want to give up. (Freud 1927, 152–3)

One can see here that, in 1927, Freud's theory of fetishism diverges from that of 1905. The child does *not* fantasize the way Little Hans had, by imagining what he called the "widdler." Now the child fantasizes about the phallus.

In addition, Freud relates this fantasy to the trauma of sexual difference. In this experience, Freud argues, following the child's observation of a woman, the (fetishist) child experienced a conflict between the weight of the unwanted perception (the absence of the penis) and the force of the contrary desire (the female phallus). Even so, the child continued to believe in the woman's phallus through the formation of a compromise, or a substitute for the female phallus: the fetish. Similar to Binet's discussions about different forms of denial of unwanted perceptions, including the substitution of memories, Freud justifies the disavowal of the perception of female genitals by affirming that the fetish functions as a substitute created by the horror of castration. He claims that the permanence of the fetish is attributable to its function as a protection against (*Schutz gegen*) the threat of castration (1927, 154). In the formation of the fetish, a process correlated with the blocking of memory in traumatic amnesia takes place: the fetish becomes a substitute retaining the last impression from the time before the traumatic sighting of the female genitals.

Consistent with his main argument in 1926, that castration is the only motive of defence, Freud in 1927 also stresses that, most likely, no men are spared the fear of castration (*Kastrationsschreck*) when confronted with female genitals. He concludes that the investigation of fetishism is hard evidence of the existence of the castration complex, and that the fright of seeing female genitals stems from the fear of castration, and not from other causes.

Strictly speaking, this solution is not new. In fact, Freud himself mentions his earlier presentation of these very claims, in his 1910 study of Leonardo da Vinci (Freud 1927, 153). Thus, it seems that Freud wrote his 1927 work on fetishism to accommodate his theoretical developments of the 1920s, and specifically his enquiries into the mechanisms of the rejection of perceptions as they applied to fetishism. This line of argument continues in the next section.

3. Freud on Disavowal, Scotomization, and Splitting in Fetishism

Freud's 1927 essay can be seen as a developmental milestone in his effort to use fetishism to reorganize his concepts. It is also from this point forward that Freud begins to revive the notion of splitting. To accomplish this, Freud first brings back his debate on mechanisms of rejection with perceptions.

Freud claims that the preservation of the infantile belief that women have a phallus occurs because the boy "refused" (*sich geweigert hat*) his perception that women do not possess a penis (1927, 153). Freud appears to be thinking of Laforgue; contradicting him, though, Freud objects to claiming that the boy "scotomizes" the perception of the lack of penis in the woman. He instead asserts that the existing psychoanalytic term "repression" already refers to this pathological process.

Before 1927, the concept of repression mainly referred to processes relating to the drive. In *Fetishism*, though, Freud employs the concept of repression in relation to affects. This move is in line with his approach the previous year where he associates the affect of anxiety with the notion of castration, integrating it with his recently revived theoretical framework of defence.

It is at this point that Freud also brings back another key element of this early framework: splitting. Freud argues that Laforgue's term "scotomization" is inadequate by pointing out that it evokes the idea that the perception has been erased entirely. Nor does the term repression work in this context either, as Freud reserves it for the destiny of affect. He therefore proposes an alternative to Laforgue's "scotomization": *disavowal* (*Verleugnung*), to describe the fate of the representation of the feared perceived reality (Freud 1927, 153–4).

In postulating an alternative to scotomization, Freud shows again the influence of Binet. Consistent with Binet's conceptualization of doubling, Freud claims that in fetishism, the perception of the absence of a penis in the female genitalia in fact persists. Binet had said that, in doubling, the subject aims to defend himself and thus "splits" his own perception of an unacceptable object through suppression. The subject can then modify the perceived object.

Freud in 1927 says that a very energetic action is undertaken to disavow the perceived reality of the absence of a penis in the female genitalia (1927, 154).

Freud then calls attention to the essential difference between neurosis and psychosis, a discussion he had begun in 1924. Freud's 1927 reassessment makes clear that, having engaged with the concept of fetishism since 1905, he has now found a suitable way to rework his theory. This new solution was to prove fundamental for Freud in continuing to discuss fetishism, at least until the 1930s.

He describes an analysis of two brothers who "scotomized" the death of their father – they disavowed it without developing psychosis. Freud compares this with the fetishist's disavowal of female castration, as in both cases, one psychic current denies a troubling reality while another accepts it. This coexistence, he argues, is made possible by splitting (*Spaltung*), a mechanism that allows contradictory currents to persist simultaneously. Splitting thus becomes central to understanding how repression and disavowal function together, particularly in cases in which psychosis does not result.

Freud treats splitting not simply as a break from reality but as a structural condition enabling parallel beliefs or attitudes. He notes that in one brother, splitting formed the basis of a moderate obsessive neurosis, a finding reminiscent of Binet's theory that doubling underlies various pathologies. Freud speculates that in a true psychosis, the current aligned with reality would vanish entirely, whereas in neurosis and fetishism, both currents persist. Returning to fetishism, Freud emphasizes the fetishist's divided stance towards female castration, as he simultaneously knows and denies it. This ambivalence, Freud suggests, reflects the dual character of the fetish object itself, echoing Binet's earlier model of the fetish as a double-sided phenomenon. In light of this book's arguments, what is striking is that splitting here is not confined to pathology. Freud presents it as a structural mechanism of the psyche, which then allows contradictory beliefs to coexist without collapsing into psychosis. Fetishism demonstrates this ordinary psychic operation. The fetishist's stance reveals not the exceptionality of perversion but rather the continuity between so-called pathological "formations" and the compromises by which everyday subjects manage conflict and ambivalence.

4. Freud on Binet on Double-Sided Fetishes

Freud's (1927) assessment of the fetishist's attitude as divided into two parts harmonizes with Binet's idea of the fetish object as capable of doubly incorporating opposites and contradictory elements. To describe how the fetish object can encompass double opposites, he refers to a case where the patient's fetish was an athletic support-belt (*Schamgürtel*) (Freud 1927, 156). This case is worth examining in greater detail.

Specifically, the supplementary information about this case makes possible the argument that, although Freud discussed the disavowal of reality and the coexistence of two contradictory currents in the fetish, the specific fetish was found in the treatment of a case of schizophrenia (psychosis) (Freud 1963, 101, 106, 108). This fetish is particularly germane to Freud's debate with Laforgue on scotomization, given that schizophrenia was the main pathology Laforgue used to discuss scotomization. In this case, arguably, Freud had sufficient reason to recognize the disengagement of the ego from the part of reality that characterizes psychosis in such situations. But with a fetish that disavows and affirms unpleasant facts of reality, this case presumably led Freud to take a more nuanced view, stating that psychosis is characterized by the disengagement of the ego from a part of reality. In this sense, the case adds to Freud's argument in favour of reintroducing splitting as a concept that would handle some of this explanatory work.

Nevertheless, in *Fetishism* Freud maintains that, in the scotomization or disavowal in psychosis, the current associated with reality would actually *disappear*. As a result, Freud's aim in isolating the fetish object was not to integrate the fetish into a nosological class, but rather, along the lines of Binet's notion of the fetish as a double-sided phenomenon, to explore the propensity of the fetish to gather opposing elements, after which he could employ the idea of splitting.

During 1926 and 1927, Freud observed increasing paranoid delusions in this patient and ultimately diagnosed schizophrenia (Freud 1963, 101, 106, 108). Given the limited therapeutic progress, he chose to focus less on diagnosis and more on the patient's "living material" (1963, 106, 108). The fetish emerged incidentally in the course of treatment (Lynn 1993, 72–3). In a letter to Pfister dated 11 April 1927, Freud noted that he had urged the patient to abstain from fetishistic masturbation, but the patient rejected the suggestion and insisted that it was unnecessary for his recovery (Freud 1963, 108). While no further correspondence on the case survives, David J. Lynn later uncovered additional records indicating that the patient viewed the shock of discovering female genital difference as the cause of his illness (Lynn 1993, 71–2).

With these arguments on the table, we can make a connection to the contradictory bifurcation (*Zwiespältigkeit*) that manifests itself in what the fetishist worships (*verehrt*) – his fetish in reality or in fantasy (Freud 1927, 157). To this Freud adds another way of reflecting on the simultaneous disavowal of reality and the recognition of castration. Tenderness and hostility can merge in the treatment of the fetish, and this corresponds to the disavowal of reality and the recognition of castration. Like before, his approach coincides with Binet's developments on doubling and the dual nature of the fetish object.

Supported by Binet's ideas, Freud was now finally able to solve the problem he had been left with in 1919: linking the Oedipus complex to fetishism. To discuss how two opposing feelings – tenderness and hostility – can coexist in the treatment of the fetish, Freud used the example of a particular kind of fetishism, that of braid-cutters (*Zopfabschneider*). Freud interprets the act of cutting a woman's braids as the enactment of castration, but without the fetishist recognizing the braid as a substitute for the female penis. Here, Freud applies the theoretical relationship between the Oedipus complex and the castration complex. The combination of tenderness and hostility towards the fetish takes place particularly when a patient has developed a strong identification with the father. This is because the child has ascribed to the father the role of castrating the woman. Thus, Freud finds a way to theoretically reconcile the Oedipus complex and the castration complex, just as the braid-cutter reconciles the two contrary propositions of "the woman still has a penis" and "my father has castrated the woman" (Freud 1927, 157).

Given the depathologization of fetishism we have been following, this example is unusually revealing. The braid-cutter's fetish practice demonstrates how contradictory attitudes, in this case belief in and denial of castration, can be sustained simultaneously within desire. Where before Freud may have seen this case as exposing a pathological incoherence, he now can understand the contradiction, intrinsic to the fetish, as integral to erotic life. We are left questioning the assumption that healthy sexuality must be internally consistent. The case shows how fetishism resists pathologization and opens a space for rethinking desire as structured by ambivalence, instead of a presupposed unity.

5. Fetishism in Freud's Works in the Late 1930s

Freud continued these developments in two works written and published in the late 1930s: *An Outline of Psychoanalysis* (1940a) and *The Splitting of the Ego in the Process of Defence* (1940b). Freud wrote them during 1937 and 1938, but they were left unfinished owing to Freud's worsening health. Both works were published posthumously in 1940. Having already confronted fetishism for more than thirty years, at the end of his life Freud acknowledged something astonishing: because of fetishism, he could now present a new psychopathological perspective on mental disorders! The following discussion contextualizes the concerns that led Freud to resume his discussion of fetishism and splitting in the late 1930s, as well as to present his new perspective on psychopathology.

In this connection we must note Freud's ongoing exploration of the consequences of the child's discovering the anatomical difference between the sexes. This is particularly true for the psychosexual development of girls (Freud 1931, 1933). He later showed that the consequences of this distinction can be linked to the limitations of the therapeutic effectiveness of psychoanalysis (Freud 1933, 250). In this sense, it is precisely the traumatic effect caused by the child's discovery of the anatomical difference between the sexes that led Freud, in the late 1930s, to assume that the synthetic function of the ego is responsible for a large number of disturbances. From this background, he presents a new theory of psychopathology by arguing the point by means of fetishism.

It was in his final works that Freud found the confidence to link the concept of splitting to the consequences of the anatomical difference. Freud's reintroduction of splitting in 1927 was a way to understand how the ego detaches itself from the external world in neurosis and psychosis. After evolving Binet's ideas on fetishism, Freud returns to Binet's conceptualization of doubling and relates it to fetishism. The result is Freud's central argument of his late theory of psychopathology.

Despite admitting his hesitations, Freud claims he is presenting a new theoretical development in his last works (1940a, 275). Indeed, *The Splitting of the Ego in the Process of Defence* expresses a return to his earlier framework of splitting and defence, based on Binet's ideas about doubling from the 1890s.

In the late 1930s we observe Freud moving even closer to Binet's conceptualization, a move that was catalyzed by Freud's theorizing on fetishism. In his paper, Freud is once again working with the idea originally developed by Binet, despite the fact that he does not refer to him. That he is using these ideas is clear enough from the fact that Freud selects fetishism as a topic of discussion, following Binet's conceptualization in *Fetishism in Love*; it is also clear that the theoretical similarities between what Freud called "splitting of the ego" and Binet's idea are prominent in Freud's works written in the late 1930s. As these similarities are crucial here, we shall analyze them carefully.

Freud's paper also presents another important theoretical parallel between his and Binet's theories. In Binet's view, subjects engage in particular attitudes of ignoring and becoming insensitive to certain perceptions and facts, subsequently experiencing the simultaneous presence of two contrary consciousnesses, wills, attitudes, characters, and sensitivities. Binet stressed these attitudes as the most frequent conditions for the doubling of the ego. In turn, Freud describes the child's attitude of disavowing reality while simultaneously recognizing danger in reality (Freud 1940a, 275). This forms two opposing reactions to the conflict, which is the essence of ego-splitting (*Ichspaltung*). To illustrate his theory, Freud recounts a case in which a young boy, seduced by an older girl, responded to the traumatic discovery of female genitalia by creating a fetish that disavowed her castration while preserving belief in his own penis (Freud 1940a, 277). Through regression he displaced value onto another part of the woman's body. Despite this defence, the boy still feared paternal punishment – evidence, Freud argues, that castration anxiety persisted.

In arguing for the central role of ego-splitting in mental illness, Freud reaffirms that the ego's pathological states were founded on a suspension or loosening of the relation between the ego and the external world. But what exactly changes in his thinking during the 1930s. Arguably, the view first articulated in his 1927 essay *Fetishism*, about splitting in fetishist disavowal, was the one that in 1938 changed his perspective on psychosis. Freud assumes that ego disorders always derive from general psychic splitting. He thus includes psychosis as a pathology that entails splitting. In fact, he admits that various cases of fetishism he had encountered served to convince him of this new perspective (Freud 1940b, 202). As we have seen many times before, fetishism again and again leads Freud to retool his approach, and it is fetishism that, in the end, compels Freud to revise his ideas on psychopathology.

Convinced by cases of fetishism, and now incorporating psychosis into his new thinking, Freud infers that the psychic splitting of the ego (*psychische Spaltung*) occurs in all cases of pathological states of the ego (1940b, 202). This conclusion considered the fact that psychic splitting occurs in all disorders: "We may probably take it as being generally true that what occurs in all these cases is a psychical split. Two psychical attitudes have been formed instead of a single one: one, the normal one, which takes account of reality, and another which under the influence of the drives detaches the ego from reality. The two exist alongside of each other" (Freud 1940b, 202). Here we see how Freud conceptualizes splitting by referencing coexisting currents, similar to what Binet had done for doubling. Freud's remark also shows that Freud is now applying splitting to all cases (*in all solchen Fällen*). Binet did something similar here as well, saying that doubling underlies different pathologies (Binet 1892, VIII, 2; Binet and Simon 1910, 119–20).

By 1938, Freud no longer classified pathologies by distinct psychic mechanisms, as he had in the 1920s. Instead, he proposed a model that distinguished them by the relative strength of the two coexisting attitudes within psychic splitting. In psychosis, the detachment from reality dominates; in neurosis, the opposing current is stronger. Freud introduced ego-splitting to capture this shift in psychopathological perspective (1940b, 202). He argues that defence mechanisms, whether rejecting external reality or inner drive demands, never fully succeed, resulting in a split ego where the weaker attitude leads to symptoms (1940b, 204). Echoing Binet's earlier view that ego doubling underlies many mental disturbances, Freud affirms the relevance of his new model, which he claims applies even to neurosis-like conditions.

In light of so many similarities, we shall soon be able to comment in great detail on the differences between Freud and Lacan's psychoanalytic theories of fetishism. Freud relies on specific models already formulated in Binet's studies. Lacan, too, engages with Binet's thinking on doubling, and his version of doubling in psychoanalysis entails a summary interpretation of Freud's discussion of splitting. In theorizing about fetishism, though, Freud refers to one set of Binet's models, while Lacan explores and further develops an alternative doubling model he gets from Binet. We shall return to these issues in the next chapter.

Let us begin wrapping up the current arguments by considering some of Freud's clinical views. Drawing on his experience with fetishist patients, Freud in 1938 addresses his clinical assessment of the relationship between the fetishist and the fetish object. He had already begun to formulate these ideas in 1920. First, Freud claims that the disavowed perception of fetishism does not remain entirely without influence, as would be expected in the psychotic separation from reality. As Freud emphasizes the strength of the psychic current linked to reality in the case of the splitting of the ego in fetishism, in his late clinical assessment on fetishism he recognized that, although the fetishist creates the fetish to avoid castration anxiety (1940b, 203), fetishists can develop the same castration anxiety as non-fetishists. In addition, Freud revises his 1927 categorization of fetishism as a type of object-choice. Freud was forced to rethink whether fetishism could actually be fully developed, or even categorized at all as a sole object-choice. He claims that the circumstance of a stronger psychic current linked to reality allows the assumption that fetishism is often only partially developed.

In this way, Freud admits that fetishism cannot be an exclusive dominating object-choice. Instead, he follows Binet and Krafft-Ebing to suggest gradual transitions of fetishism from minor to major. Fetishism, Freud asserts, can give way to normal sexual behaviour, either to a greater or lesser extent. The fetish can therefore even be restricted to a modest role in sexual behaviour: the individual may merely *allude* to the fetish. Freud concludes that in the case of fetishism, the detachment of the ego from the external world is never entirely successful (1940b, 203). This view belongs to Freud's gradually developing characterization of perversions and fetishism, where he takes them, particularly in the 1920s, as lesser abnormalities.

Freud did not frame his interest in fetishism as a means to explore the concept of perversion, but rather as a suitable object to study (*günstiges Studienobjekt*): "It must not be thought that fetishism presents an exceptional case as regards a splitting of the ego; it is merely a particularly favorable subject for studying the question" (Freud 1940b, 203). Freud does not see fetishism as a means of arguing for any specifics of perversion; rather, fetishism is for him a vehicle to defend his general theory of splitting. Freud's choice of language is crucial. By calling fetishism a "favorable subject" for study, he explicitly distances it from the realm of pathology. Now the fetish is not a disorder in its own right but rather a way to see the dynamics of splitting that shape psychic life more generally. This formulation marks a culmination in Freud's gradual depathologization of fetishism. At last, it has passed beyond a sexual perversion to be cured and instead become a theoretical resource to illuminate the structural operations of the ego.

As this chapter has shown, Freud's later use of splitting to explain various pathologies aligns with Binet and Simon's early critique of Freud's sexual aetiology. In 1910, they proposed splitting as a primary cause of disorders, which was to be an idea Freud gradually adopted as he moved away from perversion and sexuality as central explanatory models. Over time, fetishism shifted in Freud's work from a case of sexual deviance to a lens for understanding ego vulnerability. By the late 1930s, Freud had placed splitting at the heart of his psychopathology, effectively returning to the conceptual terrain of his early debates with Binet on doubling.

What is most striking about this late turn is that fetishism no longer functions as a pathological category at all. Instead, by linking it with Binet's notion of *dédoublement*, Freud repositions fetishism as a diagnostic window onto the ego's fundamental operations of splitting and disavowal. Fetishism does not merely need to be an anomalous symptom that is to be explained away, and can instead serve as a case for observing how the psyche manages contradictory currents. In this way, Freud's late writings complete the gradual withdrawal of fetishism from pathology. In the end, it stands with the normal and abnormal alike as a key to understanding psychic life.

6. Freud, Fetishism, and the Brain

Freud's late writings on fetishism, and in particular his insistence on splitting as a general mechanism of psychic life, invite further reflection beyond the boundaries of psychoanalysis. By recasting fetishism as a subject of "favorable study" for the workings of the ego, Freud transformed it into a conceptual tool for investigating how contradictory attitudes and perceptions coexist within a single subject. This emphasis on structural division, or on the mind's capacity to sustain incompatible currents without collapsing into psychosis, resonates with more contemporary findings in neuroscience.

In the decades since Freud, research on trauma, split-brain phenomena, and dissociative disorders has opened new perspectives on the brain's ability to manage, or fail to manage, conflicting streams of experience. These studies suggest that the psychic splitting Freud described can be tracked not only in the symbolic registers of clinical analysis but also in neural pathways and patterns of cortical integration. The psychoanalytic language of disavowal, doubling, and contradiction finds an unexpected parallel in the neuroscientific description of hemispheric specialization, dissociative states, and the fragmenting effects of trauma on memory and perception.

Bringing these literatures together does not require collapsing one into the other. Rather, in this section, it is shown how Freud's riddle of fetishism remains fertile for contemporary enquiry. We are beginning to see, in physiological mechanisms, how the psyche protects itself through compromise formations. The convergence of psychoanalysis and neurobiology sheds new light on Freud's late ideas for understanding the mind as both psychic and embodied. Some of this neuroscientific work is considered here to explore how Freud's views can influence and be influenced by modern evidence about the brain.

Krause-Utz and colleagues (2017), for example, survey neuroimaging and clinical findings on dissociation to show how it involves altered patterns of connectivity between cortical and limbic regions, particularly heightened prefrontal regulation of limbic reactivity. In depersonalization disorder, increased prefrontal activity dampens emotional responses and produces a state of affective detachment even as perceptual awareness remains intact. Freud's late description of fetishism as sustained by a splitting of the ego offers an analogue here: the fetishist both acknowledges and denies castration, holding contradictory currents in tension. Just as the dissociative brain sustains competing modes of processing (here, emotional numbing and heightened vigilance), Freud's fetishist maintains incompatible psychic attitudes without collapse into psychosis.

The review also emphasizes how trauma-related dissociation fragments memory, with sensory and affective traces of events encoded separately and later returning in intrusive flashbacks. Freud's account of fetishism as a compromise formation that preserves an unbearable perception in altered form anticipates this logic. In both cases, the psyche defends against overwhelming threat not by erasure but by reorganization in order to compartmentalize experience so that contradictory realities can coexist.

Most importantly, Krause-Utz and colleagues emphasize that dissociation should not be reduced to a unitary pathology but rather understood as a spectrum of adaptive responses to overwhelming affect. This perspective finds a friend in Freud's clinical observation that fetishism often brought "relief" rather than suffering, and that patients rarely sought treatment for it. If dissociation in the brain reflects an effort at psychic survival, then fetishism in Freud's sense can be read as a parallel form of adaptation. It is a mechanism that challenges the normal/pathological binary by revealing how defence itself can sustain life and desire.

Similarly, Lotfinia and colleagues (2020) review structural and functional brain alterations across psychiatric disorders, paying particular attention to dissociative symptoms. They highlight consistent evidence for abnormalities in fronto-limbic circuits, including reduced hippocampal and amygdala volumes, disrupted prefrontal connectivity, and altered activity in networks responsible for self-referential processing. These findings suggest that dissociation is best understood not as a discrete illness but as a neurobiological mode of coping with overwhelming affect, so that one may reorganize memory, perception, and self-experience in the service of psychic survival. Freud's late theory of fetishism as a product of splitting comes to mind immediately here, in the idea that dissociation and fetishism operate by holding incompatible representations together. They allow the subject to continue functioning under conditions that would otherwise overwhelm the ego.

In addition, Lotfinia and colleagues situate dissociation within a broader continuum of psychiatric phenomena and note its presence across disorders rather than as a separate nosological category. Freud anticipated precisely this kind of move in his late writings, where fetishism is not treated as a bounded perversion and instead becomes a place to understand the dynamics of splitting. In both accounts, dissociation and fetishism stand out not as pathologies but rather as windows into the fundamental strategies by which the mind, by means of the brain, sustains contradiction and defends against annihilation.

Along these lines, Lebois and colleagues (2021) show that trauma-related dissociation can be predicted from large-scale changes in brain network architecture, especially connectivity between the default mode and frontoparietal control networks. Using individualized connectivity maps, they achieved stronger predictions of dissociation severity than with group-level atlases. In non-technical parlance: dissociation manifests in *subject-specific* neural patterns, rather than in *generic* patterns. This finding echoes Freud's late treatment of fetishism, where he abandoned broad labels such as "perversion" and instead studied how individual cases disclosed the structure of denial, disavowal, and splitting.

We arrive at similar conclusions from a recent review by Modesti and colleagues (2022). They synthesize thirteen functional neuroimaging studies of dissociative disorders and find consistent alterations in prefrontal, cingulate, parietal, and temporal regions, as well as subcortical structures such as the hippocampus and caudate. Across conditions such as dissociative identity disorder, depersonalization, and dissociative amnesia, the most robust finding is prefrontal dysfunction, particularly in the regulation of emotional and autobiographical memory processes. These data support a model in which dissociation reflects not a unitary pathology but rather a reconfiguration of neural networks to manage conflict, self-processing, and trauma. At the same time, these authors note that dissociation often entails paradoxical *enhancements* as well as deficits. Patients with dissociative disorders sometimes outperform controls on tasks requiring egocentric learning or working memory, with such performance linked to hyperactivation in regions such as the cingulate gyrus and precuneus. Freud similarly observed that fetishism could provide relief and stabilization rather than dysfunction, and, in its own way, allow patients to sustain their love lives. Both perspectives challenge the purely pathological view that Freud took early in his career, or that we might take towards some fetishes now. Dissociation and fetishism show us how contradiction and fragmentation can be adaptive, and we find underlying physiological mechanisms of *resilience* rather than signs of illness. Indeed, in the neurobiology as much as in Freud's writings, pathologization and depathologization are inextricably entwined. What psychiatry and neuroscience once code as a disorder might equally be understood just as well as the psyche's ingenuity in surviving conflict.

While we might make sense of all these findings in various ways, Lopez (2025) offers a model that offers a powerful connection to Freud's psychoanalytic framework, especially its post-fetishism form. Lopez proposes that classic split-brain failures do not show a total loss of phenomenal unity. What they reveal is a layered structure to experience. There are local layers (fine-grained, object-specific contents) that can come apart, while global layers (scene gist, coarse spatial/temporal structure, summary statistics) remain unified. On this view, subjects can simultaneously experience right- and left-field stimuli together at a global level even when they cannot compare their local features. The model is underwritten by *attention* as a unity-maker. Preserved capacities for attentional agency and centrality, or for what feels phenomenally "central" versus "peripheral," can bind experiences into a single global system despite local disunities. In short: *global* unity with *local* disunity explains why people "feel normal" yet fail at classic split-brain tasks. The phenomenal unity is partial, layered, and attention-dependent.

Let us leave aside the neuroscientific jargon to see the relevance of these views. Lopez's "layered unity" model argues that even in split-brain patients, where each half of the brain seems to operate separately, there is still a kind of overall unity. The local details may be split, as with each hemisphere processing its own shapes and colours, but the broader, global picture remains joined together. This is fascinatingly close to Freud's idea of splitting in fetishism. The mind can hold two contradictory attitudes at once, without ever fully reconciling them, but still function as a whole. Just as Freud saw fetishism as revealing how psychic life can sustain incompatible beliefs and desires side by side, Lopez shows how consciousness can remain unified at one level even when divided at another. In both cases, what looks like breakdown or pathology actually exposes the layered, flexible ways in which the psyche maintains coherence. This layered view reinforces one of the major themes of this book. Splitting does not necessarily mark a descent into pathology but can rather be a way of preserving unity in the face of conflict. Freud's account of fetishism, like Lopez's model of consciousness, shows how contradiction can serve meaningful purposes. Fetishism, as with other dissociative or splitting conditions, once again unsettles the sharp divide between normality and abnormality.

Taken together, these reflections suggest that Freud's late writings on fetishism continue to offer a productive framework for thinking about division, contradiction, and adaptation. Splitting may not be a sign of failure. In some cases at least, it allows us to see how psychic life remains coherent even while sustaining opposing forces.

With this perspective established, we can now return to Freud's psychoanalytic theory itself, where the riddle of fetishism once again tests the boundaries of his conceptual system.

7. Freud's Psychoanalytic Theory and Fetishism

This chapter has examined how Freud, in the 1920s and 1930s, reoriented his theory of fetishism to address long-standing tensions in his psychoanalytic model. Whereas earlier efforts had situated fetishism within frameworks of sexual perversion or neurotic symptom formation, Freud's later writings, especially *Fetishism*, *The Splitting of the Ego in the Process of Defence*, and *An Outline of Psychoanalysis*, shift the focus away from aetiology towards structural dynamics of the ego. Fetishism became, in Freud's later work, not a deviant sexual expression to be pathologized but rather a privileged lens through which to understand psychic splitting and disavowal. This shift allowed Freud to fit fetishism within the broader defensive operations of the ego, and it marked a decisive move away from his earlier sexual aetiology. Throughout the chapter, we saw how Freud, without always naming him, returned to Binet's theory of doubling as a conceptual resource for articulating these late developments.

In reframing fetishism as a case study for investigating the ego's management of contradictory realities, Freud forged a new psychopathological model based on the relative strength of coexisting psychic currents. This model dissolved the earlier sharp distinctions between neurosis and psychosis, instead locating a continuum rooted in the ego's synthetic capacities. Fetishism served as an especially "favorable study object," enabling Freud to theorize splitting as a general condition of pathological states. In this way, Freud's late work accomplishes a significant theoretical reversal: the phenomenon once treated as an anomalous sexual perversion becomes the key to understanding the ego's fundamental vulnerabilities. Fetishism thus re-emerges not as an explanatory *endpoint*, but rather as a conceptual *bridge* linking trauma, defence, perception, and psychic structure.

Let us pause for a moment to consider the major results of our study so far. Across Chapters 3–6, this study has traced how the problem of fetishism exerted sustained pressure on Freud's evolving theories of sexuality, neurosis, perversion, and ultimately psychopathology. Chapter 3 began with Freud's early conceptualization of perversion as the unrepressed "negative" of neurosis, an idea grounded in trauma, affect, and seduction theories from the 1890s. In this phase, Freud viewed fetishism largely through the lens of adult compulsions rooted in early sexual impressions, drawing heavily on Binet's aetiological emphasis on childhood events. The theory of fetishism, at this stage, was not yet truly the riddle that Freud would later find it to be, as it aligned with his assumption that neurosis stemmed from repression and perversion from its absence.

Chapter 4 then explored how Freud's 1905 *Three Essays on the Theory of Sexuality* destabilized this early framework. By theorizing infantile sexuality as objectless and polymorphous, Freud inadvertently rendered fetishism anomalous. Fetishism's core feature is its attachment to a specific object, and that could not cohere with the new developmental model that privileged drive over object. As Freud grappled with this contradiction, he began to revise his thinking by reintroducing Binet's ideas: chance impressions, symbolic substitutions, and the influence of early external stimuli. Fetishism thus emerged as a riddle in Freud's work: one that would threaten the coherence of his newly formulated distinction between neurosis and perversion.

Chapters 5 and 6 followed the deepening of this riddle across the 1910s, 1920s, and 1930s. Chapter 5 examined Freud's efforts to relate fetishism to the Oedipus complex, especially in *A Child Is Being Beaten*. Although Freud posited that perversions, including fetishism, originated in early Oedipal dynamics, he remained unable to establish a clear mechanism linking the fetish object to parental figures. Nevertheless, Freud's ongoing dialogue with Binet's theories allowed him to position fetishism as a defensive structure built on symbolic compromise and infantile fantasy, particularly as these intersected with trauma and castration anxiety. In response to these issues, we have just finished examining, here in Chapter 6, how Freud drew again from Binet on doubling to resolve some of these tensions. Freud began to articulate fetishism not simply as a perversion but as an indicator of the ego's failure to synthesize competing psychic currents. In this formulation, fetishism becomes a privileged case for exploring the fragmentation of the ego; or, we might, say, a diagnostic "window" into broader psychopathological processes. Freud's

1927 and 1938 writings thus repurposed fetishism as a clinical and theoretical tool for understanding disavowal, compromise formation, and the instability of ego integration.

Taken together, these chapters argue that Freud never resolved the riddle of fetishism in a stable, final way. Instead, fetishism served as a generative point of tension within his theories, compelling him to revise, adapt, and even return to earlier influences such as Binet and the late-nineteenth-century sexologists. Fetishism for him was not just a marginal perversion. It became a central testing ground for Freud's efforts to theorize repression, fantasy, object-choice, and psychic defence. In tracing this arc, it has been shown how Freud's lifelong engagement with fetishism both unsettled and shaped the very foundations of psychoanalysis.

In that light, we can return to the theme of the pathologization and depathologization of fetishism, which we have seen throughout this chapter. The reversal has wider implications. By the late 1930s, Freud no longer understood fetishism as a deviation to be classified. Its new position in this theory is one that allows his rethinking of the categories of pathology and normality. It helps to destabilize the very binaries, such as healthy versus sick or normal versus abnormal, that once defined its place in psychiatry.

The next chapter returns to these late works of Freud to examine the role they played in Lacan's formulation of his psychoanalytic theory. The discussion contrasts Freud's thinking in the 1920s and 1930s, when he no longer referred to Binet's doubling when discussing splitting, with Lacan's theory from the 1930s until the 1960s. We shall see how Lacan uses Binet's concept of doubling as a point of departure in discussing the theory of splitting in Freud's later works, and how Lacan's use of Freud's thought ought to influence how we see Freud and the development of his ideas.

Chapter 7

"Fetishism" and Freud's Riddle in Jacques Lacan's Work

Having traced the evolution of Freud's theory of fetishism across more than three decades, we are now in a position to ask not only what Freud was able to say about fetishism but also what remained unsaid, unresolved, or deferred in his psychoanalytic views. In this light, the final chapter of this book turns to Jacques Lacan. This is no mere historical epilogue; Lacan is a theoretical interlocutor who directly takes up the tensions and impasses that Freud's work on fetishism left behind. Lacan's thinking does not replace Freud's, but it does explicitly depend on Freud's most difficult problems, especially those surrounding the status of the fetish object, the logic of disavowal, and the function of sexual difference in psychic life.

Lacan's engagement with fetishism allows us to see that the contradictions Freud encountered were not simply products of empirical confusion or theoretical inconsistency. They point instead to structural problems at the heart of psychoanalytic theory itself. These became problems that Lacan reframes in terms of language, signification, and the symbolic order. What Freud described as disavowal or splitting of the ego, Lacan reconceives as the subject's relation to the signifier and to castration as a constitutive lack. Fetishism, in Lacan's account, is no longer just a curious perversion or a clinical exception. It is a privileged point of access to the operations of desire and symbolic structure. In this way, Lacan does not so much solve Freud's "riddle of fetishism" as transform it into a question about the nature of the subject itself.

But this reframing came at a cost. Where Freud's shifting and sometimes contradictory accounts left open the possibility of treating fetishism as something more than pathology, or as merely an eccentricity to destabilize the notion of "normal" sexuality, Lacan's early reliance on forensic and psychiatric frameworks tended to close down that same critical potential. By filtering Freud's ambiguities through categories of perversity and criminality, Lacan reasserted fetishism as a marker of pathology and bound it more tightly to juridical and diagnostic regimes than Freud himself had done.

This chapter, then, does not depart from the central concerns of the book but rather extends them. Lacan's theory of fetishism is inseparable from his reinterpretation of Freud's most foundational concepts: the Oedipus complex, the function of the phallus, and the splitting of the ego. The persistent conceptual displacements that Freud undertook, from trauma to fantasy, from repression to disavowal, from neurosis to psychosis, reappear in Lacan's theoretical apparatus, but with a new logic and a new vocabulary. By following this transformation, we are able to see more clearly what was at stake in Freud's decades-long struggle with fetishism, and how that struggle became the ground for future psychoanalytic theorizing.

In other words, this final chapter on Lacan is not an addendum but a culmination. It demonstrates how the seemingly marginal phenomenon of fetishism has served, for both Freud and Lacan, as a touchstone for theorizing subjectivity and the structure of the unconscious. What began as an anomalous case of sexual deviation becomes, by the end of this book, a central site through which psychoanalysis reflects on its own conceptual foundations.

Unlike Freud, whose engagement with fetishism emerged from clinical and developmental concerns, Lacan's approach is shaped by conceptual and structural questions. While he begins by engaging fetishism through debates in forensic psychiatry and object-relations theory, Lacan gradually reorients the discussion. He reconceives fetishism not as a symptom to be explained but rather as a key to understanding the subject's position in language, fantasy, and desire. This chapter traces how Lacan appropriates and reworks concepts from both psychoanalysis and outside traditions to articulate a theory of the "perverse structure" and ultimately to place the fetish object at the heart of his account of human subjectivity.

To trace the conceptual distance between Freud and Lacan, this chapter follows Lacan's thinking on fetishism in roughly chronological order. It begins with Lacan's early work in psychiatry, where fetishism is treated within a forensic framework closely tied to questions of perversity and criminality. The discussion then turns to his engagement with object-relations theory and the psychoanalytic tradition more broadly. By mapping these developments, it is shown how Lacan gradually breaks from Freud's clinical and developmental model and instead retools fetishism to serve structural and conceptual aims. These concern particularly subject formation and the symbolic order.

A brief return to Freud's early thinking on perversion is essential here, though. Freud did not align fetishism with perversity in the moral or legal sense, but rather with a developmental deviation that could be integrated into his broader account of infantile sexuality and neurosis. In contrast, Lacan enters the question from within a French psychiatric tradition that treated fetishism as a pathological personality type, often invoked in legal or criminal contexts. Although Lacan initially turns to Freud's theory as a resource, the psychoanalytic tools he draws on are not the same ones that Freud used to theorize fetishism. Lacan filters Freud through his own conceptual priorities, setting the stage for a more radical reimagining of the fetish in terms of structure and desire.

Lacan begins his reflections on fetishism by surveying what he regards as Freud's central texts on the topic, with particular attention to *Three Essays on the Theory of Sexuality*. He notes that Freud repeatedly revised this text, incorporating new ideas such as ego-libido and narcissism. Lacan welcomes these additions, but his reading of *Three Essays* reflects priorities quite different from Freud's. Rather than engaging with the conceptual and developmental problems that Freud wrestled with, such as the conflict between objectless infantile sexuality and the object-fixation of fetishism, Lacan reads *Three Essays* through the lens of his earlier psychiatric interests and his emerging commitment to the object-relational tradition. This difference helps us to understand why Lacan's approach to fetishism must be treated on its own terms, a task addressed in the sections that follow.

To further frame Lacan's intervention the discussion first considers his engagement with Binet's theory of doubling. As explored in earlier chapters, Binet's work on personality splitting shaped key aspects of Freud's thinking on fetishism, especially in relation to repression and neurosis. Lacan, too, drew from Binet, but in distinct ways. His early psychiatric writings show a sustained interest in doubling as a basis for understanding perverse and dissociative psychic formations. Exploring Lacan's appropriation of Binet helps to clarify how his conceptual departures from Freud developed, and why his theory of fetishism ultimately centres less on developmental aetiology and more on the structural dynamics of subjectivity and desire.

1. Doubling, Personality, and Perversity in Lacan's Theorization of Fetishism

Scholars claim that Lacan's works published between 1932 and 1953 represent his first interactions with Freud's ideas, and thus do not say much about Lacan's own psychoanalytic ideas per se (Julien 1985, 18). During this period, Lacan's work is already evidencing a theoretical interest in fetishism. From the outset of his engagement with psychoanalysis, Lacan theorizes about fetishism as a phenomenon to be understood via the concepts of doubling of personality and perversity. In contrast, Freud did not mobilize the concepts of personality or perversity when discussing fetishism. Even Lacan's more detailed psychoanalytic theory of fetishism in the 1950s can be seen as a deepening of his initial model, which arose from explorations in forensic psychiatry. Consistent with this argument, attention is given to how the psychiatric landscape where Lacan operated determined his early interest in fetishism, just as Freud's did for him. This discussion also elucidates how this interest resulted in a theoretical framing of this phenomenon quite different from Freud's.

A crucial point to note is Lacan's attention to Binet's ideas, particularly from the 1930s to the 1950s. Considering the recurrence of Lacan's employment of doubling in his written work and seminars, it seems plausible that Binet's concept of doubling shaped Lacan's theories even before he developed his own psychoanalytic ideas. To clarify though, it is important to discuss how Lacan's approach to fetishism relies on his theoretical engagement with the concept of doubling.

In his doctoral thesis, *Paranoid Psychosis and its Relation to the Personality*, published in 1932, Lacan explored the concept of personality as a suitable vehicle for his psychiatric investigation. In fact, Lacan takes psychosis and paranoia in particular as psychogenic, that is, as linked to the function of the subject's personality (1932, 43, 54). He adds that perversions could also be explained via this psychogenic approach. Lacan then applies his psychogenic ideas to fetishism, although he does not treat perversions in any detail.

In his search for a suitable conceptualization of personality in his 1930s psychiatric explorations, Lacan's discussions echo Binet's. Lacan did not see personality as the individual conscious psychological unit, nor did he accept the concept of personal synthesis. He found support in the notion of the doubling of personality (*dédoublement de la personnalité*), acknowledging first Binet's works on the topic, followed by those of Janet and Freud. Staking his claim to a position among the traditions in psychology that define personality scientifically, Lacan writes in a footnote: "In the deliberate aim of 'protesting against the belief in the metaphysical reality and substantial unity of the soul' [...] it remains from now on inscribed in expressions that have made a fortune such as: doubling of personality. [...] (cf. the works of Binet, Janet, Freud)" (1932, 43).

This early use of doubling is revealing. Lacan acknowledges Freud's ideas as constituting an evolution of the concept of doubling, but before his systematic exploration of Freud's works, Lacan's use of doubling expresses an affinity with the conceptualization of the French neuropathological tradition (as part of the Salpêtrière school). Even though Lacan's thesis reserved a footnote to affirm adherence to Binet's concept of doubling of personality, this discussion further shows that doubling played a major role in Lacan's theorizing in the 1930s, as well as in subsequent decades, when he discussed Freud's ideas on fetishism. While we perhaps cannot say that as Binet was for Freud, so Freud was for Lacan, it is perhaps not inaccurate to note that Lacan's early use of the notion of *dédoublement* placed him within a specifically French psychiatric lineage. That lineage ran from Binet through the Salpêtrière school, and was taken up most directly by Clérambault – and this line of descent does show us a parallel between Lacan's relation to Freud and Freud's to Binet. Whereas Freud reworked Binet's concept to develop an aetiology of fetishism, Lacan inherited a framework already full of forensic concerns, where doubling of personality was tied to perversity and criminality. This inheritance marked Lacan's engagement with fetishism from the outset and shaped his theorization of perversion less as a developmental deviation, which we see in Freud, and more as a pathological structure with forensic implications.

Lacan's doctoral thesis results from work in forensic psychiatry. From 1927 to 1931, Lacan worked in the Special Infirmary of the Paris Police Headquarters, where those considered dangerous were brought for emergency treatment (Roudinesco 1997, 17). There Lacan was influenced by the ideas of his predecessors at the Special Infirmary, the French psychiatrists Ernest Dupré and Gaëtan Gatian de Clérambault. Both Dupré and de Clérambault adopted aetiological views of theoretical doctrines concerning perversity, fetishism, and paranoia (Gumpper and Haustgen 2012a, 227). In his thesis, Lacan refers to these ideas and aims, by means of the psychogenic aetiology of paranoia, to solve difficulties in constitutional theories of psychopathology (Lacan 1932, 25, 74).

Lacan's engagement with these theories is important. Scholars have noted that the differences between Freud's and Lacan's thinking on perversion are linked to the historical background of the psychiatric appropriation of the perversions Lacan refers to (Lantéri-Laura, 2012). Moreover, contemporary debate on this topic tends to investigate how Lacan's theory of the perverse structure connects to Dupré's ideas, and inevitably induces moral regard for perversions (Lantéri-Laura 2012, 185; Mazaleigue-Labaste 2014, 290; Van Haute 2016, 275). Seeing how Lacan deals with this debate therefore presents a few advantages here. For one, it clarifies Lacan's view of fetishism in his early theorizing about paranoia in the 1930s, and, as such, it allows us to better understand his psychoanalytic theorization of fetishism in the 1950s. It also elucidates Lacan's theoretical recourse to the concepts of personality and doubling. Last, it explains precisely how Freud's ideas on sexuality provide solutions to Lacan's psychiatric thinking.

Let us examine this debate, then. Unlike Freud, who sought to distinguish sexual perversion from moral perversity, Dupré approached fetishism and paranoia as expressions of the same innate disorder: a constitutional perversion of the instincts. These instincts, functioning as character traits, manifested in behaviours such as theft or violent outbursts or "paroxysms" and were seen as signs of moral degeneracy (Dupré [1912] 1925, 372, 390, 405–6). Lacan, drawing from Dupré rather than Freud, took fetishism as a key to theorizing such paroxysms psychoanalytically, framing them as *passage à l'acte* ("passage to the act"). In so doing, Lacan applied Freud's ideas on sexuality not to advance Freud's own distinctions, but to reinterpret Dupré's premises. He rejected Dupré's hereditary assumptions, arguing instead for a psychogenic view in which paranoia and fetishism result from the developmental dynamics of personality (Lacan 1932, 25, 51, 62, 98). Even so, Lacan's departure from Dupré did not free fetishism from its forensic framing. By continuing to situate fetishism within a conceptual milieu linking deviant instincts to immorality, criminality, and social danger, Lacan retained the basic assumption that fetishism belonged to the domain of pathology. In this respect his "solution" only reworked Dupré's model, without undoing its premises: fetishism was no longer hereditary degeneracy, but it did remain a sign of moral risk and a potential threat to public order. This orientation contrasts with Freud's refusal to conflate fetishism with criminality and demonstrates how Lacan's early theorizing reinscribed fetishism into psychiatric pathology rather than opening it to Freud's more ambivalent, potentially depathologizing treatment. And it is at just this point, in fact, that Lacan begins to engage with Freud's and Binet's ideas, and particularly those concerning the ego and the concept of doubling, as the foundation for his (increasingly non-Freudian) theory of perversion.

As shown in earlier chapters, Freud's theory of fetishism gradually developed alongside his view of human sexuality as object-directed. In contrast, Lacan, responding to psychiatric concerns, sought to evolve Dupré's premise that perverted instincts function as psychological traits in disorders like fetishism and paranoia. By referencing psychoanalytic ideas, Lacan (1931, 37–42, 345) was able to frame fetishism as a way to explore problems in the objectification of images. This applied particularly to the absence or distortion of that process. He focused on Freud's shifting account of the polymorphous-perverse sexual drive, and especially the move from infantile autoeroticism towards object unification. Because Freud did not theorize fetishism in terms of ego-formation or personality structure, Lacan's approach represents a distinct psychoanalytic trajectory. We shall see more of this point in this chapter.

Although Lacan formulated a psychogenic theory of personality in the 1930s as an alternative to Dupré's constitutional model, his thinking remained grounded in the French forensic psychiatric tradition that linked personality to moral danger. As Sauvagnat and Chaillou (2016, 211) point out, Dupré's notion of personality already implied a predisposition to harmful intent. Lacan's turn to Binet's concept of the doubling of personality fits this framework: he recasts fetishism as a phenomenon of divided personality, evolving psychiatric views that had treated it as morally or criminally suspect. Scholars have noted that this association persists in later thought, where fetishism remains entangled with questions of perversity and criminality (Sauvagnat and Chaillou 2016, 220–3, 229). In Lacan's theory, personality conflicts that manifest in criminal acts are interpreted as expressions of deeper psychic structures, in particular failures in ego and object formation. In what follows, the discussion examines how Lacan's early forensic interest in fetishism led him to develop the concept of perverse structure, and how this connects back to his use of ego-formation and doubling in the 1930s.

Binet's Ideas on Paranoia as Doubling of Personality in Lacan's Explorations

In his thesis, Lacan refers to the study in which Binet and Simon criticized Freud's aetiological ideas on hysteria, and where they argued for the concept of doubling. A closer look at Binet's ideas on personality and paranoia will clarify why Lacan chose the concept of the doubling of personality to develop his psychiatric and psychoanalytic ideas.

Binet and Simon (1910, 142) discussed paranoia as insanity with conscience (*folie avec conscience*) and as systematized insanity (*folie systématisée*) (216–29). They argued that paranoid subjects are not detached from external reality, and that certain forms of paranoia are nothing more than a decreased level of ability to adapt to reality. As further discussed, Lacan defines paranoia (and consequently fetishism) as a maladaptation to reality. Paranoia, Binet and Simon claimed (1910, 119–20), implies that the subject presents a doubling of personality (*dédoublement de la personnalité*). They explain that paranoiacs are "doubled" (*dédoublés*) subjects because they are in conflict with a force unfamiliar to them. Binet and Simon explain that these subjects can speak about their doubling (*dédoublement*). Particularly, they can recognize the other (*autre*) within themselves.

Whereas Freud was engaged in reshaping Binet's foundational ideas on doubling, Lacan did not follow in considering its links to the phenomena of consciousness in hysteria nor to the double unconscious perception of objects or double-faced objects. Nor did Lacan link doubling to the simultaneity of attitudes in the doubling of the ego. When Lacan centres his psychoanalytic discussion on fetishism in the 1950s, he is aware that Freud targeted his concept of splitting the ego as related to the fetish object (Lacan [1956–7] 1994, 156). Nonetheless, Lacan insists on framing fetishism as a problem of the objectification of the subject's body image. Lacan's theory of fetishism can therefore be read as a further development of his initial psychiatric conceptualization. His study of the relationship between personality, paranoia, and fetishism in the 1930s developed from Binet and Simon's conceptualization of paranoia as a doubling of personality.

Lacan connects doubling to the stages of development that culminate in the complexity of personality, which includes the consequences of the subject's (social) interactions with other individuals (1932, 132–3, 270). He notes that the subject's persecuting enemies are duplicates (*doublets*) of familiar subject prototypes. This fact leads Lacan (296) to suggest that this doubling of personality stems from the subject's early iterative identifications (*identification iterative*) with family members. Here he argues that psychosis reveals how early socialized reactions disrupt the development of vital drives, producing what he calls "pre-personal anomalies." (Lacan 1932, 243, 340). These archaic elements shape personality through identification with one's "doubles," making the formation of subjectivity inherently relational and structured by doubling. From this perspective, it is clear that Freud did not frame fetishism in terms of personality formation, as Lacan would later do.

This idea will gradually shape Lacan's approach to fetishism. Freud's ideas led Lacan to conclude the subject's iterative identification with the mother image proves that the subject deals with duplicate images in the initial stages of the formation of his personality. Considering that these assumptions mark the beginning of Lacan's interaction with Freud's ideas, we should first ask the question: What would have been the role of Freud's theory here?

Following Binet and Simon, Lacan traces pre-personal anomalies to a maladaptation in the subject's integration of internal and external realities

(Lacan 1932, 243). He interprets Freud's theory of libido development as offering an organic account of this maladaptation, particularly in the early "contact with reality" that underlies paranoid doubling of personality (Lacan 1932, 255, 257). For Lacan, the libido's successive projections onto external objects occur in early life and form the basis for such anomalies. Unlike Freud, who did not apply these ideas to fetishism, Lacan links fetishism to the failure of early libidinal projections to adapt to reality.

Lacan's Initial Approach to Fetishism

But how does Lacan view fetishism in the context of his psychiatric investigation? He associates sexual perversions with his forensic psychiatric explorations. Furthermore, he claims that in addition to the murderous intent in the paranoiacs' aggression towards their enemies, paranoiacs also engage in other immoral acts, such as robbery and slander. These behaviours represent episodic manifestations of sexual perversions (Lacan 1932, 275). But the link to criminality or immorality is evidence of not only the influence of Lacan's training in forensic psychiatry but also his willingness to apply his idea of maladaptive synthesis of personality to the understanding of the paroxysms of perversions and fetishism. It is here that Lacan draws on Freud.

To substantiate the link between aggression and perversion and his model of the anomaly of personality, Lacan (1932, 341, 355) relies on Freud's theories about the drive and psychosexual development, and on his explanation for how the aggressive drives are socialized. Lacan claims that interruptions occur in the psychic development he conceptualized as narcissistic pre-personal fixations (358). Insofar as the formation of the human self is structurally dependent on a relationship with a double, Lacan (1932, 313) understands that the formation can result in an aggressive relational modality of the personality. This modality presents a discordant synthesis related to images shaping the double: that is, images of the subject's family. This formulation is highlighted here because of how Lacan develops his psychoanalytic ideas and attempts to theorize fetishism in the same framework. To explore how the paranoid ego relies structurally on a relationship with a double, Lacan (1932, 39, 324–5) turns to Freud's ideas about the formation of the Ego ideal (*Idéal du Moi*). But Lacan does not explain how fetishism and perversions result from a maladaptation in the projection of perverse components of the drives (libido) onto reality. Indeed, as Lacan tries to fit fetishism into his theory in the 1930s, it becomes evident that his ideas on objectification refer to images of *people*, and not of the kind of fetish objects Freud had investigated and that we have seen here, such as feet, nose, hair, underwear, shoe, boot, and support-belt. In addition, although Lacan considers his theory to include fetishism, he does not make clear how the fetish object – the essential characteristic of fetishism, as we saw with Freud – can explain a *personality*-related phenomenon.

What is clear, however, is that Lacan's framework still bore the imprint of forensic psychiatry. In linking fetishism to patterns of immorality and criminality, his early model inherited psychiatry's tendency to criminalize perversion. Here again we see a distinction from Freud who, even when pathologizing fetishism, resisted treating it as synonymous with delinquency. The theoretical divergence between Freud's developmental model and Lacan's structural adaptation thus also marks a diagnostic and political divide. Freud's ambivalence left space for fetishism to be viewed as eccentric but not necessarily criminal, whereas Lacan's inheritance of psychiatric categories tied fetishism more firmly to pathology and juridical suspicion.

In this it is not an exaggeration to say that we find Lacan wrestling with the same riddle that pushed Freud in so many different directions over the decades. It is simply that the riddle pushed Lacan towards something else.

In fact, Lacan's gradual approach to fetishism in the late 1930s is a clear consequence of his ongoing theorization of the link between doubling and the formation of personality. At that time he was building on his theorization regarding these topics through Freud's psychoanalytic ideas on sexual difference, and he places fetishism as an outcome of the same discordant ego-identifications he theorized about in his psychiatric thesis: as a fixation on atypical identification forms of the narcissistic phase. According to Lacan, when the maturation of the child's genital drive happens before the subject achieves a full objectification of the image of his parents, this invariably implies a lack (*défaut, carence*) in the ego's ability to synthesize and unify images ([1938] 2001, 28, 75). Thus, Lacan is able to explain that the subject's initial relations with the images of other individuals in his family are dominated by fantasies, and then constitute the image of the ego. He further affirms that the fantasy of the phallic mother is evidence of the primordial image of the double (*imago primordiale du double*), which forms the ego function and shapes how the subject relates to other objects (28). When the early pressure of sexuality confronts the subject with this *lack* in the objectification of images, the subject can then form his ego by identifying with the fantasized form of the phallic mother ([1938] 2001, 45). Lacan claims that this process can result in sexual fetishism (*fétichisme sexuel*). He writes that "this identification of the narcissistic phase can be observed either to generate the formal demands of homosexuality or of a sexual fetishism, or, in the system of the paranoiac ego, to become objective as an external or internal persecutory agent" (Lacan [1938] 2001, 45).

In this passage we see Lacan's ongoing connection between fetishism and the model of paranoia he had developed in the 1930s. While developmental problems with the anal drive lead to an idealized objectification in paranoia that generates the double image of persecutory persons, Lacan presupposes similar problems in the development of the genital drive. An idealized (fantasized) objectification in fetishism may result, thus generating the double image of the (phallic) mother.

In light of these theoretical positions, what exactly is Lacan's conceptualization of fetishism? What does Lacan mean when he discusses fetishism as a discordant ego-identification in relation to a double image? What is the meaning of "lack" in the objectification of images in fetishism? And, bearing in mind that fetishism is a phenomenon characterized exclusively as linked to an *object*, what would then be the role of the fetish object in an anomaly of personality? These are the pertinent questions here, as, in the late 1930s, Lacan still refrains from further developing fetishism; he leaves the questions unanswered. We can therefore argue that Lacan's evolving link between fetishism and the model of paranoic disturbance of personality demonstrates his continued effort to develop an alternative to Dupré's theory. The alternative would work such that fetishism, sexual perversions, and paranoia would not be considered moral perversities stemming from predispositions of personality and character. In other words, at this point he was not looking to deepen Freud's ideas.

As explored in previous chapters, Freud struggled to theorize fetishism apart from the fetish object. He ultimately turned to Binet's insights to develop an aetiology grounded in the origin and function of the object. Lacan, by contrast, approached fetishism through the lens of forensic psychiatry, and framed it as a disturbance in personality and interpersonal patterns. While this approach echoes Freud's early attempts to treat fetishism independently of the object, Lacan similarly fails to establish a clear theoretical link between the fetish object and specific personality structures – despite fetishism being defined by attachment to non-personal objects, such as body parts or clothing.

Lacan follows Binet and Simon in relating paranoia to a doubling of personality, but he does not explicitly extend this framework to fetishism. Although he gestures towards such a connection, as he views fetishism as a response to the failure to objectify the maternal image in early development, his 1930s model lacks the conceptual tools to explain fetishism as a synthetic anomaly tied to genital drives and maternal doubling. Only later, through the psychoanalytic tradition of object-relation, would Lacan attempt to theorize this lack of objectification.

In the next section, it is shown how Lacan continued to develop his version of doubling within psychoanalysis, by applying it to his evolving understanding of fetishism.

Lacan's Psychoanalytic Model of Doubling

In pursuing his exploration of doubling and personality, Lacan elaborated a theorization of doubling and discussed the imaginary constitution of the ego. Lacan's choice to theorize problems in the objectification of the ego is crucial in differentiating between his own theoretical challenges with fetishism, and those Freud faced. Lacan's approach to objectification does not refer to sexual objects like those that characterize fetish objects. Rather, it refers to the objectification of the image of the ego and the image of persons.

At the outset of Lacan's psychoanalytic thinking in the 1950s, he generalizes the psychoanalytic relevance of this doubling in the subject's personal synthesis. In this he builds on his psychiatric theory of the 1930s, that is, by connecting doubling to Freud's ideas on the role of libido and aggressive drives in the formation of the ego (narcissism). In the 1950s, Lacan includes neurosis in his theoretical exploration ([1953] 1978, 294–6): this is a corresponding model arguing for narcissistic problems during psychosexual development, leading to doubling.

Lacan ([1953] 1978) elaborates on the doubling of the subject (*dédoublement du sujet*) (303). He claims that insofar as the Oedipus complex lies at the heart of every psychoanalytic experience, it can be assumed that neurosis always involves a doubling (*dédoublement*) in the subject's function. For, in neurosis, Lacan says, despite subject's striving to avoid the internal division of his ego, in a close (narcissistic) relation with his sexual partner the subject's beloved person (love object) doubles (*dédoublé*) (300). This doubling occurs because the relationship between the neurotic subject and his or her love partner is established on a narcissistic identification. Besides being amorous to his beloved, then, the narcissistic identification with his sexual partner is also a mortal one. Lacan puts it this way: "In this very special form of narcissistic doubling lies the drama of the neurotic" (Lacan [1953] 1978, 300). On these grounds Binet's concept of doubling set a foundation for Lacan's theorization, from the time of his initial interaction with Freud's ideas. This concept later served as the basis for Lacan's notion of narcissistic doubling, and in the 1950s shaped his discussion of Freud's splitting.

In his writings and seminars, Lacan ([1954–5] 1978, 312) turns to the discussion of Freud's ideas about splitting as a form of doubling of the ego (*dédoublement du Moi*) in psychoanalysis (1955, 338, 343). He notes that the psychoanalytic relevance of his view by claiming that the imaginary function of the human ego is diverted to narcissistic relations. This fact, Lacan states, has consequences for human subjectivity when this is conceptualized as an internal doubling (*dédoublement interne*) (343) of existence, of which sexual perversion is the most clinically evident form.

The discussion in this section has demonstrated that Lacan sees fetishism differently from Freud. Freud's efforts to explain the origin of the fetish object have previously been discussed through an exploration of Binet's initial ideas. Here we see that Lacan, unlike Freud, views fetishism as a personality-linked phenomenon characterized by specific patterns of relating to other individuals. And yet, despite this difference, fetishism still pushed Lacan, as it did Freud, to not only sharpen but also change some of his most fundamental ideas.

Indeed, by understanding fetishism from this perspective, Lacan found no reason to discuss the role of the fetish object in his theorization. Until 1950, Lacan was still unable to elaborate a theory that linked the existence of the fetish object to something that could be a fetishist disturbance of personality, or to the specificity of fetishist patterns of interaction with other individuals.

2. Lacan's Debate on Fetishism with Object-Relation Theory

This was not always to be the case, however. In 1956, Lacan finally attempts to solve the problem created by fetishism in his theory. His strategy is to develop the psychoanalytic approach of the object-relation. In doing so, Lacan falls back on his previous (psychiatric) ideas, where he had conceptualized perversion as a perversity.

During 1956 and 1957, in his Seminar IV called "The object-relation," Lacan ([1956–7] 1994, 11–13, 77) took up the subject of fetishism and aimed to conceptualize this phenomenon as one of the "Freudian structures." He did so in the context of developing a structural theory, mainly by contributing to the psychoanalytic perspective of object-relation. Some background will help here. In the 1940s and 1950s, various psychoanalyst scholars elaborated on the psychoanalytic line of thought of object-relations, which was based on Freud's psychoanalytic views. This line of thought focuses on the child's development of the ego from the perspective of the child's relationship with other people in its environment (Greenberg and Mitchell 1983, 12). It also examines how the child assimilates images, especially those of the mother. This process subsequently determines the formation of the child's own body image and personality. Accordingly, in his theory of fetishism Lacan specifically engages in a discussion about the ideas of object-relation with psychoanalytic authors trained in this way of thinking. These scholars saw fetishism and the fetish object as a pathological phenomenon during development. Lacan finds in these authors ideas similar to those he had already been forming about fetishism. In this context he also applies his model of doubling.

In Seminar IV, Lacan ([1956–7] 1994, 12–13, 17, 62) builds on his earlier view of fetishism as a narcissistic disturbance in the subject's adaptation to reality, particularly through the relation with the image of others. Drawing on object-relation theorists such as Greenacre (1955), who linked fetishism to mutual mirroring between mother and child, Lacan argues that this relationship is marked by a dual, conflict-ridden identification with the maternal image. He introduces his theory of the lack of object to explain this dynamic: the child compensates for the perceived absence of the mother's phallus by constructing a phallic image. Fetishism, for Lacan, becomes an imaginary way of accessing this lacking object. He links this process to his earlier model of doubling, now reframed as a structural feature of the child's relationship to the mother. According to Lacan, fetishism emerges as the child identifies with the mother's imagined phallus and produces a doubled maternal image. This doubling, Lacan claims (71, 83–4), constitutes a narcissistic and perverse attempt to repair the maternal deficiency. Thus, fetishism appears as a psychic structure rooted in an idealized, mirrored relationship with the mother.

To better understand Lacan's reasoning on this complicated issue, the discussion next considers how he read other thinkers in this context.

Fetishism as an Object-Relation Phenomenon

Even as late as 1956, Lacan was still unable to position the role of the fetish object in a presupposed fetishist personality phenomenon, or in fetishist patterns of interactions with other individuals. Here, then, two points are discussed: the ideas formulated from the object-relation perspective on fetishism, which allowed Lacan to present, finally, a new theory of fetishism; and also the ideas about fetishism he receives from the object-relation theorists, which take fetishism as a privileged phenomenon to theorize about perversion in terms of perverse and fetishist structure.

When theorizing about fetishism in greater detail, Lacan referred to the ideas about the infantile origin of the fetish object set by psychoanalyst authors who address the topic as part of the object-relation approach. Lacan's interaction with these ideas as well as his resulting explanations offer him several advantages. First, he can understand fetishism as a phenomenon related to personality and interpersonal relationships in terms of a lack in the objectification of images. Second, he can characterize fetishism in line with assumptions like that of the psychiatric conceptualization of perversity. Third, he is able to conceptualize fetishism as a paradigm of perversion (this is the idea of "perverse structure"). Let us develop these points.

In thinking about fetishism as an object-relation phenomenon, Lacan (1956–7, 25, 34–5, 127) highlights the influential object-relation concept of the *transitional object*. This idea was first formulated by British psychoanalyst Donald Woods Winnicott. Exploring the development of personal (personality) and interpersonal relationships patterns, Winnicott (1953) coined the concept of the transitional object to designate material objects, like pieces of cloth or plush toys, that a child assigns a special value during the early months and years of life. He assumed that transitional objects allow the child to advance in shifting from the earliest oral relationship with the mother's breasts to a step of differentiating itself (ego) from its mother. There is an important connection to Lacan here. Before Lacan proposed his theory of lack of object in fetishism, Winnicott had already said that fetishism occurs because of a "gap" in infantile development, when the child becomes aware of reality in the relationship with the mother. He had also postulated fetishism as a mode of complementing and filling this gap, which would otherwise not take place in the normal outcome of psychic development. Winnicott (1953, 96–7) had further conceptualized fetishism as leading the individual to *continue* the infantile experience of the transitional object, persisting into adult sexual life in the form of a fetish.

Bearing in mind that the fetish is a delusional image of a maternal phallus, Winnicott thus claims that fetishism exists as an urge to bridge a developmental gap that would maintain the continuity of the individual's experience with respect to a transitional object in adult life. Here is where things are crucial for Lacan. It is my view that, when aiming to contribute to Winnicott's theory of fetishism as filling a gap, Lacan defended (1956–7, 53–7, 84–5, 108) the idea that the fetish has a function in the frustration the child encounters in its relationship with the mother. That function is to complement the relation between the subject and the lack of the object (here, the mother deprived of the phallus). In his subsequent conceptualization of fetishism, Lacan also relies on Winnicott's discussion on the types of personal and interpersonal relationship patterns characterizing fetishism.

Winnicott further details the fetishist's urge to fill the developmental gap in the transitional field as involving the use of falsehoods and lying ("Pseudology"), in addition to thieving (Winnicott 1953, 97). Lacan, in turn, states that while identifying with the object the mother lacks (the phallus), fetishists create a deceptive object (*objet trompeur*) in their relationship with the mother: a false representation of themselves with respect to the mother, in order to try to deceive (*tromper*) her desire (Lacan 1956–7, 194). Lacan situated the fetishist in what he called the imaginary "luring" (*leurrante*) relation with the mother. The fetishist maintains a position in relation to the mother to "delude" (*leurrer*) her desire. According to Lacan, this position is structured within the framework of fetishism because it is the only position from which the relation of the fetishist to his object can be properly articulated (Lacan [1956–7] 1994, 224–5).

In connection with Lacan's arguments on fetishism and the mother's lack, we can now deal with Lacan's conceptualization of the perverse structure and the fetishist structure. In this context, Lacan's reading of Freud's late works on fetishism focused on isolating perversions as a clinical category, and then selecting fetishism as a privileged subject to develop the notion of the perverse structure and the fetishist structure (Lacan [1956–7] 1994, 145, 157). Whereas Freud, at least in his later works, did not place fetishism within the main nosological categories at all and, in his 1927 essay, made no mention of perversion, Lacan took the opposite approach. He addressed Freud's works on fetishism to develop a psychopathological framework for understanding perverse structure as a subjective position. From this perspective, fetishism is no longer a pathological variation, as it is in Freud's theory, but rather a general structure. Rather than categorizing fetishism within any nosology class, Freud considered it to be an acceptable eccentricity. Thus, is it that when Lacan conceptualizes and characterizes perverse structure and fetishist structure, he does so based on ideas not from Freud's works, but rather from those of psychoanalytic thinkers who adhere to the object-relations tradition.

One of these thinkers is the American psychoanalyst Phyllis Greenacre, who was mentioned briefly above. It is worth deepening our understanding of how Greenacre's work influences Lacan.

Fetishism as a Paradigm of Perversion in Lacan's Theory

Considering Lacan's interest in Greenacre's ideas, a closer look at her conceptualization of fetishism will reveal parallels to Lacan's earlier ideas. Prior to Lacan, Greenacre (1953, 85; 1955, 189) saw in fetishism a paradigm for characterizing perversions in general. For her, fetishism allows an understanding of the interrelation between different types of perversion. She argued that fetishism stems from disturbances during the transitional object phase, when visual and oral-aggressive components of the drive fail to integrate properly (Greenacre 1955, 191). As a result, fetishism reflects a weakness in ego structure rooted in disrupted early visual identifications with the mother (Greenacre 1953, 79, 85–6, 89).

As a result, Greenacre argues that in fetishism and other perversions there is a strong visual identification with a phallic mother, which creates instability of the body image and subsequent feminine identification. The fetishist in adult life can then stabilize his (sexual) identity only through the use of the fetish (1955, 188, 191). Taking fetishism as a paradigm for characterizing perversions, Greenacre claims that the same is true in transvestitism.

Along with Greenacre and others, Lacan ([1956–7] 1994, 126, 161) agrees that, in perversion, the valorization of the image and the imaginary dimension is prevalent. Lacan contributes to the debate by arguing the theory of lack of object. Likewise, in aiming to apply the theory to fetishism, Lacan (154) comments on Freud's late works on the topic. This is, in fact, the strategy for interpreting Freud's ideas on the fetish as representing the phallus as absent from the mother – the so-called "symbolic phallus." Owing to the child's frustration with the object, the subject remains in a state of imaginary relationship to the mother; and so, in fetishism, the subject assumes a permanence of that which is unseen and beyond the object (*au-delà de l'objet*), that is, the imaginary phallus of the mother ([1956–7] 1994, 119, 154).

In this sense, Lacan claims that the fetishist identifies with the phallus the mother lacks ([1956–7], 86). Staying close to Greenacre, Lacan conceptualizes what he calls the "fetishist structure" (*structure fétichiste*) (166) as a type of pathological object-relation where the subject identifies itself with the mother or, more generally, with a female character or some kind. Lacan also claims that the subject veils the lack of the mother: the fetishist, through his fetish object, effectively overcomes the lack of mother in the image of the other female. This process of overcoming characterizes perversion and the fetishist structure. This further characterizes fetishism as an "exemplary perversion" (184), as Lacan puts it. Unlike Freud, but similarly to Greenacre, Lacan claims that the fetishist structure constitutes a general nosological class. In making this move, Lacan decisively shifted fetishism into the terrain of formal psychopathology. Freud had consistently hesitated to classify fetishism within a nosological scheme and left it in an ambiguous position that, however pathologizing, still allowed for the possibility of treating it as eccentric variation rather than categorical disorder. Lacan, by contrast, aligned himself with the object-relations tradition and Greenacre's paradigm of perversion, and so transformed fetishism into a diagnostic type. This solidification narrowed the interpretive flexibility that Freud's approach had permitted and reinforced a clinical consensus that fetishism was not merely unusual but definitively pathological. Lacan writes, "fetishism is in effect a class that nosologically includes all sorts of phenomena whose affinity or kinship with fetishism is indicated to us in some way by our intuition" (Lacan [1956–7] 1994, 161).

Lacan conceptualizes fetishism not in Freud's terms but rather through the lens of object-relation theory, treating it as a central model for theorizing perversion more broadly. This contrasts sharply with Freud's approach. Building on Greenacre's ideas, Lacan further identifies relational patterns specific to fetishism, extending his earlier psychiatric view of fetishism as a form of perversity.

Just as Lacan's predecessors in forensic psychiatry, Greenacre also assumed that fetishism is associated with manifestations of perversity and instability of character. She (1955, 189) claims that this connection leads fetishists to aggression and to acting out. When commenting on Greenacre's stance and the work of other authors belonging to the object-relation tradition, Lacan finds support for discussing the mode of the fetishist relations as an identification with women, which identification implies aggressiveness, destruction, and even murder. He states:

> In short, we find an alternation of identifications in the amorous relations with the object which organize this cycle in the fetishist. Identification with the woman [...] the imaginary phallus of the primordial experiences of the oral-anal stage, centered on the aggressivity of the sadistic theory of coitus – and, in fact, many of the experiences which analysis brings to light show an observation of the primitive scene perceived as cruel, aggressive, violent, indeed, murderous. [...] The child is delivered up to the bipolar oscillation of the relation between two irreconcilable objects, which in any case ends in an outcome that is destructive, indeed murderous. (Lacan [1956–7] 1994, 160)

Whereas Freud reworked Binet's aetiological ideas about fetishism in terms of the trauma of sexual difference, Lacan ([1956–7] 1994, 153) sees the differentiation between the sexes as a symbolically ordered relation, and one that disciplines inter-human relations through *interdicts*, like the law of incest. In this sense, Lacan interprets Freud's idea of castration as an interdict of prohibitive laws. According to Lacan, perversion is characterized by a symbolic reduction resulting in a de-subjectified intersubjective relation. He thus confirms fetishism as a perverse structure: in the fetishist object-relation, the object takes the place of the lack, and Lacan takes the fetish object as devoid of any subjective, intersubjective, and trans-subjective properties. He claims that the fetishist identification with the mother or other woman demonstrates a de-subjectified symbolization. It is here that, aiming at characterizing this symbolization, Lacan argues for the "paroxysms of perversions." ([1956–7] 1994, 85, 162)

According to Lacan, because perversion shows a mode of relation going beyond the image of the other, perversions manifest themselves at their greatest degree of intensity, or during these "paroxysms." The paroxysms of perversions are not symbolically ordered; they are considered to be *passage à l'acte* (passage to the act) ([1956–7] 1994, 163). It is during these occurrences of *passage à l'acte* that perversion provides access to the other by going beyond the other's image. Immediately Lacan then connects the notion of *passage à l'acte* to fetishism. Although he gives no examples, he affirms that delinquent acts (*actes délinquants*) are equivalents of fetishism (163). Thus, it is that Lacan finally explains the paroxysms of fetishism in accordance with the doctrines of perversity, in line with the tradition of forensic psychiatry. By equating fetishistic acts with delinquency, Lacan reinscribed fetishism into the orbit of criminal pathology. What Freud had often described as a peculiar but tolerable eccentricity now became, in Lacan's hands, an index of forensic risk. This alignment reveals how the theoretical stakes of fetishism for Lacan were, just as for Freud, both diagnostic and political. Where Freud's ambivalence opened the possibility of depathologization, Lacan's adoption of psychiatric categories closed it off. He then positioned fetishism squarely within the logic of perversity and criminalization.

3. The Fetish as a Model of the Object of Human Desire in Lacan's Thinking

It is now time to consider how Lacan framed his theory of fetishism in relation to the notion of a perversion, for it is here that we see the most important aspect of the Freud–Lacan relation with respect to fetishism: Lacan attempts to explore fetishism as separate from the particulars of the fetish object.

The analysis turns to the 1960s, when, in exploring fetishism as a theoretical model of human desire, Lacan examines the objectification of the action causing the subject's desire for the object. Unlike Freud, Lacan sees the phenomenon of fetishism less as a sexual practice and more as a product of theories of perversity that aim to explain immoral as well as criminal acts.

Various scholars (Assoun 1994, 118–20) have noted that Lacan's interest in the fetish object heralded the re-emergence of the question of the *object* in psychoanalysis. But since Lacan starts discussing the fetish from theoretical references that are no longer understood to be psychoanalytic, a somewhat different argument is pursued here. Two claims are made. First, Lacan's undertaking of such a theorization can again be read as further developing ideas present in the contemporary psychiatric landscape. And, second, that theorization engages with ideas of the same psychoanalytic thinkers Lacan had previously debated when discussing fetishism. In continuing to discuss the fetish as a model of human desire, Lacan is extending his previous theory of paroxysm and "passage to the act" to fetishism and perversion.

Lacan ([1956–7] 1994, 194) famously called fetishism the "perversion of perversions," positioning it as the paradigm case for understanding perversion more broadly. But he also deepened its significance by linking it to the structure of human desire. In the 1950s, Lacan reframed fetishism as central to object-relations, describing it as an illusory relation to the object of desire ([1956–7] 1994, 158). He saw fetishism as revealing a fundamental dynamic: the subject constructs a fetish object to symbolize a missing element, and specifically the lack represented by the feminine phallus ([1956–7] 1994, 154–5). This object, while not the true object of desire, becomes indispensable, then mediating the subject's relation to both the world and their own desire. Fetishism thus models how desire operates through symbolic substitution. This makes it, for Lacan, a key to understanding the very dynamics of human longing.

Let us say a bit more about what is at issue here. Starting in the late 1950s, as Lacan continued to develop this theory, he changed his view of fetishism from a radical perversion of human desires (Lacan [1957–8] 1998, 76) to a more generalized approach ([1958–9] 2013, 370). As a model of the object of desire, the fetish in the perverse structure demonstrates the functioning of the object in terms of desire's absolute condition (Lacan [1958] 1966, 682; [1962–3] 2004, 122). Lacan claims that the object of desire has a function in the association of subject and fantasy. Furthermore, the object takes the place of that which the subject is symbolically deprived of, namely the phallus. Given that the fetish symbolizes the phallus, the object of human desire, in general, has a fetishistic character. Thus, Lacan is able to claim that the fetishization of human objects (*fétichisation des objets humains*) lies at the root of human relations: the fetish is a fundamental dimension of the human world. In the years that followed, Lacan deepened the link between the fetish and the idea of the "lack" in the objectification of human desire; his goal was to devise a theory addressing the limitations of the subjective symbolization of human desire.

There is a problem, though. In this view Lacan equated delinquent acts and *passage à l'acte* with acts of fetishism, but from the early 1960s onwards, he never offered any examples. For Lacan, as for Freud, fetishism was a phenomenon linked to an object, frequently a piece of clothing or part of the body. As such, there yet remains a question: how are the actions of the fetishist structure, such as delinquent acts and *passage à l'acte*, explained on this way of thinking, considering the presence of the fetish object?

In my view, Lacan's strategy for answering this question was to explore a direction opposite to Freud's. As we have seen in previous chapters, the riddle of fetishism in Freud's theorizing appeared *after* he began to view the phenomenon as distinct from its object. To solve this problem, Freud turned to Binet on fetishism and sought an aetiological theory to explain the origin of the fetish object. To make this happen, Freud gradually applied concepts from his theory of neurosis, such as fantasy, idealization, and overvaluation, as well as symbolization and memory – all of which concern the object. Lacan, in contrast, does not explain the actions of the fetishist structure by focusing on how the fetish comes to be fantasized, overvalued, idealized, symbolized, or remembered. On the contrary, in fact, Lacan does not opt for an aetiological theory of how the fetish object originated, formed, or came to be chosen in the fetishist structure at all. He instead maintains the view that fetishism is a singular topic with which to theorize about processes preceding the formation or choice of the fetish.

The more Lacan says about fetishism, the more his thinking diverges from that of Freud. In reality, as part of Lacan's theory of the cause of desire, he identifies fetishism as a vehicle for understanding actions that concern pre-subjective processes. In the 1960s, Lacan begins to see the fetish as a prerequisite for the subject to perform de-subjectivized actions towards the object. The argument here acknowledges the influence of Lacan's previous psychiatric training, as well as his reasons for turning to theories other than Freud's psychoanalytic ideas. From that perspective we can understand much better why Lacan directs his attention to fetishism, and in particular to pre-subjective issues (which in the 1960s he termed the "cause of desire"). ([1962–3] 2004, 122).

An exploration of fetishism from the perspective of non-subjectivized actions towards the object had already been undertaken within the psychiatric landscape before Lacan approached fetishism that way. Like Lacan, his predecessors in forensic psychiatry did not follow Freud's long-standing efforts to formulate a psychoanalytic aetiology of fetishism that introduced the fetish object. Lacan and his predecessors preferred to position fetishism as a way to explain criminal and immoral acts, which would be understood from the perspective of pathological, involuntary, uncontrollable, and non-subjectivized processes leading to actions towards objects.

To integrate all of these points, we must see how Lacan developed this theory in the 1960s. He did it by way of the infamous "object *a*." Some scholars (Assoun 1994, 118–20) claim that Lacan's interest in the fetish foreshadows his development of "object *a*" as the lacking object causing desire in the human subject. By introducing his concept of "object *a*," Lacan's theory of the causality of human desire addresses limitations in the domain of human subjectivity ([1962–3] 2004, 119, 120–7, 140; Vanheule 2011, 125). In connection with these points, Lacan approaches the fetish object as a means of addressing the limitations of human subjectivity, that is, by perceiving the cause of desire ("object a") in terms of processes *independent of the formation or choice of the fetish.* As Lacan introduces his concept of "object *a*" and begins to discuss his idea of cause of desire (*cause du désir*), he takes the fetish as a model of an object prior to any subjective internalization. From there he can claim that the fetish as such unveils the nature of the *object* as the *cause* of desire. He states:

> The notion of cause belongs to this outside, the locus of the object, prior to any internalization. [...] To give an image of it, it is not by chance that I am going to use the fetish as such, because this is where the veil is drawn back on the dimension of the object as cause of desire. (Lacan [1962–3] 2004, 122)

In other words, even if Lacan recognizes the fetish as an external object, when he views the fetish as the object *causing* the desire, he theorizes it as prior to subjective interiorization. Consistent with the argument here, which uncovers his affiliations to theoretical traditions other than Freud's psychoanalytic work, it can be argued that Lacan's ideas about the (fetishist) dimension of the object of desire also differ from Freud's ideas on fetish and perversion. In this case, Lacan's conceptualization conforms to the French psychiatric tradition to which he belonged. In the development of his theory of subjectivity, Lacan discusses fetishism from his native psychiatric perspective, as an evolution of the conceptualization of personality doubling. This reasoning culminates in his elaboration of the notions of fetishist and perverse structures.

In the background of Lacan's discussion of the fetish as the cause of desire, he postulates another (psychiatric) conceptualization of doubling *not* associated with the images influencing the subject's personality. This conceptualization of doubling reflects the subject's uncontrollable impulses towards desire.

In the 1930s, after developing a psychogenic theory of personality doubling in opposition to Dupré's model of constitutional perversity, Lacan turned to the work of de Clérambault, as noted above a psychiatrist at the Paris Police Infirmary, to further refine his ideas. In 1946, Lacan drew on de Clérambault's concept of mental automatism, or the intrusion of involuntary, alien motor, and sensory-affective processes, as a key influence on his own notion of psychic structure and causality. These automatisms, which include psychomotor symptoms and verbal impulses, were seen as foundational to the development of mental disorders. Lacan's engagement with this theory marks a significant divergence from Freud's debate with Binet on doubling. De Clérambault, who had studied doubling at the Salpêtrière and discussed it with Binet and Simon, defined mental automatism as a splitting or "scission" of the ego and personality, often using terms such as *dédoublement* and *double* to describe the phenomenon.

Lacan's divergence from Freud becomes even more pronounced when he moves beyond theorizing fetishism as a perverse structure and begins framing the fetish as a model for the cause of desire, or again "object *a*." Some scholars argue that Lacan increasingly linked this concept to de Clérambault's theory of mental automatism (Vanheule 2018; Gumpper and Haustgen 2012b). While most studies of this influence focus on Lacan's theory of psychosis, its relevance for understanding fetishism is highlighted here. Given Lacan's forensic training, which associated fetishism with perversity and criminal behaviour, his adoption of de Clérambault's model helps to clarify how involuntary, alien psychomotor impulses – the mental automatisms – could ground his theory of desire. Fetishism, in this view, becomes a key to understanding the compulsive and embodied dimensions of desire, which expands Lacan's earlier framing of fetishism in terms of paroxysm, *passage à l'acte*, and delinquency.

Freud never characterized fetishism in terms of mental automatisms, and this absence is a key difference between his theory and Lacan's. While Freud's focus remained on the fetish's connection to the sexual drive, and particularly its ties to early erotic impressions or sensory modalities such as smell and taste,

Lacan reframes the issue through the lens of French psychiatry and object-relations theory. In this context, mental automatism becomes the bridge linking the fetish, the cause of desire ("object *a*"), and the subject's enactment of that desire by acting out. Notably, Lacan's discussion of fetishism as linked to the cause of desire bypasses Freud's actual writings on the topic. Instead, Lacan draws selectively on Freud's broader concepts, such as "auto-eroticism," to describe a pre-subjective emergence of desire where the ego is not yet formed. Even when citing Freud, Lacan reorients the ideas towards his own goals: rather than building on Freud's careful aetiological account of fetishism, he extracts language to support a theory in which the fetish functions as a structural marker of desire's logic.

This is how Lacan identifies the fetish as the vehicle for conceptualizing "object *a*," that is, not as having specific sexual features or for aetiological reasons, but rather as capable of demonstrating desire prior to the processes of subjectification. Lacan writes:

> What is desired? It's not the little item of footwear, nor the breast, nor anything else with which you can embody the fetish. The fetish causes desire. Desire goes off to hook on wherever it can. It is not absolutely necessary for her to be wearing the little shoe. (Lacan [1962–3] 2004, 122)

The object that causes desire is something that the subject steals away (*que se dérobe*) ([1962–3] 2004, 121, 127). Here, Lacan discusses the "object *a*" that causes desire as *acting out*, specifically through acts of theft. This characterization is crucial, as we shall see.

Lacan ([1962–3] 2004, 149) reinforces his view that the fetish reveals the object as the cause of desire by drawing on Greenacre's theory of acting out. Greenacre (1953, 86; 1955, 188–9, 193–4) had characterized fetishism as both a form of perversity and a character disorder, emphasizing that acting out, especially with kleptomania and aggression, was a hallmark of the fetishist's character. Lacan adopts this framework. Greenacre's understanding of acting out also shares features with de Clérambault's concept of mental automatism: both describe a disconnect between verbal intention and bodily expression, manifested as involuntary impulses or tensions. De Clérambault had developed this concept through his study of women arrested for theft, by which he was able to link mental automatisms to impulsive acts such as stealing. Lacan extends the model and interprets the fetishist's desire and behaviour as expressions of a pre-subjective automatism. This reliance on the language of automatism hints at how deeply Lacan's structuralist theorizing remained tied to forensic psychiatry. By grounding fetishism in theft, compulsion, and impulsive acts, he cast it less as a neutral mode of desire than as a pathological drive with the potential to erupt beyond the subject's control. Even as Lacan recast Freud's riddle in the vocabulary of structure and desire, he inherited from Dupré and de Clérambault a diagnostic framework to tether fetishism to pathology and juridical doubt. The critical potential that Freud's ambiguities had opened – of viewing fetishism as eccentric rather than pathological – was once again narrowed, and this time perhaps inescapably so. By referencing Greenacre and analysing cases of kleptomania in women, Lacan ([1962–3] 2004, 168, 170–1, 372, 385) argues that acting out provides insight into how the fetish, as a displaced object, structures desire before the ego is fully formed.

Earlier in his career, Lacan aligned his thinking on psychic causality and structure with de Clérambault's psychogenic views. But by the mid-1950s, as he turned to fetishism, Lacan shifted away from both psychogenesis and organogenesis to develop a structural theory of psychoanalysis that emphasized concepts such as perverse and fetishist structures. In this framework, the genesis of fetishism becomes less central, as Lacan treats fetishism not as a developmental outcome but as a paradigmatic structure rooted in object-relations. This move distances Lacan from Freud, who, as shown throughout this book, persistently sought an aetiology of fetishism – he developed accounts of fantasy, repression, memory, and symbolization in dialogue with Binet's ideas. Lacan, in contrast, rejects explanatory accounts of origin and instead theorizes the fetish as an object structuring desire through its absence. This contrast highlights a core tension between Freud's developmental and aetiological focus and Lacan's structuralist model grounded in pre-subjective dynamics. As many scholars have noted (Lantéri-Laura 1994; Casanova 1987; Dimitriadis 2014), Lacan's theory of "object *a*" crystallizes this shift: the fetish becomes not an object formed through psychic history, but a structural placeholder in the triadic registers of the symbolic, imaginary, and real.

Lacan's concept of "object *a*" signals the irreducibility of human desire to any single subjective register. As early as the 1950s, he positioned fetishism as a privileged phenomenon that articulates the symbolic, imaginary, and real, or the three registers of human reality (Lacan and Granoff 1956). By the 1960s, Lacan had fully developed the fetish as a model of pre-subjective desire, shaped by the lingering influence of de Clérambault's psychiatry. This approach complements the broader argument of this book: unlike Freud and his predecessors, who struggled to isolate the phenomenon of fetishism from its object, Lacan reframes fetishism *through the structure of desire itself*, and most specifically through the subject's impulsive and uncontrollable relation to the fetish.

Decades earlier, de Clérambault had described similar processes in his forensic studies on "erotic passion for fabrics" (*la passion érotique des étoffes*), which he characterized as automatisms – reflexive, impulsive sexual responses to texture, detached from fantasy, memory, or personal attachment. In this context, de Clérambault also drew on Krafft-Ebing's *Psychopathia Sexualis*, explicitly comparing his own observations with Krafft-Ebing's case material to delimit what he called "intermediate perversions" between typical fetishism and erotic passion for fabrics (de Clérambault 1908, 709). By aligning his forensic studies with Krafft-Ebing's taxonomic framework, de Clérambault narrowed the more open-ended possibilities Freud and his predecessors had glimpsed in fetishism to reinscribe the phenomenon within a diagnostic lineage that emphasized pathology and perversity. Lacan inherits this framing and uses it to theorize fetishism as rooted in non-subjectivized structures, rather than as a developmental outcome linked to the object. In so doing, he takes fetishism in a direction quite distinct from Freud, as he emphasizes action and structural causality over symbolic content and psychic history.

It is also significant that de Clérambault's case material, and Lacan's subsequent uptake of it, carried a distinctly gendered inflection. Forensic psychiatry tended to construe women defendants and patients as pathological subjects of erotic compulsion while presenting men as the paradigmatic fetishists whose desires attached to women's bodies and attire. Lacan's reliance on this tradition reinforced a set of assumptions in which pathology and gender were deeply intertwined. If Freud's writings left open a space where fetishism might be viewed as an eccentricity rather than a crime, Lacan's inheritance of forensic psychiatry reproduced the gendered stereotypes that tied fetishism to perversity and criminality. This is an association that later views would work to correct, but the original association shows us the limits of what Lacan might be able to show in this respect. Because he took on the tradition of forensic psychiatry and the criminalization of fetishes, he could not transcend the gendered assumptions in which those views emerged.

Before Lacan turned to Freud's concept of autoerotism to theorize pre-subjective desire, de Clérambault had already described fetishistic automatisms involving a compulsive, impersonal attraction to fabrics, or what Shera (2009, 158) terms "autoerotic." This early framing, rooted in Lacan's forensic training, cast fetishism as tied not to sexual pleasure, as in Freud, but rather to instinctual, non-subjectivized acts. This shift allowed Lacan to see fetishism as a path to a different form of gratification. He then conceptualized it as *jouissance*.

By the 1950s, Lacan was already equating fetishism with delinquent acts and arguing that perverse paroxysms defy symbolic order. In the 1960s he expanded this view and presented fetishism as a model for acting out that disrupts the symbolic function of law. This disruption produces *jouissance* – a form of satisfaction exceeding pleasure, overwhelming the subject and fracturing both symbolic and imaginary structures (Lacan [1962–3] 2004; Fink 1995; Vanheule 2011). Here, fetishism becomes a privileged site for Lacan's broader theory of desire as dislocation.

In fact, de Clérambault's conceptualization of a sexual object derived from fetishism that does *not* function as a substitute for the male body is relevant to the overarching arguments of this entire book. It was shown that, in *Three Essays*, Freud initially conceptualized fetishism by considering the genital zone as one of several erogenous zones, thus demonstrating that the sexual drive attaches itself to various objects. After *Three Essays*, though, the concept of fetishism led Freud to modify his theory and discuss sexuality from the perspective of the trauma of sexual *difference*, finally giving central role to the idea of the genital zone. Freud did so by progressively ascribing a specific meaning to Binet's aetiology of fetishism and theorizing the defence against castration in fetishism. Unlike Freud's theory, Lacan's view on fetishism, when viewed as a return to de Clérambault's ideas and concepts, leads to a conceptualization of *jouissance* as an experience *not* framed as sexual pleasure. Indeed, after crediting de Clérambault's notion of mental automatism as grounding his structural theory of psychopathology (Lacan 1966, 65), Lacan ultimately specifies, as de Clérambault did before him, via the erotic passion for fabrics, a type of female *jouissance* that transcends sexual difference by negating the relevance of the phallus (Lacan [1972–3] 1975, 69). Here Lacan describes female *jouissance* as a doubling of *jouissance* (Aflalo 2012, 7–8; Pesenti-Irrmann 2006, 65, 68; Pickmann 2004, 201).

Considering Lacan's interaction with Freud's theory of fetishism in the discussion of these arguments, we can now much more clearly evaluate the differences between the two thinkers. We can argue that Lacan's theorization of fetishism, even when referencing Freud's later works on the topic, does *not* align with Freud's thinking at the time. These differences arise for three main reasons. First, Lacan views fetishism through the lens of forensic psychiatry, where theories of perversity established conceptual links between sexual deviance, pathology, and criminality. In adopting categories shaped by Dupré and de Clérambault, Lacan positioned fetishism not as a potential critique of "normal" sexuality, as Freud's ambivalence sometimes allowed, but rather as a condition legible within juridical and psychiatric frameworks. This orientation reinforced the pathologization, and even the criminalization, of fetishism, as it bound the idea more tightly to notions of danger, delinquency, and perversity. Second, Lacan's theory of fetishism was developed in the context of the psychoanalytic tradition of object-relations. And, third, Lacan discusses the fetish object in service to his theory on subjectivity and his theory on the object of human desire – topics not discussed by Freud.

Freud's struggle to define fetishism, moving as he does between repression, displacement, symbolism, and aesthetic idealization, revealed a persistent conceptual instability. As later thinkers have noted, this instability may be intrinsic to the phenomenon itself. Anselm Jappe (2020), for instance, has argued that fetishism ultimately transcends its Freudian sexual framework to become a defining structure of modern capitalist subjectivity. Drawing on Freud but also Marx, Jappe links commodity fetishism to pathological narcissism, suggesting that both reflect an inability to perceive objects (including people) as possessing autonomous reality. In capitalism, as in the narcissistic psyche, the external world becomes a mere extension of the desiring subject, with its reality effaced by projections of value or self. Freud's difficulty in stabilizing the fetish concept may thus reflect not only internal contradictions in his theory, but a broader cultural transformation where a form of fetishism has become not a deviance but a *norm*.

This broader transformation also sheds light on why Lacan, in revisiting Freud's theory, elevated fetishism to a privileged position within psychoanalytic thought. For Lacan, the fetish is not a failed repression or an isolated anomaly. It is a structural response to the absence at the heart of subjectivity itself. The fetish object covers over a constitutive lack, a gap introduced by the symbolic order and embodied most forcefully in castration anxiety. In this sense, Lacan anticipates the kind of reading Jappe advances: fetishism becomes not an exception to normative psychic development but rather its formal support. Where Jappe sees a society organized around the fetishized logic of abstract value and narcissistic projection, Lacan sees a subjectivity structured around the disavowal of loss through object-substitution. Both accounts point to the same conclusion: the fetish is not marginal or pathological, but central; this remains the case whether in connection to capitalist social relations or to the formation of the desiring subject.

But this centrality carries a double edge. For Freud, and for later critics such as Jappe, the instability of fetishism opened space to critique the idea of "normal" sexuality, suggesting that what counted as pathological might in fact be constitutive of subjectivity or social life. Lacan, however, inherited a forensic framework that constrained this potential. By embedding fetishism within the nosology of perverse structures, he generalized its significance while simultaneously foreclosing its depathologization. The fetish is therefore central in Lacan's theory, yes, but central precisely *as a pathology*, rather than as a challenge to the category of "pathology" itself. Freud's failure to domesticate fetishism may thus signal not theoretical weakness but an early encounter with a structure that psychoanalysis and social theory would later recognize as foundational.

This chapter has shown that Lacan's theory of fetishism is not a departure from the core concerns of psychoanalysis but a radical reworking of its foundations. Beginning with Lacan's early psychiatric engagements, and particularly his appropriation of Binet's theory of doubling and his forensic training under Dupré and de Clérambault, the chapter traced how Lacan framed fetishism not as a sexual anomaly to be explained but as a structural feature of personality, desire, and subjectivity. Over time, Lacan moved from a forensic and psychogenic model of perversion to a structural psychoanalytic theory where fetishism reveals the dynamics of identification, lack, and symbolic substitution. Drawing on object-relations theory and especially the work of Greenacre and Winnicott, Lacan reconceived the fetish as a privileged expression of the subject's relation to the phallus and the image of the other. By the 1960s, fetishism becomes, in Lacan's work, a theoretical tool for articulating his concept of "object *a*," the structural placeholder for what eludes symbolization and grounds human desire.

In the broader context of the book, this chapter provides a fitting culmination to the historical and conceptual trajectory traced across earlier chapters. Where Freud struggled to develop a coherent theory of fetishism – we have seen him many times oscillating between models of trauma, repression, disavowal, and symbolic compromise – Lacan transforms the riddle Freud could never solve into a structural question about the nature of the subject and the logic of desire. This final analysis shows that the tensions and blind spots in Freud's theory were not accidental but rather indicative of deeper impasses that Lacan explicitly thematized. Importantly, Lacan does not return to Binet in the same way Freud did. Rather than using Binet's work to build an aetiology of the fetish object, Lacan uses it to theorize subjectivity itself as structured by doubling, lack, and misrecognition. In this way, the chapter reinforces the book's central claim: that fetishism, far from being a marginal or anomalous phenomenon, has been a crucial testing ground for the conceptual development of psychoanalysis from its earliest formulations through its structuralist transformations.

Conclusion

In this conclusion, I review the central arguments of this study and discuss their implications. I also reflect on the significance of these findings. This study has traced Freud's evolving theory of fetishism through the lens of Alfred Binet's influence, arguing that Binet's ideas offer the clearest context for understanding Freud's ongoing efforts to refine psychoanalytic thinking in dialogue with nineteenth- and early twentieth-century neuropathology. By revisiting Freud's writings in chronological order, the book shows how his conceptual struggles with fetishism reflect an attempt not to break with, but rather to adapt and evolve, frameworks inherited from figures such as Binet and Richard von Krafft-Ebing.

In 1905, Freud's portrayal of fetishism as part of normal sexual development marked a departure from rigid diagnostic norms, but not a wholesale rejection of prior sexological theories. On the contrary, Freud's claim that perversion should be de-pathologized echoed Binet's earlier efforts to reframe fetishism as continuous with ordinary sexuality. Over time, Freud moved towards viewing fetishism as a minor pathology – an eccentric but manageable form of sexual expression. His late work reflects a clinical tolerance for fetishism while embedding it firmly within the framework of neurosis. Against recent interpretations that cast Freud as a forerunner of sexual pluralism, this book has argued that Freud's thinking on fetishism remains deeply rooted in the scientific and conceptual frameworks of French neuropathology, shaped above all by Binet. The trajectory of Freud's theory, from early aetiological models to his final reflections on ego-splitting, reveals not a rupture but rather a sustained development of Binet's foundational ideas.

At the same time, this study has traced how Freud's theory oscillates between pathologizing and depathologizing impulses. It shows fetishism to be a phenomenon that continually unsettles the line between the normal and the abnormal. This tension has been the backdrop for much of our discussion, as Freud's vacillations and Lacan's reformulations reveal how psychiatry and psychoanalysis alternately closed down and reopened possibilities for depathologizing fetishism.

By subsuming perversion within the domain of ordinary sexual development, Freud rendered it a concept without pathological weight. Across the following decades, he increasingly aligned with Binet's thinking, eventually treating fetishism as a benign eccentricity or minor clinical issue. Although Freud framed fetishism in neurotic terms, his final stance marked it as an acceptable deviation and not a significant disorder. This position runs counter to contemporary claims that Freud anticipated a modern pluralism of sexual practices. Instead, Freud's theory remains rooted in the scientific frameworks of French neuropathology, shaped most decisively by Binet. His gradual Oedipalization and neuroticization of fetishism reflects a deepening, and not at all a rejection, of that inheritance.

Tracing Binet's influence on Freud has helped to clarify a central question: does Freud's theory of fetishism imply that human sexuality is independent of an object? While Freud's early work linked fetishism to the aim of the sexual drive, his later writings reveal a sustained effort to rethink this in terms of object-choice. Over time, Freud increasingly adopted Binet's ideas, particularly around early impressions and psychic doubling, to build a psychoanalytic aetiology of the fetish object. Ultimately, Freud came to understand human sexuality as fundamentally object-related. The fetish object became central to his revisions of trauma theory and to his revival of the concepts of defence and splitting.

This trajectory also suggests an important direction for future research: examining how Freud's understanding of sexual function came to depend on mechanisms of splitting and defence. Freud's claim that the fetish does not wholly displace normative object-choice hinges on his theory of splitting, which is a psychological mechanism he borrowed, in effect, from Binet's earlier work on doubling. By the end of his career, Freud had returned to Binet's ideas to shape a theory of fetishism that anchored psychopathology in the dynamics of a divided ego.

The influence of Binet's concept of doubling extends beyond Freud to Lacan, whose early psychoanalytic work similarly reflects an effort to develop ideas rooted in French forensic psychiatry. As shown in the previous chapter, Lacan's engagement with fetishism and doubling reveals a shared intellectual lineage with Freud, shaped by Binet's conceptual legacy. Future research might further explore these parallel developments, offering deeper insight into how Binet's thinking shaped both Freud's and Lacan's views on fetishism and perversion.

In this work, we ought to consider the importance, not yet fully recognized, of Lacan foreclosing the critical potential that Freud's ambiguities had opened. Where Freud's oscillations sometimes destabilized the boundary of normal sexuality, Lacan's reliance on forensic psychiatry put fetishism again within categories of perversity and criminality. The scope for depathologization has thus narrowed.

In connection with this difference, though more broadly, this study has shown that both Freud and Lacan used fetishism to formulate key claims about human psychosexual development. Their theories diverge in crucial ways, however. Freud challenged established psychiatric distinctions between normal and pathological sexuality, while Lacan reasserted those older associations between perversion, immorality, and criminality. In so doing, Lacan overlooked Freud's most significant contribution to theorizing fetishism, which was his attempt to dismantle normative boundaries around sexual behaviour.

Whereas Freud grappled for decades with the nature and origin of the fetish object, and ultimately positioned it as a defensive formation tied to splitting and the preservation of the subject's relation to the sexual drive, Lacan reframed fetishism not as a question of the object itself but rather as a structural feature of human desire. Drawing on both French forensic psychiatry and object-relation theory, Lacan treated the fetish not as a fixed object of sexual overvaluation but as a placeholder for an absent, unrepresentable object (the "object *a*") that animates desire. This move effectively displaced the fetish's object-intrinsic character, making it less about the content of the object and more about its function within a symbolic and imaginary economy. In so doing, Lacan shifted the meaning of fetishism from a question of pathological attachment to a broader psychoanalytic model of how subjectivity and desire are structured around lack.

Even in his final formulations, Freud seems to have left unresolved whether fetishism should be taken as a harmless eccentricity or a diagnosable condition. This indeterminacy, as we have seen in Lacan and as we shall see below in other authors, allowed later readers to seize on fetishism either to reinforce psychiatric nosologies or to challenge them by questioning whether the category of pathology itself could be meaningfully sustained.

This same conceptual inheritance, which so strongly features the instability and power of the fetish as a site of disavowal, has also shaped later cultural theory. Laura Mulvey, writing in the wake of feminist film theory and semiotics, argued that Freud's model of fetishism provided a crucial tool for understanding how the erotic spectacle of femininity in cinema operates as a form of ideological defence. Like Jappe (2020), Mulvey (1993) sees fetishism not as an isolated psychological perversion, but rather as a structural condition of cultural life. This condition connects the Freudian mechanisms of substitution and denial with the Marxist critique of commodity fetishism. In both cases, disavowal allows the subject to "know very well" while still "believing all the same," manifesting a logic underpinning not only the fetishist's investment in a bodily substitute but also the viewer's fascination with cinematic glamour or the consumer's attachment to pristine commodities. Mulvey's analysis of cinema's "aesthetics of disavowal" (1993, 7) reinforces the broader claim that fetishism functions as a structural bridge between psychic defence, cultural production, and political economy – a bridge that Freud was the first to glimpse but could not fully cross. Lacan would attempt to do so as well, by means of subjectivity and desire.

The afterlife of fetishism as a conceptual tool extends beyond psychoanalysis and aesthetics, and into even the foundations of economic theory. Desmond McNeill (2020) has recently argued that Marx's notion of fetishism is not a historical curiosity but in fact remains central to understanding how value is constructed and misrecognized in contemporary capitalism. Like Freud, Marx described fetishism as a structure of disavowal, one that masks the true origins of meaning, whether in labour or in childhood perception. The notion projects them onto a misleading surface. McNeill emphasizes that this mystification is not incidental, but rather constitutive of how economic systems function, as value becomes detached from production and reified in abstract signs such as money or price. This conceptual affinity with Freud's account of the fetish object, understood as a substitute that both conceals and reveals an underlying trauma, further supports the view that fetishism marks the point where systems of psychological meaning break down. It reveals their dependence on symbolic sleight-of-hand by means of "scientific" categories inherited from prior generations, whose internal contradictions have never been fully worked out. Freud may have located the problem in sexual development, but the resonance of his insights across aesthetics, economics, and theory indicates to a deeper structural instability that no single discipline can fully contain. Clearly, then, there is far more work to do here.

As we have seen in many places throughout this book, this instability also opens the opportunity to make fetishism a key point of engagement for queer and trans theory. There it would serve as a lens for examining the limits of psychoanalytic categories themselves. The fetish object, always excessive and never quite assimilable to traditionally normative accounts of desire, resists the developmental teleology underpinning much of Freud's sexual theory. Its refusal to signify straightforwardly, which creates some of the riddle we have been following, is simultaneously a theoretical advantage for those who might view gender and sexuality not as fixed endpoints but rather as improvisational and affectively charged negotiations with a traditional hierarchical order. A trans reading in particular could explore how the fetish might be reimagined not as a symptom of failed psychical development but rather as a creative and adaptive structure that permits desire to persist in the face of disavowed or unspeakable truths – unspeakable by a binary normativity, that is. As a result, from this perspective, fetishism would not simply interrupt Freud's system. It would reveal forms of life and meaning that exceed the binaries, such as male/female and normal/perverse, on which that system was built.

Stepping back from these points regarding other fields, this book has traced the conceptual evolution of fetishism in Freud's work. I have argued that his enduring struggle to theorize the phenomenon cannot be understood in isolation from the influence of Alfred Binet and the broader context of French neuropathology. Freud's persistent return to the question of the fetish object – what it is, how it forms, and what psychic function it serves – demonstrates a long-standing effort to rework Binet's ideas within the framework of psychoanalysis. He was not radically breaking with his predecessors; Freud adapted and extended Binet's model of doubling and mental splitting and translated these into a psychoanalytic vocabulary centred on repression, defence, and the dynamics of the sexual drive. As a result, Freud's theory of fetishism became a crucial testing ground for many of his major innovations, from the theory of infantile sexuality to the later structural model of the psyche.

The trajectory of Freud's work on fetishism also illuminates the development of psychoanalysis itself, as it moves from early explorations of perversion towards more intricate accounts of ego-formation, symbolic substitution, and the mechanisms of desire. That same trajectory reveals how Freud's thinking remained anchored in a nineteenth-century medical-psychological discourse, even as it gave rise to a new discipline. This book has argued that Freud's framing of fetishism, despite its eventual shift from pathology to eccentricity, continued to rely on a view of the fetish object as a response to psychic conflict and shaped by defence and repression. In contrast, Lacan's structuralist reworking of the concept displaced the object as such and treated fetishism instead as a paradigmatic expression of how desire is organized around lack. This divergence reveals not just a theoretical difference between Freud and Lacan but also a shift in how psychoanalysis itself conceptualized the relation between sexuality, objecthood, and subjectivity.

Taken together, the results of my analyses reinforce, in various ways, the insight that the history of theorizing fetishism is not only about conceptual refinements within psychoanalysis but also about the broader struggle over whether sexuality should be framed in pathological terms *at all*. The ambivalences in Freud, and the corresponding closures in Lacan, both demonstrate how fetishism presses against the medicalization of desire. Then and now, it is a privileged site for reconsidering the meaning of pathology and normality in human sexuality. These questions continue to surround us today.

Understanding the development of Freud's theory of fetishism, as well as its transformation in Lacan, helps us to grasp a deeper methodological and conceptual divide in the history of psychoanalysis. At stake is not merely how fetishism is classified or explained, but what kind of object it is: whether it retains intrinsic meaning as a relic of early experience, as in Freud, or becomes an empty marker of structural absence, as in Lacan. By following this evolution across decades of psychoanalytic and psychiatric thought, this book has demonstrated how a single, often marginal, phenomenon – here, fetishism – has served as a crucible for the formation of broader theories of sexuality, subjectivity, and mental life. These results matter not just for the history of psychoanalysis but also for the conceptual history of the human sciences. They show how questions of desire and pathology are inseparable from the epistemological frameworks in which they are theorized.

References

Adams, Parveen. 2002. "Of Female Bondage." In *Between Feminism and Psychoanalysis*, edited by Teresa Brennan, 247–65. Abingdon: Taylor & Francis.

Aflalo, Agnès. 2012. "Des amours et des femmes. Des homosexuelles en analyse." *La Cause du Désir* 81, no. 2: 83–7. https://doi.org/10.3917/lcdd.081.0083.

Alexander, Franz. 1954. "Interview with Franz Alexander Conducted by Kurt Robert Eissler, January 16, 1954." The Sigmund Freud Collection. Manuscript Division, Library of Congress, Washington, D.C.

Alvarado, Carlos S. 2010. "'Divisions of Personality and Spiritism' by Alfred Binet (1896)." *History of Psychiatry* 21, no. 4 (December): 487–500. https://doi.org/10.1177/0957154X10380513.

Apter, Emily. 2018. *Feminizing the Fetish: Psychoanalysis and Narrative Obsession in Turn-of-the Century France.* Ithaca, NY: Cornell University Press.

Assoun, Paul-Laurent. 1994. *Le fétichisme*. Paris: Presses universitaires de France, 2008 (coll. "Que sais-je?"), 128 p.

Atkinson, James Jasper. 1903. *Social Origins and Primal Law*. London: Longmans, Green & Co.

Binet, Alfred. 1888a. "Le Fétichisme dans L'Amour." In Études de Psychologie Expérimentale. Bibliothèque des Actualités Médicales et Scientifiques. Paris: Octave DOIN Éditeur.

Binet, Alfred. 1888b. "Les Théories Modernes de la Génération et de l'Hérédité." *Revue Philosophique de la France et de l'Étranger* 26: 529–59. https://www.jstor.org/stable/41074977.

Binet, Alfred. 1889b. "La Vision Mentale." *Revue Philosophique de la France et de l'Étranger* 27: 337–73. https://www.jstor.org/stable/41075043.

Binet, Alfred. 1890a. *On Double Consciousness: Experimental Psychological Studies*. Chicago, IL: Open Court.

Binet, Alfred. 1890b. "Compte Rendu de Pierre Janet, l'Automatisme Psychologique (1889)." *Revue Philosophique de la France et de l'Étranger* 29: 186–200.

Binet, Alfred. 1892. *Les Altérations de la Personnalité*. Paris: Félix Alcan Éditeur.

Binet Alfred. 1895. "La Peur chez les Enfants." *L'Année Psychologique* 2: 223–54. https://doi.org/10.3406/psy.1895.1536.

Binet, Alfred, and Charles Féré. 1887. *Le Magnetisme Animal.* Paris: Félix Alcan Éditeur.

Binet, Alfred, and Théodore Simon. 1910. "Définition des principaux états mentaux de l'aliénation" *L'Année Psychologique* 18: 61–317.

Blass, Rachel. 2017. "Understanding Freud's Conflicted View of the Object-Relatedness of Sexuality and Its Implications for Contemporary Psychoanalysis." In Deconstructing Normativity? Re-Reading Freud's 1905 Three Essays, edited by Philippe Van Haute and Herman Westerink, 6–27. London: Routledge, Taylor & Francis Group.

Campbell, Jan. 2000. *Arguing with the Phallus: Feminist, Queer, and Postcolonial Theory: A Psychoanalytic Contribution*. London: Zed Books.

Casanova, Bernard. 1987. "Qu'il n'y ait Pas de Psychogenèse." *Littoral* 22: 25–31.

Charcot, Jean-Martin, and Valentin Magnan. 1882. "Inversion du Sens Génital." *Archives de Neurologie* 3, no. 4: 53–60.

Davidson, Arnold I. 1987. "How to Do the History of Psychoanalysis: A Reading of Freud's Three Essays on the Theory of Sexuality." *Critical Inquiry* 13, no. 2 (Winter): 252–77. https://www.jstor.org/stable/1343491.

Davidson, Arnold I. 1990. "Closing Up the Corpses: Diseases of Sexuality and the Emergence of the Psychiatric Style of Reasoning." In *Meaning and Method: Essays in Honor of Hilary Putnam*, edited by George Boolos, 295–325. Cambridge: Cambridge University Press.

Dean, Tim. 2009. *Unlimited Intimacy: Reflections on the Subculture of Barebacking*. Chicago, IL: University of Chicago Press.

De Brosses, Charles. 1760. *Du culte des Dieux Fétiches, ou Parallèle de l'ancienne Religion de l'Égypte avec la Religion actuelle de Nigritie*. Paris: [publisher not identified].

De Clérambault, Gaëtan Gatian. 1908. "Passion Érotique des Étoffes chez la Femme." In *Oeuvre Psychiatrique*, 683–715. Paris: Presses Universitaires de France.

De Clérambault, Gaëtan Gatian. 1910. "Discussion de la Communication de Binet et Simon: Sur la Nécessité d'une Méthode Applicable au Diagnostic des Arrièrés Militaires." In *Annales Médico-Psychologiques*, 127. Paris: Masson Éditeurs.

De Clérambault, Gaëtan Gatian. 1920. "Automatisme Mental et Scission du Moi (1)." In *Oeuvre Psychiatrique*, 457–67. Paris: Presses Universitaires de France.

De Clérambault, Gaëtan Gatian. 1924a. "Définition de l'Automatisme Mental (1)." In *Oeuvre Psychiatrique*, 492–4. Paris: Presses Universitaires de France.

De Clérambault, Gaëtan Gatian. 1924b. "Les Psychoses Hallucinatoires Chroniques." In *Oeuvre Psychiatrique*, 495–526. Paris: Presses Universitaires de France.

De Vleminck, Jans. 2010. "Sexuality, Psychoanalysis, and Philosophy – An Introduction." In *Sexuality and Psychoanalysis: Philosophical Criticisms. Figures of the Unconscious*, edited by Jans de Vleminck and Eran Dorfman, 9–17. Leuven: Leuven University Press.

Dimitriadis, Yorgos. 2014. "Les Positions de Jacques Lacan sur la Psychogenèse et la Question du Déficit des Fonctions Organiques." *Cliniques Méditerranéennes* 89: 281–94. https://doi.org/10.3917/cm.089.0281.

Dupré, Ernest. [1912] 1925. "Les perversions instinctives." In Pathologies de l'imagination et de l'émotivité, 357–427. Paris: Payot.Eilenberger, Hans-Georg. 2020. "Freud and Merleau-Ponty on the (Sexual) Experience of the Child." *Philosophy Today* 64, no. 1: 137–57.

Ellenberger, Henri. 1970. *The Discovery of the Unconscious; The History and Evolution of Dynamic Psychiatry*. New York: Basic Books.

Fink, Bruce. 1995. *The Lacanian Subject: Between Language and Jouissance*. Princeton, NJ: Princeton University Press.

Fischer-Homberger, Esther. 2004. *Die Traumatische Neurose: Vom Somatischen zum Sozialen Leiden*. Gießen: Psychosozial Verlag.

Foschi, Renato, and Elisabetta Cicciola. 2006. "The Notion of 'Double Consciousness' in Alfred Binet's Psychological Experimentalism." *Physis: Rivista Internazionale si Storia della Scienza* 43, no. 1–2: 363–72.

Foucault, Michel. 1979. *The History of Sexuality I: The Will to Knowledge*. London: Allen Lane.

Foucault, Michel. 2003. *Abnormal: Lectures at the Collège de France 1974-1975*. New York: Picador.

Frazer, James George. 1910. *Totemism and Exogamy. A Treatise on Certain Early Forms of Superstition and Society*. Vol. 4. London: Macmillan.

Freud, Sigmund. 1886. "Report on My Studies in Paris and Berlin." In The Standard Edition of the Complete Psychological Works of Sigmund Freud, Vol. 1 (1886–1899): Pre-Psycho-Analytic Publications and Unpublished Drafts, 3–15. London: Hogarth Press.

Freud, Sigmund. [1888a] 1990. "Brain." In A Moment of Transition: Two Neuro-scientific Articles by Sigmund Freud, edited by Mark Solms and Michael Saling, 39–87. London: Routledge.

Freud, Sigmund. 1888b. "Hysteria." In *The Standard Edition of the Complete Psychological Works of Sigmund Freud, Vol. 1 (1886-1899): Pre-psycho-analytic Publications and Unpublished Drafts*. London: Hogarth Press.

Freud, Sigmund. 1888c. "Preface to the Translation of Bernheim's Suggestion." In *The Standard Edition of the Complete Psychological Works of Sigmund Freud, Vol. 1 (1886-1899): Pre-psycho-analytic Publications and Unpublished Drafts*, 73-87. London: Hogarth Press.

Freud, Sigmund. 1889. "Review of August Forel's Hypnotism." In The Standard Edition of the Complete Psychological Works of Sigmund Freud, Vol. 1 (1886–1899): Pre-Psycho-Analytic Publications and Unpublished Drafts, 89–102. London: Hogarth Press.

Freud, Sigmund. 1890. "Psychical (or Mental) Treatment." In *The Standard Edition of the Complete Psychological Works of Sigmund Freud, Vol. 7 (1901-1905): A Case of Hysteria, Three Essays on Sexuality and Other Works, 281-302*. London: Hogarth Press.

Freud, Sigmund. 1892–3. "A Case of Successful Treatment by Hypnotism." In *The Standard Edition of the Complete Psychological Works of Sigmund Freud, Vol. 1 (1886-1899): Pre-psycho-analytic Publications and Unpublished Drafts, 115-128.* London: Hogarth Press.

Freud, Sigmund. 1893b. "Some Points in a Comparative Study of Organic and Hysterical Paralyses." In *The Standard Edition of the Complete Psychological Works of Sigmund Freud, Vol. 1 (1886-1899): Pre-psycho-analytic Publications and Unpublished Drafts, 57-172.* London: Hogarth Press.

Freud, Sigmund. 1894. "The Neuro-Psychoses of Defence." In *The Standard Edition of the Complete Psychological Works of Sigmund Freud, Vol. 3 (1893-1899): Early Psycho-Analytic Publications, 41-61.* London: Hogarth Press.

Freud, Sigmund. 1895a. "Mecanismo de las Representaciones Obsesivas y las Fobias." In *Textos Inéditos y Documentos Recobrados. Traducción, Introducción y Notas de Fernando Gabriel Rodrígüez y Mauro Vallejo, 71-84.* Medellín, Barranquilla: Editorial Universidad de Antioquia y Editorial Universidad del Norte.

Freud, Sigmund. 1895b. "On the Grounds for Detaching a Particular Syndrome from Neurasthenia under the Description 'Anxiety Neurosis'." In *The Standard Edition of the Complete Psychological Works of Sigmund Freud (1893-1899): Early Psycho-Analytic Publications, 85-115.* London: Hogarth Press.

Freud, Sigmund. 1895c. "Obsessions and Phobias: Their Psychical Mechanism and their Aetiology." In *The Standard Edition of the Complete Psychological Works of Sigmund Freud, Vol. 3 (1893-1899): Early Psycho-Analytic Publications, 69-82.* London: Hogarth Press.

Freud, Sigmund. 1895d. "A Reply to Criticisms of My Paper on Anxiety Neurosis." In *The Standard Edition of the Complete Psychological Works of Sigmund Freud, Vol. 3 (1893-1899): Early Psycho-Analytic Publications,* 123-139. London: Hogarth Press.

Freud, Sigmund. 1895e. "Project for a Scientific Psychology." In *The Standard Edition of the Complete Psychological Works of Sigmund Freud, Vol. 1 (1886-1899): Pre-psycho-analytic Publications and Unpublished Drafts, 281-391.* London: Hogarth Press.

Freud, Sigmund. 1895f. "Besprechung von A. Hegar, Der Geschlechtstrieb; Eine sozialmedizinische Studie." In *Gesammelte Werke. Nachtragsband. Texte aus den Jahren 1885-1938.* Frankfurt am Main: Fischer.

Freud, Sigmund. 1896a. "Further Remarks on the Neuro-Psychosis of Defence." In *The Standard Edition of the Complete Psychological Works of Sigmund Freud, Vol. 3 (1893-1899): Early Psycho-Analytic Publications,* 162–185. London: Hogarth Press.

Freud, Sigmund. 1896b. "Heredity and the Aetiology of the Neurosis." In *The Standard Edition of the Complete Psychological Works of Sigmund Freud, Vol. 3 (1893-1899): Early Psycho-Analytic Publications,* 143-156. London: Hogarth Press.

Freud, Sigmund. 1896c. "The Aetiology of Hysteria." In *The Standard Edition of the Complete Psychological Works of Sigmund Freud, Vol. 3 (1893-1899): Early Psycho-Analytic Publications*, 187-221. London: Hogarth Press.

Freud, Sigmund. 1898. "Sexuality in the Aetiology of the Neuroses." In *The Standard Edition of the Complete Psychological Works of Sigmund Freud, Vol. 3 (1893-1899): Early Psycho-Analytic Publications*, 259-285. London: Hogarth Press.

Freud, Sigmund. 1899. "Screen Memories." In *The Standard Edition of the Complete Psychological Works of Sigmund Freud, Vol. 3 (1893-1899): Early Psycho-Analytic Publications*, 299-322. London: Hogarth Press.

Freud, Sigmund. [1905a] 2016. *Three Essays on the Theory of Sexuality: The 1905 Edition*, translated by Ulrike Kistner, edited by Phillippe Van Haute and Herman Westerink. London: Verso.

Freud, Sigmund. 1905b. "Fragment of an Analysis of a Case of Hysteria." In *The Standard Edition of the Complete Psychological Works of Sigmund Freud, Vol. 7 (1901–1905): A Case of Hysteria, Three Essays on Sexuality and Other Works, 1-122.* London: Hogarth Press.

Freud, Sigmund. 1905c. "Three Essays on the Theory of Sexuality." In *The Standard Edition of the Complete Psychological Works of Sigmund Freud, Vol. 7 (1901–1905): A Case of Hysteria, Three Essays on Sexuality and Other Works*. London: Hogarth Press.

Freud, Sigmund. 1906a. "My Views on the Role of Sexuality in the Aetiology of the Neuroses." In *The Standard Edition of the Complete Psychological Works of Sigmund Freud, Vol. 7 (1901-1905): A Case of Hysteria, Three Essays on Sexuality and Other Works*. London: Hogarth Press.

Freud, Sigmund. 1906b. "Psychoanalysis and the Establishment of the Facts in Legal Proceedings." In *The Standard Edition of the Complete Psychological Works of Sigmund Freud, Vol. 9 (1906-1908): Jensen's "Gradiva" and Other Works*. London: Hogarth Press.

Freud, Sigmund. 1907a. "Delusions and Dreams in Jensen's Gradiva." In *The Standard Edition of the Complete Psychological Works of Sigmund Freud, Vol. 9 (1906-1908): Jensen's "Gradiva" and Other Works, 1-96.* London: Hogarth Press.

Freud, Sigmund. [1907b] 1974. "Scientific Meeting on January 23, 1907." In *Minutes of the Vienna Psychoanalytic Society. Vol. I. 1906-1908*, edited by Herman Nunberg and Ernst Federn, 81–91. New York: International Universities Press.

Freud, Sigmund. 1908a. "'Civilized' Sexual Morality and Modern Nervous Illness." In *The Standard Edition of the Complete Psychological Works of Sigmund Freud, Vol. 9 (1906-1908): Jensen's "Gradiva" and Other Works*. London: Hogarth Press.

Freud, Sigmund. 1908b. "On Sexual Theories of Children." In *The Standard Edition of the Complete Psychological Works of Sigmund Freud, Vol. 9 (1906-1908): Jensen's "Gradiva" and Other Works*, 205-226. London: Hogarth Press.

Freud, Sigmund. 1908c. "Hysterical Phantasies and Their Relation to Bisexuality." In *The Standard Edition of the Complete Psychological Works of Sigmund Freud, Vol. 9 (1906-1908): Jensen's "Gradiva" and Other Works*. London: Hogarth Press.

Freud, Sigmund. 1908d. "Creative Writers and Day-Dreaming." In *The Standard Edition of the Complete Psychological Works of Sigmund Freud, Vol. 9 (1906-1908): Jensen's "Gradiva" and Other Works,* 141-154. London: Hogarth Press.

Freud, Sigmund. 1908e. "Family Romances." In *The Standard Edition of the Complete Psychological Works of Sigmund Freud, Vol. 9 (1906-1908): Jensen's "Gradiva" and Other Works,* 235-242. London: Hogarth Press.

Freud, Sigmund. 1908f. "The Sexual Enlightenment of Children." In *The Standard Edition of the Complete Psychological Works of Sigmund Freud, Vol. 9 (1906-1908): Jensen's "Gradiva" and Other Works*. London: Hogarth Press.

Freud, Sigmund. 1908g. "Character and Anal Erotism." In *The Standard Edition of the Complete Psychological Works of Sigmund Freud, Vol. 9 (1906-1908): Jensen's "Gradiva" and Other Works*. London: Hogarth Press.

Freud, Sigmund. 1908h. "Obsessive Actions and Religious Practices." In *The Standard Edition of the Complete Psychological Works of Sigmund Freud, Vol. 9 (1906-1908): Jensen's "Gradiva" and Other Works*. London: Hogarth Press.

Freud, Sigmund. [1909a] 1988. "On the Genesis of Fetishism." In *Freud and Fetishism: Previously Unpublished Minutes of the Vienna Psychoanalytic Society*, edited and translated by Louis Rose. *Psychoanalytic Quarterly* 57, no. 2 (April): 147–66.

Freud, Sigmund. 1909b. "Analysis of a Phobia in a Five-Year-Old Boy." In *The Standard Edition of the Complete Psychological Works of Sigmund Freud, Vol. 10: Two Case Histories ("Little Hans" and the "Rat Man"),* 1-150. London: Hogarth Press.

Freud, Sigmund. 1909c. "Notes Upon a Case of Obsessional Neurosis." In *The Standard Edition of the Complete Psychological Works of Sigmund Freud, Vol. 10: Two Case Histories ("Little Hans" and the "Rat Man")*. London: Hogarth Press.

Freud, Sigmund. 1909d. "Zur Genese des Fetischismus." In *Ernst Federn & Gerhard Wittenberger. Aus dem Kreis um Sigmund Freud: Zu den Protokollen der Wiener Psychoanalytischen Vereinigung,* 10-22. Frankfurt am Main: Fischer.

Freud, Sigmund. 1910a. "Leonardo da Vinci and a Memory of his Childhood." In *The Standard Edition of the Complete Psychological Works of Sigmund Freud, Vol. 11: Five Lectures on Psycho-analysis, Leonardo da Vinci and Other Works*. London: Hogarth Press.

Freud, Sigmund. 1910b. "Five Lectures on Psycho-analysis." In *The Standard Edition of the Complete Psychological Works of Sigmund Freud, Vol. 11: Five Lectures on Psycho-analysis, Leonardo da Vinci and Other Works*. London: Hogarth Press.

Freud, Sigmund. [1910c] 1974. "Scientific Meeting on March 9, 1910." In *Minutes of the Vienna Psychoanalytic Society. Vol. II. 1908-1910*, edited by Herman Nunberg and Ernst Federn, 445–51. New York: International Universities Press.

Freud, Sigmund. 1913a. "Totem and Taboo." In *The Standard Edition of the Complete Psychological Works of Sigmund Freud, Vol. 13: Totem and Taboo and Other Works,* 1-162. London: Hogarth Press.

Freud, Sigmund. [1913b] 1974. "Scientific Meeting on April 9, 1913." In *Minutes of the Vienna Psychoanalytic Society. Vol. IV. 1912–1918*, edited by Herman Nunberg and Ernst Federn, 185–6. New York: International Universities Press.

Freud, Sigmund. [1914a] 1974. "A Case of Foot Fetishism." In *Minutes of the Vienna Psychoanalytic Society. Vol. IV. 1912-1918*, edited by Herman Nunberg and Ernst Federn, 243–6. New York: International Universities Press.

Freud, Sigmund. [1914b] 1974. "Ein fall von fußfetischismus." In *Protokolle der Wiener Psychoanalytischen Vereinigung*, vol. 4, edited by Herman Nunberg and Ernst Federn, 236–9. Frankfurt am Main: Fischer.

Freud, Sigmund. 1915. "Repression." In *The Standard Edition of the Complete Psychological Works of Sigmund Freud, Vol. 14: On the History of the Psycho-Analytic Movement, Papers on Meta-psychology and Other Works,* 141-158. London: Hogarth Press.

Freud, Sigmund. 1916–17. "Lecture 22 – Some Thoughts on Development and Regression – Aetiology." In *The Standard Edition of the Complete Psychological Works of Sigmund Freud, Vol. 15: Introductory Lectures on Psychoanalysis (Parts I and II),* 339-357. London: Hogarth Press.

Freud, Sigmund. 1918. "The Taboo of Virginity (Contributions to the Psychology of Love III)." In *The Standard Edition of the Complete Psychological Works of Sigmund Freud, Vol. 11: Five Lectures on Psycho-analysis, Leonardo da Vinci and Other Works.* London: Hogarth Press.

Freud, Sigmund. 1919. "A Child Is Being Beaten: A Contribution to the Study of the Origin of Sexual Perversions." In *The Standard Edition of the Complete Psychological Works of Sigmund Freud, Vol. 17: An Infantile Neurosis and Other Works,* 175-204. London: Hogarth Press.

Freud, Sigmund. 1920. "The Psychogenesis of a Case of Homosexuality in a Woman." In *The Standard Edition of the Complete Psychological Works of Sigmund Freud, Vol. 18: Beyond the Pleasure Principle, Group Psychology and Other Works,* 145-172. London: Hogarth Press.

Freud, Sigmund. 1921. "Group Psychology and the Analysis of the Ego." In *The Standard Edition of the Complete Psychological Works of Sigmund Freud, Vol. 18: Beyond the Pleasure Principle, Group Psychology and Other Works.* London: Hogarth Press.

Freud, Sigmund. 1922. "Some Neurotic Mechanisms in Jealousy, Paranoia and Homosexuality." In *The Standard Edition of the Complete Psychological Works of Sigmund Freud, Vol. 18: Beyond the Pleasure Principle, Group Psychology and Other Works.* London: Hogarth Press.

Freud, Sigmund. 1923a. "The Ego and the Id." In *The Standard Edition of the Complete Psychological Works of Sigmund Freud, Vol. 19: The Ego and the Id and Other Works,* 1-66. London: Hogarth Press.

Freud, Sigmund. 1923b. "The Infantile Genital Organization of the Libido: An Interpolation into the Theory of Sexuality." In *The Standard Edition of the Complete Psychological Works of Sigmund Freud, Vol. 19: The Ego and the Id and Other Works*, 139-146. London: Hogarth Press.

Freud, Sigmund. 1924a. "Neurosis and Psychosis." In *The Standard Edition of the Complete Psychological Works of Sigmund Freud, Vol. 19: The Ego and the Id and Other Works,* 147-154. London: Hogarth Press.

Freud, Sigmund. 1924b. "The Loss of Reality in Neurosis and Psychosis." In *The Standard Edition of the Complete Psychological Works of Sigmund Freud, Vol. 19: The Ego and the Id and Other Works,* 181-188. London: Hogarth Press.

Freud, Sigmund. 1925. "Negation." In *The Standard Edition of the Complete Psychological Works of Sigmund Freud, Vol. 19: The Ego and the Id and Other Works,* 233-240. London: Hogarth Press.

Freud, Sigmund. 1926. "Inhibitions, Symptoms and Anxiety." In *The Standard Edition of the Complete Psychological Works of Sigmund Freud, Vol. 20: An Autobiographical Study, Inhibitions, Symptoms and Anxiety, Lay Analysis and Other Works,* 77-178. London: Hogarth Press.

Freud, Sigmund. 1927. "Fetishism." In *The Standard Edition of the Complete Psychological Works of Sigmund Freud, Vol. 21: The Future of an Illusion, Civilization and its Discontents, and Other Works,* 153-158. London: Hogarth Press.

Freud, Sigmund. 1931. "Female Sexuality." In *The Standard Edition of the Complete Psychological Works of Sigmund Freud, Vol. 21: The Future of an Illusion, Civilization and its Discontents, and Other Works,* 123-146. London: Hogarth Press.

Freud, Sigmund. 1933. "Lecture 33 – Femininity." In *The Standard Edition of the Complete Psychological Works of Sigmund Freud, Vol. 22: New Introductory Lectures on Psycho-Analysis and Other Works*, 112-135. London: Hogarth Press.

Freud, Sigmund. 1937. "Analysis terminable and interminable." In *The Standard Edition of the Complete Psychological Works of Sigmund Freud, Vol. 23: Moses and Monotheism, An Outline of Psycho-Analysis and Other Works,* 209-254. London: Hogarth Press.

Freud, Sigmund. 1940a. "An Outline of Psychoanalysis." In *The Standard Edition of the Complete Psychological Works of Sigmund Freud, Vol. 23: Moses and Monotheism, An Outline of Psycho-Analysis and Other Works*, 139-208. London: Hogarth Press.

Freud, Sigmund. 1940b. "Splitting of the Ego in the Process of Defense." In *The Standard Edition of the Complete Psychological Works of Sigmund Freud, Vol. 23: Moses and Monotheism, An Outline of Psycho-Analysis and Other Works*, 271–278. London: Hogarth Press.

Freud, Sigmund. 1972. *Gesammeltewerke: Chronologischgeordnet. 19 Bände*. London: Imago.

“”Freud, Sigmund. 1985. *The Complete Letters of Sigmund Freud to Wilhelm Fliess 1887-1904,* edited and translated by Jeffrey Moussaieff Masson. Cambridge, MA: Harvard University Press.

Freud, Sigmund. 1986. *Briefe an Wilhelm Fließ 1887-1904*. Frankfurt: S. Fischer.

Freud, Sigmund. 2015. *Sigmund Freud Gesamtausgabe (Originalausgabe ed., Bibliothek der Psychoanalyse). 23 Bände*. Gießen: Psychosozial Verlag.
Freud, Sigmund. 2025. *Schriften zum Fetischismus*, edited by Victor Blüml and Matthias Schmidt. Göttingen: Vandenhoeck & Ruprecht.
Freud, Sigmund, and Josef Breuer. 1893. "On the Psychical Mechanism of Hysterical Phenomena: Preliminary Communication." In *The Standard Edition of the Complete Psychological Works of Sigmund Freud, Vol. 2 (1893-1895): Studies on Hysteria*, 1-17. London: Hogarth Press.
Freud, Sigmund, and Josef Breuer. 1895. "Studies on Hysteria." In *The Standard Edition of the Complete Psychological Works of Sigmund Freud, Vol. 2 (1893-1895): Studies on Hysteria*. London: Hogarth Press.
Freud, Sigmund, and Oskar Pfister. 1963. *Psychoanalysis and Faith*: The Letters of Sigmund Freud and Oskar Pfister. Edited by E. L. Freud and H. Meng. Translated by E. Mosbacher. New York: Basic Books.
Freud, Sigmund, and Carl Jung. 1974. *The Freud/Jung letters: The Correspondence between Sigmund Freud and C. G. Jung*, edited by William McGuire. New Jersey: Princeton University Press.
Freud, Sigmund, and René Laforgue. 1977. "Correspondence 1923-1937." In *Nouvelle Revue de Psychanalyse*, no. 15, 251–314. Paris: Editions Gallimard.
Gallop, Jane. 1982. "Lacan's 'Mirror Stage': Where to Begin." *Substance* 11–12: 118–28. https://doi.org/10.2307/3684185.
Gay, Peter. 1988. *Freud: A Life for Our Time*. New York: W. W. Norton.
Greenacre, Phyllis. 1950. "General Problems of Acting Out." *Psychoanalytic Quarterly: IV* 19, no. 4: 455–67.
Greenacre, Phyllis. 1953. "Certain Relationships between Fetishism and Faulty Development of the Body Image." *Psychoanalytic Studies of the Child* 8, no. 1: 79–98. https://doi.org/10.1080/00797308.1953.11822762.
Greenacre, Phyllis. 1955. "Further Considerations Regarding Fetishism." *The Psychoanalytic Study of the Child* 10, no. 1: 187–94. https://doi.org/10.1080/00797308.1955.11822555.
Greenberg, Jay, and Stephen Mitchell. 1983. *Object-Relations in Psychoanalytic Theory*. Cambridge, MA: Harvard University Press.
Gumpper, Stéphane, and Thierry Haustgen. 2012a. "Gaëtan Gatian de Clérambault (1872-1934) - I. Sa Vie et Son Œuvre." *Annales Médico-Psychologiques* 170, no. 3: 224–30.
Gumpper, Stéphane, and Thierry Haustgen. 2012b. "Gaëtan Gatian de Clérambault (1872-1934) II. Son Héritage Psychiatrique." *Annales Médico-Psychologiques* 170, no. 5: 358–63. https://doi.org/10.1016/j.amp.2012.05.004.
Hacking, Ian. 1995. *Rewriting the Soul: Multiple Personality and the Sciences of Memory*. Princeton, NJ: Princeton University Press.
Hell, Daniel. 2001. "Eugen Bleulers Herkunft, Kindheit und Jugend – Hintergrund für seine Lehre." In *Eugen Bleuler – Leben und Werk*, edited by Daniel Hell, Christian Scharfetter, and Arnulf Möller, 19–27. Bern: Huber.

Hirschmüller, Albrecht. 2003. "Zur Vor- und Frühgeschichte des Perversionsbegriffs." In *Jahrbuch der Psychoanalyse: Beiträge zur Theorie, Praxis und Geschichte*, 115-133, vol. 46. Stuttgart: Frommann-Holzboog Verlag.

Høgh-Olesen, Henrik. 2018. "Aesthetics and Fetishism: Key Stimuli and Power Objects." *Evolutionary Studies in Imaginative Culture* 2, no. 2: 200–11.

Iacono, Alfonso Maurizio. 2016. *The History and Theory of Fetishism*. New York: Palgrave Macmillan.

Janet, Pierre. 1889. *L'Automatisme Psychologique: Essai de Psychologie Expérimentale sur les Formes Inférieures de l'Activité Humaine*. Paris: Alcan.

Jappe, Anselm. 2020. "Fetishism and Narcissism – The Base of Capitalism?" *Estudios de filosofía* 62: 165–73.

Julien, Philippe. 1985. *Le Retour à Freud de Jacques Lacan: L'application au miroir.* Paris: Epel Éditions.

Jung, Carl G. 1902. *Zur Psychologie und Pathologie sogenannter occulter Phänomene: eine psychiatrische Studie*. Leipzig: Druck and Verlag von Oswald Mutze.

Jung, Carl G. [1904] 1970. "On Hysterical Misreading." In *Jung, Carl, G. Collected Works of C. G. Jung*, vol. 1, 2nd. ed., 89–92. Princeton, NJ: Princeton University Press.

Kaan, Heinrich. [1844] 2016. *Psychopathia Sexualis*, edited by Benjamin Kahan, translated by Melissa Haynes. New York: Cornell University Press.

Kern, Stephen. 1975. "The Prehistory of Freud's Theory of Castration Anxiety." *Psychoanalytic Review* 62, no. 2: 309–14.

Kerr, John. 1993. *A Most Dangerous Method: The Story of Jung, Freud, and Sabina Spielrein.* New York: Alfred A. Knopf.

Klein, Alexandre. 2011. "La correspondance d'Alfred Binet avec Théodore Flournoy: témoignage inédit d'une collégiale amitié." *Bulletin de psychologie*, no. 513: 239–50. https://doi.org/10.3917/bupsy.513.0239.

Krafft-Ebing, Richard von. 1877. "Ueber gewisse Anomalien des Geschlechtstriebs und die klinisch-forensische Verwerthung derselben als eines wahrscheinlich functionellen Degenerationszeichens des centralen Nervensystems." *Archiv für Psychiatrie und Nervenkrankheiten* 7: 291–312. https://doi.org/10.1007/BF01969552.

Krafft-Ebing, Richard von. 1888. *Psychopathia sexualis mit besonderer Berücksichtigung der conträren Sexualempfindung. Eine klinisch-forensische Studie. Dritte vermehrte und verbesserte Auflage*. Stuttgart: Verlag von Ferdinand Enke.

Krafft-Ebing, Richard von. 1889. *Psychopathia sexualis mit besonderer Berücksichtigung der conträren Sexualempfindung. Eine klinisch-forensische Studie. Vierte vermehrte und theilweise umgearbeitete Auflage*. Stuttgart: Verlag von Ferdinand Enke.

Krafft-Ebing, Richard von. 1890a. *Psychopathia sexualis mit besonderer Berücksichtigung der conträren Sexualempfindung. Eine klinisch-forensische Studie. Fünfte vermehrte und theilweise umgearbeitete Auflage*. Stuttgart: Verlag von Ferdinand Enke.

Krafft-Ebing, Richard von. 1890b. *Neue Forschungen auf dem Gebiet der Psychopathia sexualis: eine medicinisch-psychologische Studie*. Stuttgart: Verlag von Ferdinand Enke.

Krafft-Ebing, Richard von. 1891. "Ueber Fetischismus Eroticus." *Wiener Medizinische Blätter* 14: 400–2, 432–4.

Krafft-Ebing, Richard von. 1892. *Psychopathia sexualis mit besonderer Berücksichtigung der conträren Sexualempfindung. Eine klinisch-forensische Studie. Siebente vermehrte und theilweise umgearbeitete Auflage*. Stuttgart: Verlag von Ferdinand Enke.

Krafft-Ebing, Richard von. 1893a. *Psychopathia Sexualis: With Especial Reference to Contrary Sexual Instinct: A Medico-legal Study.* (Authorized translation of the 7th German edition (1892).) Philadelphia; London: F.A. Davis Co.

Krafft-Ebing, Richard von. 1893b. *Lehrbuch der Psychiatrie auf klinischer Grundlage - für praktische Ärzte und Studierende. Fünfte vermehrte und verbesserte Auflage*. Stuttgart: Verlag von Ferdinand Enke.

Krafft-Ebing, Richard von. 1895. *Nervosität und neurasthenische Zustände*. Wien: Alfred Hölder.

Krafft-Ebing, Richard von. 1896. "Zur Suggestionsbehandlung der Hysteriagravis." *Zeitschrift für Hypnotismus* 4, no. 1: 27–31.

Krafft-Ebing, Richard von. 1899. "Zum Fetishismus." In *Arbeiten aus dem Gesamtgebiete der Psychiatrie und Neuropathologie*, issues 1–4, 169–74. Leipzig: Johann Ambrosius Barth.

Krause-Utz, Annegret, Christian Schmahl, Ruth Lanius, and Martin Bohus. 2017. "Dissociation and Alterations in Brain Function and Structure: Implications for Borderline Personality Disorder." *Current Psychiatry Reports* 19: 6.

Lacan, Jacques. [1932] 1980. *De la psychose paranoïaque dans ses rapports avec la personnalité*. Paris: Seuil.

Lacan, Jacques. [1938] 2001. "Les complexes familiaux dans la formation de l'individu." In Autres écrits, 23–84. Paris: Seuil.

Lacan, Jacques. [1953] 1978. "Le Mythe individuel du névrosé ou poésie et vérité dans la névrose." Ornicar? no. 17–18: 290–307. Paris: Éditions du Seuil.

Lacan, Jacques. [1954–5] 1978. Le séminaire de Jacques Lacan, Livre II: Le moi dans la théorie de Freud et dans la technique de la psychanalyse, 1954–1955. Paris: Seuil.

Lacan, Jacques. [1955] 1966. "Variantes de la cure-type." In Écrits, 323–62. Paris: Éditions du Seuil.

Lacan, Jacques. [1955–6] 1981. *Le Séminaire Livre III: Les psychoses*. Paris: Éditions du Seuil.

Lacan, Jacques. [1956–7] 1994. *Le Séminaire Livre IV: La relation d'objet*. Paris: Éditions du Seuil.

Lacan, Jacques. [1957] 1966. "L'Instance de la Lettre dans l'Inconscient ou la Raison depuis Freud."

In *Écrits,* 493-528. Paris: Éditions du Seuil.

Lacan, Jacques. [1957–8] 1998. *Le Séminaire Livre V: Les formations de l'inconscient.* Paris: Éditions du Seuil.

Lacan, Jacques. [1958] 1966. "Remarque sur le Rapport de Daniel Lagache." In *Écrits*, 647-695. Paris: Éditions du Seuil.

Lacan, Jacques. [1958–9] 2013. *Le Séminaire Livre VI: Le Désir et son Interprétation.* Paris: Éditions du Seuil.

Lacan, Jacques. [1962–3] 2004. *Le Séminaire Livre X: L'Angoisse*. Paris: Éditions du Seuil.

Lacan, Jacques. 1965–6. "Le Séminaire de Jacques Lacan, Livre XIII: L'Objet de la Psychanalyse." (Unpublished typescript.) Accessed 5 February 2020. http://staferla.free.fr/S13/S13.htm.

Lacan, Jacques. 1966. "De nos antécédents." In Écrits, 65–72. Paris: Éditions du Seuil.

Lacan, Jacques. [1968–9] 2006. *Le Séminaire Livre XVI: D'un Autre à l'Autre*. Paris: Éditions du Seuil.

Lacan, Jacques. [1972–3] 1975. *Le Séminaire Livre XX: Encore*. Paris: Éditions du Seuil.

Lacan, Jacques. [1975–6] 2005. *Le Séminaire Livre XXIII: Le Sinthome*. Paris: Éditions du Seuil.

Lacan, Jacques, and Wladimir Granoff. 1956. "Fetishism: The Symbolic, the Imaginary, and the Real." In *Perversion: Psychodynamics and Therapy*, edited by Sandor Lorand and Michael Balint, 265–76. New York: Gramercy.

Lantéri-Laura, Georges. 1994. "Proceso y Psicogénesis en la Obra de J. Lacan." In *Litoral: Antecedentes Lacanionos, 16*, 25–43. Córdoba: E.D.E.L.P., École Lacanienne de Psychanalyse.

Lantéri-Laura, Georges. 2012. *Lecture des Perversions: Histoire de Leur Appropriation Médical.* Paris: Economica Anthropos.

Lebois, Lauren A. M. *et al.* 2021. "Large-Scale Functional Brain Network Architecture Changes Associated with Trauma-Related Dissociation." *American Journal of Psychiatry* 178: 123–34.

Lopez, Azenet. 2025. "A Layered Unity Model of Split-Brain Consciousness." *Philosophical Studies* 182: 2159–90.

Lotfinia, Shahab, Zohre Soorgi, Yoki Mertens, and Judith Daniels. 2020. "Structural and Functional Brain Alterations in Psychiatric Patients with Dissociative Experiences: A Systematic Review of Magnetic Resonance Imaging Studies." *Journal of Psychiatric Research* 128: 5–15.

Lynn, David. J. 1993. "Freud's Psychoanalysis of A. B., a Psychotic Man, 1925–1930." Journal of the American Academy of Psychoanalysis 21, no. 1: 63–78.

Matory, J. Lorand. 2018. *The Fetish Revisited: Marx, Freud, and the Gods Black People Make*. Durham, NC: Duke University Press.

May-Tolzmann, Ulrike. 1996. *Freuds fruhe klinische Theorie (1894-1896): Wiederentdeckung and Rekonstruktion.* Tubingen: Edition Diskord.

Mazaleigue-Labaste, Julie. 2014. *Les Déséquilibres de l'Amour. La Genèse du Concept de Perversion Sexuelle, de la Révolution Française à Freud*. Paris: Ithaque.

McNeill, Desmond. 2020. *Fetishism and the Theory of Value: Reassessing Marx in the 21st Century*. London: Palgrave Macmillan.

Modesti, Martina Nicole, Ludovica Rapisarda, Gabriela Capriotti, and Antonio Del Casale. 2022. "Functional Neuroimaging in Dissociative Disorders: A Systematic Review." *Journal of Personalized Medicine* 12: 1405.

Moskowitz, Andrew. 2006. "Pierre Janet's Influence on Bleuler's Concept of Schizophrenia." Paper presented at *The First Symposium of the Pierre Janet Gesellschaft, Freiburg, Germany, June 3-4, 2005*, edited by Peter Fiedler. Lengerich: Pabst Science Publishers.

Muller, John P. 1982. "Ego and Subject in Lacan." *Psychoanalytic Review* 69, no. 2: 234–40.

Müller, Max. [1878] 2002. "Is Fetishism a Primitive Form of Religion?" In *The Essential Max Müller: On Language, Mythology, and Religion*, edited by Jon R. Stone, 193–229. New York: Palgrave Macmillan.

Mulvey, Laura. 1993. "Some Thoughts on Theories of Fetishism in the Context of Contemporary Culture." *October* 65 (Summer): 3–20.

Nicolas, Serge. 2000. "L'école de la Salpêtrière en 1885." In *Psychologie et Histoire*, 165-207, vol. 1. Paris: Université Paris Descartes.

Oosterhuis, Harry. 2000. *Stepchildren of Nature: Krafft-Ebing, Psychiatry, and the Making of Sexual Identity.* Chicago, IL: University of Chicago Press.

Oosterhuis, Harry. 2012. "Sexual Modernity in the Works of Richard Von Krafft-Ebing and Albert Moll." *Medical History* 56, no. 2 (April): 133–55. https://doi.org/10.1017/mdh.2011.30.

Parfitt, Anthony (2007). "Fetishism, Transgenderism, and the Concept of 'Castration'." *Psychoanalytic Psychotherapy* 21, no. 1: 61–89. https://doi.org/10.1080/02668730601181119.

Pesenti-Irrmann, Marie. 2006. "La Mère et le Féminin." *La Clinique Lacanienne* 11, no. 1: 65–75. https://doi.org/10.3917/cla.011.0065.

Pickmann, Claude-Noële. 2004. "Colette Soler: Ce que Lacan Disait des Femmes. Étude de Psychanalyse." *Figures de la psychanalyse* 10, no. 2: 200–6. https://doi.org/10.3917/fp.010.0200.

Piéron, Henri. 1954. "Histoire succincte des Congrès internationaux de Psychologie." *L'année Psychologique* 54, no. 2: 397–405.

Redmond, Jonathan D. 2013. *Ordinary Psychosis and The Body: A Contemporary Lacanian Approach*. Basingstoke: Palgrave Macmillan Publishers.

Rey-Flaud, Henri. 1994. *Comment Freud inventa le fétichisme … et réinventa la psychanalyse*. Paris: Payot Bibliothèque scientifique.

Rocha, G. M. 2010. "O estético e o ético na psicanálise: Freud, o sublime e a sublimação." PhD diss., Universidade de São Paulo.

Rosolato, Guy. 1967. "Étude des perversions sexuelles à partir du fétichisme." In *Le Desir et la Perversion*, 7-52. Paris: Éditions du Seuil.

Roudinesco, Elizabeth. (1997). *Jacques Lacan: His Life and Work*. New York: Columbia University Press.
Safatle, Vladimir (2010). *Fetichismo: Colonizar o Outro*. Rio de Janeiro: Civilização Brasileira.
Sauvagnat, François, and Cedric, Chaillou. 2016. "Criminalité, Perversité, Perversion: Une Mise au Point." In *Incidences (Inter)Subjectives de la Perversion*, edited by Patrick Martin-Mattera, 203–32. Toulouse: Érès.
Scharfetter, Christian. 1999. *Dissoziation, Split, Fragmentation: Nachdenken über ein Modell.* Bern: Huber.
Shamdasani, Sonu. 2003. *Jung and the Making of Modern Psychology. The Dream of a Science.* Cambridge: Cambridge University Press.
Shera, Peta. 2009. "Selfish Passions and Artificial Desire: Rereading Clérambault's Study of 'Silk Erotomania'." Journal of the History of Sexuality 18, no. 1: 158–79.
Smith, William Robertson. 1889. *Lectures on the Religion of the Semites*. London: Adam and Charles Black.
Spruiell, Vann. 1979. "Freud's Concepts of Idealization." *Journal of the American Psychoanalytic Association* 27, no. 4 (August): 777–91. https://doi.org/10.1177/000306517902700402.
Stotz-Ingenlath, Gabriele. 2000. "Epistemological Aspects of Eugen Bleuler's Conception of Schizophrenia in 1911." *Med Health Care Philos* 3: 153–9. https://doi.org/10.1023/A:1009919309015.
Strachey, James, ed. and trans. 1962. *The Standard Edition of the Complete Psychological Works of Sigmund Freud*, Vol. 2 (1893–1895): Studies on Hysteria. London: Hogarth Press.
Sulloway, Frank Jones. 1983. *Freud, Biologist of the Mind: Beyond the Psychoanalytic Legend*. New York: Basic Books.
Timms, Edward, ed. 1995. *Freud and the Child. Woman: The Memoirs of Fritz Wittels*. New Haven, CT: Yale University Press.
Van Haute, Phillipe. 2016. "Lacan Meets Freud? Patho-Analytic Reflections on the Status of the Perversions in Lacanian Metapsychology." *Studies in Gender and Sexuality* 17, no. 4: 274–84. https://doi.org/10.1080/15240657.2016.1236547.
Van Haute, Phillipe, and Herman Westerink. 2016. "Introduction: Hysteria, Sexuality, and the Deconstruction of Normativity – Rereading Freud's 1905 Edition of Three Essays on the Theory of Sexuality." In *Freud, S. Three Essays on the Theory of Sexuality: The 1905 Edition*, translated by Ulrike Kistner, edited by Phillipe van Haute and Herman Westerink, xiii–lxxvi. London: Verso.
Van Haute, Phillipe, and Herman Westerink. 2017. "Introduction: Excavating a theory of sexuality." In *Deconstructing Normativity? Re-Reading Freud's 1905 Three Essays*, 1-5. London: Routledge, Taylor & Francis Group.
Van Haute, Philippe, and Herman Westerink. 2021. *Reading Freud's Three Essays on the Theory of Sexuality*: From Pleasure to the Object. London; New York: Routledge.

Vanheule, Stijn. 2011. *The Subject of Psychosis: A Lacanian Perspective.* Basingstoke: Palgrave Macmillan.

Vanheule, Stijn. 2018. "From de Clérambault's Theory of Mental Automatism to Lacan's Theory of the Psychotic Structure." *Psychoanalysis and History* 20: 205–28. https://doi.org/10.3366/pah.2018.0259.

Westerink, Herman. 2017. "Freud's Discussion with Psychiatry on Sexuality, Drives and Objects in *Three Essays*." In *Deconstructing Normativity? Re-Reading Freud's 1905 Three Essays*, 28–43. London: Routledge, Taylor & Francis Group.

Winnicott, Donald Woods. 1953. "Transitional Objects and Transitional Phenomena – A Study of the First Not-Me Possession." *International Journal of Psycho-analysis* 34, no. 2: 89–97.

Wolf, Theta. 1973. *Alfred Binet*. Chicago, IL; London: University of Chicago Press.